Ernst Bloch a·ies

Bloomsbury Studies in Continental Philosophy

Bloomsbury Studies in Continental Philosophy presents cutting-edge scholarship in the field of modern European thought. The wholly original arguments, perspectives and research findings in titles in this series make it an important and stimulating resource for students and academics from across the discipline.

Other titles in the series

Adorno, Heidegger, Philosophy and Modernity, Nicholas Joll
Between the Canon and the Messiah, Colby Dickinson
Castoriadis, Foucault, and Autonomy, Marcela Tovar-Restrepo
Deconstruction without Derrida, Martin McQuillan
Deleuze and the Diagram, Jakub Zdebik
Deleuze and the History of Mathematics, Simon B. Duffy
Derrida and the Future of the Liberal Arts, edited by Mary Caputi and Vincent J. Del Casino, Jr
Derrida, Badiou and the Formal Imperative, Christopher Norris
Derrida: Ethics Under Erasure, Nicole Anderson
Emmanuel Levinas, Abi Doukhan
From Ricoeur to Action, edited by Todd S. Mei and David Lewin
Immanent Transcendence, Patrice Haynes
Jean-Luc Nancy and the Question of Community, Ignaas Devisch
Levinas, Storytelling and Anti-Storytelling, Will Buckingham
Lyotard and the 'figural' in Performance, Art and Writing, Kiff Bamford
Michel Henry, edited by Jeffrey Hanson and Michael R. Kelly
Performatives After Deconstruction, edited by Mauro Senatore
Post-Rationalism, Tom Eyers
Rethinking Philosophy and Theology with Deleuze, Brent Adkins and Paul R. Hinlicky
Revisiting Normativity with Deleuze, edited by Rosi Braidotti and Patricia Pisters
The Time of Revolution, Felix Ó Murchadha

Ernst Bloch and His Contemporaries

Locating Utopian Messianism

Ivan Boldyrev

Bloomsbury Academic
An imprint of Bloomsbury Publishing Plc

B L O O M S B U R Y
LONDON • OXFORD • NEW YORK • NEW DELHI • SYDNEY

Bloomsbury Academic
An imprint of Bloomsbury Publishing Plc

50 Bedford Square	1385 Broadway
London	New York
WC1B 3DP	NY 10018
UK	USA

www.bloomsbury.com

BLOOMSBURY and the Diana logo are trademarks of Bloomsbury Publishing Plc

First published 2014
Paperback edition first published 2015

© Ivan Boldyrev, 2014

Ivan Boldyrev has asserted his right under the Copyright, Designs and Patents Act, 1988, to be identified as Author of this work.

From Russian Studies in Philosophy 49, no. 4 (Spring 2011): 65 – 95. English translation copyright © 2011 by M. E. Sharpe, Inc. Used by permission. All Rights Reserved. Not for reproduction.

Excerpts from The Spirit of Utopia by Ernst Bloch, translated by Anthony A. Nassar. Copyright © 2000 by the Board of Trustees of the Leland Stanford Jr. University. All rights reserved. Used with the permission of Stanford University Press, www.sup.org.

All rights reserved. No part of this publication may be reproduced or transmitted in any form or by any means, electronic or mechanical, including photocopying, recording, or any information storage or retrieval system, without prior permission in writing from the publishers.

No responsibility for loss caused to any individual or organization acting on or refraining from action as a result of the material in this publication can be accepted by Bloomsbury or the author.

British Library Cataloguing-in-Publication Data
A catalogue record for this book is available from the British Library.

ISBN: HB: 978-1-4725-1176-8
PB: 978-1-4742-4206-6
ePDF: 978-1-4725-0534-7
ePub: 978-1-4725-1206-2

Library of Congress Cataloging-in-Publication Data
A catalog record for this book is available from the Library of Congress

Typeset by Deanta Global Publishing Services, Chennai, India

Contents

Acknowledgements		vi
Introduction		1
1	Ernst Bloch's Philosophical Prose	7
2	Heidelberg's Apostles: Bloch Reading Lukács Reading Bloch	39
3	Eschatology and Messianism: Bloch with Buber, Landauer and Rosenzweig	91
4	The Form of the Messianic: Bloch and Benjamin	113
5	The Void of Utopia and the Violence of the System: Bloch contra Adorno	167
Conclusion: Drawing the Utopian Line		179
Bibliography		183
Index		197

Acknowledgements

Nothing in the lines traditionally reserved for the acknowledgements can adequately express my gratitude to the people who helped me conceive and finalize this book. Therefore, I name them following a venerable tradition and as a sign of the greatest appreciation I could give of their engagement and generosity. First of all, Alexander Koryagin and Sam Dolbear should be mentioned: they transformed a Russian text into a (hopefully) readable English one. A meticulous and ungracious job of translating, in its desperate attempt to mend together incommensurabilities of different languages, can only be partly redeemed by reference to Benjamin's famous idea of Adamic language. Dmitry Bugai should be thanked for showing me why Bloch and Lukács are still of interest today; Nikita Kharlamov helped greatly in providing the missing sources and reassuring the author that this seemingly endless work is worth completing. I also should thank my wife Alena for her (im)patience that strongly motivated me. Ralf Becker, Alexey Boldyrev, Kirill Chepurin, Alexander Filippov-Chekhov, Christoph Gödde, Artemy Magun, Julia Matveev, Yury Selivanov, Hans-Ernst Schiller, Itta Shedletzky, Helen Stuhr-Rommereim and many others helped in various ways and I am extremely grateful to all of them. Finally, National Research University Higher School of Economics (Moscow) made available the best resources at its disposal: money (as a grant for writing a Russian version of this book) and – somewhat synonymously – time (by providing me with an excellent teaching assistant).

Introduction

It is tempting for an author to begin with a statement that the subject matter at hand is becoming more and more 'relevant', and arousing ever more interest. 'Fashionable' could also stand here, if the intellectuals did not shy away from such words. A lack of current concern with a topic could be equally well utilized as an argument in its favour. After all, any book should justify its existence. But, I believe, it should not be done at the outset. Any act of reading is a credit of attention given to the author, and, as any credit, it is essentially temporal in nature. One should take time, and who am I to assure the reader of the book's usefulness and relevance? Only with time will it be possible for the reader to formulate an ultimate judgement.

Ernst Bloch (1885–1977), a prominent German thinker of the past century, is currently not a 'hot' topic, neither in the Anglo-Saxon world nor in Europe. However, he is not completely forgotten, and today we witness some renewal of interest in his philosophy (the best evidence is the new volume: Thompson and Žižek 2013). What is Bloch known for and why do his collected works still stand among the philosophical classics in the Berlin State Library? His influential standpoints are the theory of utopian consciousness; a resolute inclination to merge aesthetics and politics; the rehabilitation of hope; and an atheistic conception of Christianity. But in the landscape of contemporary theory he is staying somewhere in the shadow of his contemporaries; besides, after some critique, his status as a part of the canon is ambiguous, and the outcome of re-appropriating his work is uncertain – as well as the upshot of this particular book.

In it I reconstruct the contexts of Bloch's philosophy and show how various implicit and explicit debates with Georg Lukács, Walter Benjamin and Theodor Adorno made a profound impact on Bloch's utopian messianism. In particular, these controversies shed light on the contradictions and paradoxes of a utopian philosophy of history. What is the time (and timing) of utopia? Should we intentionally keep its coming vague and push away the utopian horizon? Or is utopia, as Bloch seems to suggest, a part of our imperceptible experience *here and now*? These questions were important both for Benjamin's vision of history and for Adorno's critical theory. Bloch was certainly among their most important interlocutors, and these polemic exchanges were landmarks that determined the direction of the utopian thought. His literary experiences and his engagement in aesthetic debates were also fundamental for this intellectual edifice. Bloch's relevance in many respects is due to his unprecedented philosophical style that self-consciously asserts itself as a way of reshaping social reality while resolving certain problems of messianic doctrine and redeeming his precarious 'open system' philosophy. Aesthetic dimension therefore provides both substance and justification for the utopian.

The book also contributes to clarifying some widespread perceptions of Bloch and his philosophical project. Concentrating on his early works (*The Spirit of Utopia* and *Traces*), it elucidates the ideas behind various aspects of this project (in part pronounced by Bloch himself) – such as 'revolutionary gnosis' or 'messianism'. Rather than merely dealing with Bloch as a Marxist with a dubious past, I emphasize the influences that various religious traditions (such as gnosticism) and authors (such as Martin Buber) exerted on him.

The first chapter sets the scene by briefly sketching Bloch's intellectual biography. It outlines his major influences and introduces the core ideas: his theory of utopia, metaphysics of the lived instant, early philosophy of subjectivity, ontology of the *Not-Yet-Being* and his social philosophy, particularly the notion of non-contemporaneity. The chapter attempts to identify the form of Bloch's philosophical writing and proposes viewing him as an author who devised his own poetics. As an interlude, I compare Bloch with Heidegger on some key points: the philosophy of the instant, the assessment of technology, and time. (This material was conceived as an introduction to Bloch, but it is surely recommendable to refer also to other good English-language sources, such as Geoghegan (1996), as well as to the German ones, of which the most recent and comprehensive is the monumental *Bloch Dictionary* (Dietschy et al. 2012)).

The chapter ends with a preliminary discussion of the contradictions and questions inherent in Bloch's theory of utopia. What is the end of utopia? And what does it mean for a utopia to end? How could one conceive of this eternal halt? Is it possible to identify the aim of a utopian movement (that would correspond to the end of history)? What type of thinking allows us to be critical, avoids ideological fetishism, while envisioning a better life? These are clearly the questions to ask when confronting Bloch's texts and his debates with contemporaries.

Chapter 2 deals with Georg Lukács, who was a close friend of Bloch when both were members of the Max Weber circle in Heidelberg. Its historical argument revolves around Bloch's early critique in which their later disagreements manifest in the debates on Expressionism in the 1930s are recognizable. Bloch confronts Lukács's praising of form and his Nietzschean conception of the tragic hero with his utopian vision of art as pre-appearance (*Vor-Schein*) transcending the static limits of form. These two ways of aesthetic thinking are further explicated by drawing on Lukács's *Theory of the Novel*, also indirectly criticized in *The Spirit of Utopia*. Indeed, I contend, much of Bloch's early work may be regarded as explicit or implicit reaction to Lukács.

Bloch's reception of *History and Class Consciousness* was organized along the lines of the totality concept. Bloch's insightful critique of totalization paired with the new ideas inherited from Lukács's Hegelian Marxism is at stake here. Bloch appropriated both the dialectics of history and the idea of *praxis* as the major constituents of utopian philosophy and the elements of its justification. However, he went further, and claimed that modern (expressionist) art also had performative powers capable of influencing the social reality.

Another common theme significant both for Bloch's philosophy of hope and for Lukács's literary criticism was the comparison of Goethe's *Faust* and Hegel's *Phenomenology of Spirit*, the two key texts dealing with the emerging historical consciousness of modernity. Decisive for my discussion is Faust's desire to become a representative of all mankind. Here, I argue, one can find a kind of revolutionary philosophy of history, with Faust as a utopian character who paves his way through the conflicts of historical life armed with Hegel's dialectical optimism. Other motifs invoked by Bloch (both in *The Principle of Hope* and in the *Tübingen Introduction to Philosophy*) are shared by Hegel and Goethe – including the dialectical journey, negativity and the critique of formalism – and also discussed as parts of an approach that merges literary imagery and philosophical argument. In addition, this approach also mimics Bloch's own philosophical strategy discussed in Chapter 1: to be a philosophical writer and to think poetically (*fabelnd denken*). In general, the chapter discusses the forms of justification that literary imagery gives to utopian philosophy: as a tragic performance, as a novelistic discourse of lost totality, and as a messianic, dialectical journey that embraces the whole of humanity.

Chapter 3 clarifies the contexts of the mystic and eschatological elements that influenced Bloch's thinking. It analyses how the ideas drawn from various religious traditions and the pathetic style of Bloch's early works were intertwined, subsequently considering some of the gnostic metaphors that inspired his early texts (the soul languishing in the iron cage of the material world, the new God to come, the radical negation of the existing order). They are further accompanied by apocalyptic ideas of the new kingdom that appears after the annihilation of the present world. I show that Bloch's eschatology was a part of the overall cultural landscape of his time and indeed was ubiquitous, both in expressionist literature and in philosophical treatises. I further place this work in the context of contemporary ideas common among the Jewish intellectuals of that time (Buber, Landauer, Rosenzweig, Scholem), such as the idea that God and the world have a common destiny, and that they depend on each other in the movement of world history. But Bloch's apocalyptic stance also had Christian origins that should be exposed as well. All in all, his philosophy, while dependent in many respects on Jewish and Christian traditions, still cannot be categorized under any of these labels, but rather reshapes them and goes beyond confessional and religious meanings.

Furthermore, this chapter prepares the ground for a discussion of Bloch and Benjamin. Messianism being the main focus of this discussion, at the end of the chapter I delineate paradoxes of messianic thinking. These include the problems of human action and responsibility that are blocked by the appearance of Messiah, the role of historical development in messianism, the uneasy relations between mystic and eschatological conceptions of time also present in Bloch's texts, and the notion of collectivity implied in a philosophy of the messianic kingdom. A number of difficulties arise, including the lack of moral grounding for eschatological philosophy, the intensely delicate balance of the present and the feeling of historical time, uncertainty concerning the time of the coming, and the ambiguous status of the subject welcoming the messianic moment (a soul in its unique individuality or a religious community in its joint devotional practice). These issues create a context of messianic philosophy advanced by both Bloch and Benjamin, and are illustrated through Bloch's own texts.

Messianic thinking was a key component of Bloch's project of utopian philosophy, but it was no less important for Walter Benjamin. Chapter 4 seeks to uncover the uneasy relationship between Bloch and Benjamin that combined friendship, mutual admiration and sometimes rivalry and jealousy.

After scrutinizing various biographical details I deal with Benjamin's *The Theological-Political Fragment* and discuss various affinities between his rejection of the linear teleological perspective on historical development and Bloch's metaphysics of instant. Against the background of 'Jewish' and 'Kantian' origins of Benjamin's intention to disavow a link between worldly events and the coming of the messianic kingdom, Bloch's appropriation of Kantian and neo-Kantian ideas appears to be very complex and differentiated.

This discussion helps specify in what sense we may consider utopian philosophy as teleology, as well as the role that teleology plays in the utopian discourse. It also brings to light the fatal inconsistency of Bloch's philosophical project: if Bloch and Benjamin (who explicitly stated his indebtedness to Bloch's *Spirit of Utopia* in the *Fragment*) believe that the Messiah cannot be borne by profane history and that His coming is fully unexpected and breaks any links with mundane life, then what is the meaning of utopian anticipation? What exactly is anticipated? Do we perhaps corrupt a utopian ideal by anticipating it? These are the questions here.

Other common themes in Bloch's and Benjamin's messianic theology – the anarchistic rejection of state power and the radical break with the authority of transcendence – complement the picture. Their common manner of looking into the depths of ordinary experience as well as their appreciation of montage and allegory are further emphasized. In this comparison, Bloch is shown to be closer to a more traditional Hegelian-Marxist style of thinking, with its utopian imagery serving as a system of signs that anticipates a future liberation. His criticism of both Benjamin and Adorno boils down to the alleged lack of real dialectical mediations and excessive aestheticism.

Bloch and Benjamin were secular mystics who found their inspiration in everyday life as well as in the simple objects that for them were materializations of both bourgeois culture and mythical powers. The main metaphorical underpinnings of their mystical prose were the ideas of imperceptible displacement necessary for establishing the messianic kingdom, the transmigration of souls and self-encounter in Bloch, and the concept of sudden awakening in Benjamin.

I also consider in detail their notions of the relationship between the past and the present. Bloch used the concept of non-contemporaneity for dealing with the actuality of the past, and Benjamin, in his theses *On the Concept of History*, deployed the concept of *Jetztzeit* (now-time) in a similar way. These similarities and differences are decisive in dealing with the paradoxical structures of messianism. Is the Messiah part of the present, or should He come at the end of history and constitute its consummation? What relationship does messianic philosophy maintain with the past? Is it able to avoid eternal repetition of mythical time? These are the questions we have to face if we want to come to terms with utopian philosophy of history.

The problem here is that the new vision of history is dependent upon this linear historicist (or Hegelian) account so heavily criticized by Rosenzweig and Scholem as well. Bloch and Benjamin seem to reject both mystical transcendence – for its incompatibility with their historical sense – and the Christian idea of gradual historical evolution. They were revolutionaries, and their Marxist inspiration added another component to their messianism. They inherited the idea of active participation in history from Lukács that is also difficult to reconcile with messianic waiting. Projectivity, active collaboration in order to achieve some social goals, and the construction of the very goals one may achieve are at odds with the transcendent nature of a messianic kingdom.

The final chapter traces the relationships between Bloch and Adorno and seeks to reinterpret the problems of utopian and messianic philosophy discussed thus far in the context of Adorno's critical thinking. Despite all political and philosophical divergences and sometimes harsh controversies, Adorno remained faithful to the utopian style of thought and to the general revolutionary appeal of Bloch's early writings. His review of the 1959 edition of *Traces* serves as a good starting point to reflect on the inner deficiencies of Bloch's utopian philosophy, as well as on Adorno's own philosophical doctrine.

Adorno criticizes the dialectical 'consumption' of utopian material in Bloch's texts, the idea that various experiences merely reflect a more general utopian goal. This totalization is considered inappropriate, and Adorno seeks to separate Bloch the poet from Bloch the systems-builder. I argue, however, that Adorno's own theory always verged on paradox and tried to escape the dichotomy between nihilism and a positive totalizing meta-narrative. Therefore, what really fascinated Adorno was Bloch's ability to find a deep meaning in the literary gesture of appearance (*Schein*), deceit and false utopia, a fake that nevertheless conveys a revolutionary message.

After this short overview, some methodological remarks are in order. Any historian of philosophy who is engaged in speculation would face two extreme options in his or her work.

The first would be to imitate the style of one's own 'hero' to the point in which the differences become indiscernible. Most often it is the case in which the tautology is not productive at all, but rather dull and sometimes repulsive.

The second option would be a detached analysis, putting together historical details and aiming at a complete and possibly faithful reconstruction. This narrative is most often equally repetitive and indigestible. The exceptions are rare and only prove the rule. Enthusiastic writers and more academically inclined scholars pretend both to produce something new *and* to provide an ingenious interpretation. If in this book I fail to find a third way, I hope to show, at least, why Bloch's philosophy still deserves attention, and will do this by both drawing on its contexts and engaging in a dialogue with utopian thinking.

And yet – could such a work nevertheless be considered a vain exercise mixing up learning, erudition and quotemanship, a redundant piece of prose retelling the texts written by someone who told us everything he wanted anyway? I would readily have similar doubts, were they not sometimes raised on behalf of a 'genuine', 'authentic' philosophical experience, an experience of sovereign and free thought, creativity, etc. – particular formulations depending on the tradition and intellectual horizons to which the critic belongs. But this position raises even more doubts with me. And the most apparent issue to be emphasized here is the absolute necessity to become familiar with the ideas of others – not just in order to come to grips with some problem, but to the end that this problem *could emerge at all*. It is commonplace to think that the problems haunting philosophers do not exist outside the space of philosophical traditions, classical texts and their interpretations. But this also implies that the reproaches of the type: 'All you argue is to be found already in Plato/Aristotle etc. etc.' are nonsense: *you never find in them anything like that,* and the limit case reminding of the decisive role played by the speaking from and out of a historical situation would be the notorious Pierre Menard, author of the *Quixote*, portrayed by Borges. Any philosophical effort, any undertaking is an interpretation of the already existing meanings, and it would be strange to assert that a 'real' philosopher does not need any upholders in the shape of references to previous texts and ideas. Even a genius never does without these noble crutches. Moreover, any simple action of ours or everyday event cannot occur outside the mediating domain of meanings and concepts, or philosophy, if you will. Concepts, words and meanings influence our life and become part of our destinies and our bodies, philosophy being a privileged way to navigate in this space.

Hence, a strict opposition of the 'true' philosophy and 'secondary' interpretations is most often misleading. It does not mean, however, that a useless erudition is oxymoronic. The question is, rather, of the successful hermeneutics: whether the constellation of meanings has been found, which could gain relevance for – and, hence, find a response in – our common forms of life and thought.

Populating the book with many philosophers I did not mean, however, to provide more or less comprehensive biographies. The aim was, rather, to give an account of some important ideas and discussions of which Bloch was a part. After all, as Paul Valéry noted in his letter on Mallarmé, 'rien toutefois dans l'examen de nos productions qui intéresse plus philosophiquement l'intellect et le doive plus exciter à l'analyse que cette modification progressive d'un esprit par l'œuvre d'un autre' (1957, p. 634).

In the times when the fragmentation and departmentalization in the *Geisteswissenschaften* has become comparable with that of the sciences and when, say, only Benjamin studies comprise hundreds of papers and monographs – it is extremely easy to disturb an expert. Be it as it may, I tried to achieve the most natural degree of extensiveness and detail, for any of the points could lead beyond the reasonable limits. The question of the endpoint turns into the problem of the context: what dimensions should its account possess to make the picture adequate to the epoch and ideas that are dealt with? One has to make recourse to one's own feeling dictated by the *time* in which one lives – this persistence within time is the only incontestable advantage of the author.

1
Ernst Bloch's Philosophical Prose

A brief intellectual biography

Unlike his childhood friend, Lukács, Bloch, though being a radical thinker, never radically changed his views.[1] Between his first and last major works there is a long path that could characterize the central events of European intellectual and political life. Bloch's life followed the rhythm of his philosophy: a systolic-diastolic movement of 'assembling' oneself and of the *explicatio* described by Nicholas of Cusa, the encyclopaedic unfolding of this thought and its realization in the farthest limits of the cultural and historical universe (Holz 1975, p. 103).

Bloch was born in Ludwigshafen in 1885. Despite this being distanced from philosophy, he communicated with the eminent thinkers Ernst Mach, Theodor Lipps, Eduard von Hartmann and Wilhelm Windelband (at that time it was possible to instigate dialogues with famous philosophers). Between 1905 and 1906 he studied philosophy under Lipps in Munich, where he met Max Scheler and other phenomenologists of the Munich school; he then continued his studies under Oswald Külpe in Würzburg in 1907–08 (where he also took physics and musical theory as minors), only to move to Berlin to Georg Simmel between 1908 and 1911 and to Heidelberg to Max Weber between 1912 and 1914.

Even though Bloch's dissertation *Critical Reflections on Heinrich Rickert and the Problem of the Modern Theory of Knowledge* (published in Ludwigshafen in 1909, partially reprinted in 1978: TL, pp. 55–107) was written within Simmel's circle, by the time of the first edition of *The Spirit of Utopia*, Bloch was criticizing his teacher for being too subjective and emotional, failing to grasp the rhythm of his subject, to find solid ground for his argument (GU1, pp. 246–7). Bloch was discontented with Simmel's relativism, he called him the maybe-thinker (in German it sounds quite derogatory – *Veilleichtsdenker*) and sarcastically said that relativism is too strict a characteristic for Simmel (PA, p. 57). Nevertheless, it was Simmel and Weber from whom Bloch had inherited an analysis of the crisis of contemporary culture, the conflict between the intellectuals and the new technical bourgeoisie, and a critique of a civilization powered by the onslaught of reason.

In his dissertation Bloch argued contra to the neo-Kantians that the historical process is not predetermined, emphasizing the role of exceptional personalities and great (unpredictable) events in history. Its final call is for a new metaphysics: one that 'not only forms the domain of inquiry for the general world-view, but also deepens the lived present down to the total knowledge, containing both the darkness of the first principle and the indication of the mystical outcome to which things should be led in their process' (Bloch 1909, p. 77; cited by Münster 1982, p. 50). These words express the essence of Bloch's lifelong philosophical project.

Like many intellectuals of his epoch, Bloch was deeply affected by the revolutionary events in Russia. During World War I he lived in exile in Switzerland, where he began research on the Swiss utopias and reform programmes for Weber's journal *Archiv für Sozialwissenschaft und Sozialpolitik*. In the 1920s Bloch went to Berlin, where he became acquainted with Bertolt Brecht, Alfred Döblin, Walter Benjamin and Theodor Adorno and became (together with Döblin and Brecht, as well as Johannes Becher, Max Brod, Robert Musil, Erwin Piscator, Ernst Toller and others) a member of the writers' *Group 1925*. He frequently left Berlin for Southern Europe and Africa.

When the Nazi came to power Bloch was deprived of his German citizenship due to his Jewish roots and anti-fascist views, only to leave for Switzerland in 1933, and after roaming around Europe in the meantime, emigrating to the United States in 1938. Before emigration he had published *The Spirit of Utopia* (1918, 2nd edition – 1923), *Thomas Müntzer as Theologian of Revolution* (1921), the collection of essays, stories and aphorisms *Traces* (1930), and the social-political and philosophical-ideological work *Heritage of Our Times* (1935).

Some of the titles themselves are quite telling. Bloch's first book – *The Spirit of Utopia* – refers both to Weber and Montesquieu. *Thomas Müntzer* was partially written as a pendant to Weber's famous work *The Protestant Ethic and the Spirit of Capitalism*. At the same time, Weber's idea of the interplay between religious and social-economic forms of thought and social organization is also realized in Bloch, but in a different way: as a connection between mystical atheism and proletarian revolution (Bolz 1987, p. 305).

Traces (Spuren) bears witness not only of Bloch's fascination with Karl May's adventure novels, whose heroes track wild animals and Indians, but also of the Latin word for hope – *spes* or *spero* (Weissberg 1992, p. 35). Bloch is, of course, concerned with the metaphysical traces, the traces of sudden insights and new ideas found in everyday life; traces that contain both a hint of a solution, a longing for a quest, and an uncertainty as to what this quest might lead to.

In the United States he wrote his *opus magnum* – three volumes entitled *The Principle of Hope* (published in 1954–59), a monograph *Subjekt-Objekt: Commentaries on Hegel* (1949) and a book *Natural Law and Human Dignity* (published in Bloch's complete works in 1961). After his return to the GDR in 1949, Bloch became a professor at the University of Leipzig, and then, after his emigration to West Germany in 1961, taught in Tübingen until his death in 1977. In 1959–78 the West German publisher *Suhrkamp* issued 17 volumes of his work.

Bloch's political views can be characterized as being broadly left/social-democratic; and always vehemently anti-fascist. When *The Principle of Hope* was published in 1959 in West Germany, it was perceived as opening a dialogue between the East and the West, while Bloch himself passed for the main philosopher of the GDR. Nevertheless Bloch had already come into conflict with the East German government by 1957. After the erection of the Berlin wall in 1961, he was forced to stay in West Germany, where publishers cautiously deleted his references to Stalin in *The Principle of Hope*. Bloch's radicalism and communist convictions were attractive to the revolutionary youth movements of the 1960s, when he continued his political and social work, engaging with Rudi Dutschke and writers from the *Group 47*.

As early as the late 1910s, readers were taken by Bloch's prophetic style – both in writing and in speech. Despite all his declared humanism, he was quite an authoritarian thinker. Even in his voice (retained on several recordings) there is something of a *Führer*, a strictness and uncompromising severity, which won the hearts of some, but frightened others (Weber among them).[2] It probably reflected a well-known propensity, which is characteristic of the relationship between intellectuals and power: a constant desire for inversion, the aspiration of intellectuals – even the most radical, those most distanced from conformism and opportunism – to take power, to gain authority, to subdue, mesmerize or lead the way. Admittedly, Bloch has also paid tribute to Soviet propaganda, glorifying the communist state in the 1940s and 1950s. But he became neither the official ideologist of the GDR, nor a dissident: he was forced to leave by those who – quite correctly – did not regard his views as wholly orthodox. The GDR for Bloch could not have become a country of 'realized' utopia, for the philosophy of hope compels one to never be satisfied with the current state of affairs and fight for freedom in every instant. Besides, Bloch was always a marginal figure – both with regard to orthodox Marxism and to the right, and even more to scientific streams of philosophy. It is both tragic and inevitable that Bloch and Lukács – the ones who imported a stream of revolutionary emancipation to philosophy – were forced out of the intellectual mainstream into the communist bloc.

An important factor in Bloch's intellectual evolution was *Expressionism*,[3] which defined both his aesthetic views and his literary style. Like the Expressionists, early Bloch was suspicious of nature and of the external world in general. One of the most representative expressionist poets, Georg Heym, in his anthology *The Eternal Day* (1911), describes nature as *Die Heimat der Toten* (*The Home of The Dead*) – a landscape is penetrated by images of death, the idyll is deliberately destroyed, replaced by images of chaos and decay – for instance, in the poems '*Der Baum*' (from *Umbra Vitae*) or '*Die Tote im Wasser*'. Bloch describes nature as a dungeon, a coffin, from which the soul is trying to escape in search of new revelations (GU2, p. 208). Nevertheless, both Heym and Gottfried Benn, despite their infinite contempt for bourgeois life, were much further away from Bloch than politically engaged 'left-wing' Expressionists (like early Becher and Toller). Bloch who openly aspired to be *the* philosopher of Expressionism, shared with Expressionists a conviction that it is necessary to completely destroy the modern world, for that is the only way to renew it.

Bloch's language is difficult, and at times deliberately enigmatic. Many passages require supplementary commentaries, and his literary style, like that of any other apocalyptic writer, does not really contribute to 'the clarity of philosophical distinctions' (Bulgakov 1993, p. 395). But when this philosophy unfolds – in aesthetics, in politics, in a dialogue with the contemporaries – it undoubtedly becomes clearer, as we begin to understand what constitutes its meaning and purpose. In *The Principle of Hope*, Bloch develops his philosophy of utopia and provides a compendium of utopian motives (in music, literature, religion and politics). Some authors even compare the structure of Bloch's magnum opus to *The Phenomenology of Spirit*: Bloch opens his work with a description of expectation and anticipation of the future, then (in the 2nd volume) political, religious and literary utopias are analysed, and towards the end of the book the idea of utopian philosophy is expounded with respect to the forms of the 'absolute spirit': in art, religion and philosophy (Widmer 1974). *The Tübingen Introduction in Philosophy* envisions a specific ontology *without being*, before being itself can be found – suggesting an ontology of the *Not-yet*. This is an attempt to reformulate dialectical materialism in the spirit of the *naturphilosophic* speculation of Bruno, Goethe and the German romanticists.

Bloch, the 'Marxist Schelling' (Habermas 1971), systematically laid out this project in his last book *Experimentum Mundi* (1975). By building a system of categories, he once again demonstrated that his thinking worked against the grain of systematic thought. Recalling the philosophical explorations of his youth, Bloch once cited his early passage:

> In systems . . . thoughts are like tin soldiers; one can set them up as one likes, but they will never win an empire. Our philosophy has always been suspended from grammatical hooks or from the systematic of exhausted old men; science takes the root of life, art raises it to a power, and philosophy? Our blood must become as the river, our flesh as the earth, our bones like the mountains, our brain like the clouds, our eye like the sun. (S, p. 70; T, p. 49)

Bloch was familiar with and quite receptive towards the old traditions of Western thought. He was deeply influenced by Aristotle and medieval Aristotelianism (in 1952 he published a book entitled *Avicenna and the Aristotelian Left*), Neoplatonism and the Jewish and Catholic mystics of the Middle Ages. Hegel's dialectic was an absolute authority to him, and from the very beginning the conceptual schemes of Eduard von Hartmann are evident in his work (Christen 1979, p. 170ff.).[4] Bloch even wrote several historical books, in which he tried to reinterpret the philosophy of the past, transforming it into his own schema. In particular, he investigated the development of materialist ideas (*The Problem of Materialism*, 1972) and Hegel's system (*Subjekt-Objekt*, 1949). Bloch actually did not consider his philosophy to be entirely original:

> All freedom movements are guided by utopian aspirations, and all Christians know them after their own fashion too . . . from the exodus and messianic parts of the Bible. In addition, the merging of have and have-not constituted by longing and hope, and by the drive to reach home again, has in any case been burrowing in great philosophy. Not only in Plato's Eros, but also in the far-reaching Aristotelian concept of matter . . . and in Leibniz's concept of tendency. Hope acts unmediatedly in the Kantian postulates of moral consciousness, it acts in a world-based, mediated way in Hegel's historical dialectic. (PH, p. 17; PHE, p. 7f.)

Bloch also suggested an anthropological interpretation of religion (*Atheism in Christianity*, 1968) thus anticipating contemporary discussions in radical theology and 'theology of action' (Munich 2008, see also Moltmann 1964).

One would fail to give a satisfactory characteristic of Bloch's philosophy without mentioning his special relationship with music rooted within the canon of Western aesthetics. Music most clearly expresses the transient nature of the 'fulfilled instant', which 'flowered . . . as sight, as clairvoyance, the visible world, and also God's traces in the visible world disintegrated' (GU2, p. 198; SU, p. 156). In music we rid ourselves of the visual images we are accustomed to in everyday life; sound opens to us the inner, pure part of the soul. Music is the most 'dynamic' of arts, it manifests the immediacy of the subjective experience, it carries out instantaneous transitions, one can both plunge into the abyss and soar towards the sky, even the most insignificant theme can become crucial. The immediacy of the perception of music conjures the Pythagorean harmony of the spheres, the horns of the Apocalypse and those who heed the Word, without seeing God. By no accident Bloch considers music the utopian medium *par excellence* that preserves duration, enables one to live from the inside out, which, in utopian terms, constitutes the inner restlessness of being (see further Vidal 2010, Korstvedt 2010).

The musical experience also defines the way in which Bloch cultivates the utmost sensitivity to the insignificant objects in *The Spirit of Utopia*. The coexistence with art, the attempt to see and hear things and sounds in their imperceptible, inconspicuous existence, leads him to try and find behind them the future utopian community and an encounter with oneself.

In the late writings the primary aesthetic category is no longer appearance (*Schein*), but anticipatory illumination (*Vor-Schein*), the search for real, latent possibilities of the world, a Faustian experiment. The objective content of art always refers to something undisclosed, transcending its own limits. This is precisely the meaning of allegory and other symbolic forms. It is not the artist, but the world itself that transcends its boundaries. The concept of anticipation in the late Bloch is an entirely immanent category, and this explains the necessity of an 'objective' utopian hermeneutics, where the act of artistic creation itself is rooted in the utopian drive – as one of the primary features of consciousness.

Bloch's philosophy combined insights of avant-garde art, creative Marxism and mystical gnosis, and the academic interest to it is by no means accidental. Most commentators agree that Bloch did not create an overreaching philosophical system, but nevertheless his style and the direction of his thought exerted a significant effect both on the outlook of his contemporaries (Lukács, Benjamin, Brecht, Adorno, Siegfried Kracauer) and the subsequent philosophical tradition. Bloch influenced Emmanuel Lévinas, while Herrmann Hesse, Eric Hobsbawm, Helmut Schelsky, Jean-François Lyotard, Fredric Jameson, Umberto Eco, Gianni Vattimo and even Joseph Ratzinger commented on his work on various occasions. Significant authors of the twentieth century like Thomas Mann, his son Klaus, as well as Erich Fromm and Henri Michaux were also careful readers of Bloch.

The key topics of Bloch's philosophy – theory and history of utopia, conception of non-contemporaneity, problems of humanistic Marxism, eschatological philosophy of history, atheistic conception of Christianity, rehabilitation of *Naturphilosophie*, new version of leftist aesthetics and politics – have become part of European culture in 'great time', to use Bakhtin's dictum. Bloch has been a standard reference figure for the scholars dealing with utopia as a fundamental concept in philosophy and social theory, the role of the Weimar Republic in the constitution of modernity, and the forms of German-Jewish intellectual interactions. In fact, Bloch was among the first in the twentieth century to give new meaning to the concept of utopia. Today his work is not just a reminder of a half-forgotten philosophical-theological or political discussion, but an outstanding landmark of its time – a monument, and yet, at the same time, a vivid philosophy.

Utopia as concept and form of life

As early as *The Spirit of Utopia* Bloch established the domain of his philosophical inquiry. One could speak of a certain intellectual intention, sometimes identified with certain real forms of consciousness – *a dialectically rendered drive towards the future*. The 'philosopher of the October revolution'[5] associates this intention with the 'concrete', becoming utopia, not one that is by definition unrealistic, but with actual possibility, one that yearns for realization. In his characterization of the 'concrete' utopia he refers to a famous definition of communism from *The German Ideology*: 'Communism is for us not a *state* of affairs which is to be established, an *ideal* to which reality [will] have to adjust itself. We call communism the *real* movement which abolishes the present state of things' (Marx 1998, p. 57).

Utopia is concrete because, unlike the 'abstract' one (which Bloch sometimes refers to as utopianism), it is rooted in objective reality, dialectically mediated by an external. Utopian thinking is not just a theory of the world, it is always already revolutionary: 'Revolutions realise the oldest hopes of mankind: for this very reason they imply, demand the ever more precise concretion of what is intended as the realm of freedom and of the unfinished journey towards it' (PH, p. 206; PHE, p. 188). Bloch often quoted Franz Baader:

> It is a basic prejudice of human beings to believe that what they call a future world is a thing created and completed for man, which exists without him like a ready built house which man only needs to enter, whereas instead that world is a building of which he is himself the architect, and which only arises through him. (PH, p. 923; PHE, p. 789)

This passage clearly shows the basic tenets of Bloch's thinking. Utopia underlies a creative human attitude towards the world, being thus a foundation of all culture. In *The Principle of Hope* Bloch develops an account of *utopian function* without either reducing or opposing utopia to ideology, as it was done by his contemporary Karl Mannheim. Utopia – as Bloch and his student Burghart Schmidt (1985, pp. 127–8) succinctly put it – is a 'ferment', which contains both a critical attitude towards the existing ideological constructs and institutions, and an image of the future world, indispensable to ethics or sociality. However, utopia always remains indefinite, resists schematization; it never puts any constraints on the search for new goals (Ueding 2009, p. 161), forever projecting into the future. By contrast, ideology is not just an established, a realized utopia, every ideology always has a utopian 'surplus', something above the *status quo*. Utopian consciousness is characterized by a particular 'melancholy of fulfilment' (PH, p. 348ff.), dissatisfaction even at the point where everything might have been achieved.

Bloch notes that metaphysics must be directed towards an *expectation* of utopia, a longing for utopia that, unrelated to determinate *content*, is driven by art. As a 'displaced prophetic gift' (GU2, p. 150; SU, p. 116), as a medium, a space between the empirical and the transcendent, art is an integral element of the apocalyptic project, a movement towards the liberation and redemption of humanity. This is the reason why both the artist and the spectator or reader can legitimately attempt to find their true selves there. Bloch's thinking, abundant with reoccurring tropes, appears as allegory, overgrown and spread out in every direction.

In *The Spirit of Utopia* neither nature nor society can aspire to become the space of liberation; utopia is foremost an event of the inner world (GU2, p. 201), collecting 'itself to accept every longing for God-likeness' and fulfilling it 'in the omega, as the alpha finally made good – without domination, with congregation, without this world, with the Kingdom' (GU2, p. 272; SU, p. 216). In Bloch's later work utopia became a dream of a better life, a call for social reform and an unalienated *natural* process, none reducible to technology. A teleological, speculative, qualitative, as opposed to quantitative vision of nature is the origin of Bloch's later utopian ideal – where labour, in the words of Benjamin's *Theses* on the philosophy of history, 'far from exploiting nature, is capable of delivering her of the creations which lie dormant in her womb as potentials' (IER, p. 259).

Nature in Bloch appears at the same time as an aesthetic phenomenon that needs to be deciphered by utopian hermeneutics. But the beauty of nature is possible because it reflects subject-object mediation, and not merely because of subjective or arbitrary judgement. The anticipatory illumination of being-as-utopia occurs not only in art, but also in nature, which is symbolic and requires interpretation. The working subject paves its way through history, but also animates nature, becoming a 'subject-nature' (*Natursubjekt*), the basis of vitality and dynamism (PH, p. 786).

This is how (deliberately making Hegelian overtones) Bloch describes nature, often calling it *matter*:

> Matter is a seething bosom of substance, that in the beginning somehow begets, that is – develops, illuminates and forms itself. What seethes, ferments is a subject of the matter, and a flower or a fruit emerging out of it on the dark and difficult way of the process is a substance of this subject. (M, p. 375)

Such a doctrine of nature echoes Marx's rendering (in *The Holy Family*) of Böhme and the Böhmean idea of a qualitative, intense, passionate drive of matter.

This is not to be understood in a sense that the human in Bloch is wholly defined by nature: he preserves the free creative act as a basis of human existence. Animals and plants, although being a part of nature, lack the ability to shape their future. Materialism in its primitive sense is meaningless for Bloch, he is rather a *realist* in the spirit of later Schelling (Christen 1979, p. 193f.). Devoid of the subject, the transition from the postulative, projective possibility to actual realization of utopia is impossible (Schiller 1991, p. 86).

Thus, the utopian consciousness in Bloch is concrete not only because it has to take into account the objective conditions and forms of being, but also because natural reality also exists in the utopian mode of dynamic anticipation and realization of new possibilities, breathing the air of a different world. As Novalis once said, 'a man never speaks alone, the universe speaks as well – the infinity of languages' (1999, p. 500). Utopia in Bloch is a chance of speaking, a capacity to utter amidst the dumb and dull landscape of ordinary life. It is an unfinished process of establishing a correspondence between subject and world, an intrusion of the utopian reality, which is *ethical* by nature, into the tautology of the mundane, a productive and active principle of human existence.

Metaphysics of the instant

To be able to hear and understand what the 'nature' or the unforeseen points in the decorations you conceived hint at. To be able to hear the whisper of the combined editing strips, of the shots, which, on the screen, live a plastic life of their own, at times extending far beyond the limits of the imagination that has begotten them – is a great blessing and a great art.

Sergei Eisenstein. Twelve Apostles.

Bloch's utopian messianism necessitates a particular metaphysics, different from that of the Greeks in that it sought not beginnings, but ends (Landmann 1982, p. 171f.); not foundations, but perspectives, formed out of the traces of everyday experiences (Ueding 2009, p. 42). After a phenomenological training, and having carefully studied Simmel, Bloch set out to reinterpret this experience and, in an attempt to avoid excessive abstraction, he discovered *the instant.*

The experience of the instant, or moment, is first of all the absence of any experience, for the essence of the instant lies in its darkness; it is transient and is experienced indirectly. The darkness of the lived instant is for Bloch an aspect of the existential human condition; thus it is an anthropological, and not just an epistemological, category; and its significance lies in the fact that the essential determination of an individual remains hidden both for herself and for those around her. Notably, in the later period, Bloch hesitates to label his philosophy as anthropology, deeming this to be an unjustified narrowing of the subject, *pars pro toto* (Landmann 1975, p. 182)

An individual does not have an organ to comprehend her own self, she remains within a blind spot of her own perception, running into what Sartre calls 'the prereflexive cogito' (Blumentritt 1999). The closer something is to us, the more opaque it is to our consciousness. This is both true in spatial terms – an eye cannot see itself – and, what is of particular interest, in terms of time: this concerns the numinous instant of *Now* (*Jetzt*), that which is continuously lived with us. 'But the now itself ultimately remains the most dark in which we each find ourselves as experiencing beings. The Now is the place where the immediate hearth of experience in general stands, stands in question' (PH, p. 312; PHE, p. 287). More so:

> the darkness of the just lived moment illustrates precisely this Not-Having-Itself of the realizing element. And it is in fact this still unattained aspect in the realizing element which primarily also overshadows the Here and Now of something

realized ... what is realized is brilliant and slightly in shadow at the same time, because in the realizing element itself there is something that has not yet realized itself. (PH, p. 221; PHE, p. 193)

The dark instants can form a long chain of abstract, repetitive, mundane moments of life (after all, time itself consists only of instances), accompanied by a vague feeling of estrangement – being alien to oneself. But the instant becomes an event, which produces a rupture in homogeneous time, in order to gain an affective meaning. Bloch combines the mystical sense of the instant as a falling out of time into eternity, the fullness of times: 'Not time but the moment as that in time which does not belong to it, communicates with eternity in which alone perfect joy has its measure' (PH, p. 1548; PHE, p. 1310), – and the idea of the *Now*-instant, imperceptible, dark, but comprising the true nature of time, for time is the way out of this darkness (EM, p. 104).

An instant is an event at the beginning of world history; it always started anew. In the *Tübingen Introduction*, Bloch conceives the temporal origin of the world not as genesis, or time before any time, but in actuality: in the time that is most immanent to the present, and closest to us (TE, p. 275).

The rupture of the event is marked by the corresponding individuation of objects. Darkness of the instant is perceived in the usually unapparent objectivity – due to its extreme proximity: 'the last other world is our nearest this-world, our most immanent nearness' (PH, p. 1534; PHE, p. 1298).

But what exactly constitutes this event, where can we discover it? Bloch often locates the instant as an experience of happiness one wants to prolong, like a sudden encounter, a feeling of recognition, a moment of revolutionary decision, *kairos*, a historical counterpoint. He particularly emphasizes the feeling of *wonder* before the transience of the instant: in the instant philosophical subjectivity is constituted, thus serving as a starting point of philosophical experience, like a lens gathering different rays: the ethics of the blessed, the good life, creative experience and an existential comprehension of time.

The metaphysical interpretation of the instant starts with the search for the substantial core of identity or the self, to which the will to witnessing, to being present, is attributed. The conditions and the texture of the instant turn into symbols showing the way towards the solution. It is to this solution that Bloch's philosophy is directed in its entirety: he strives to enter into this immediacy and to be commensurate to it – philosophically, politically and aesthetically. The torn pulse of these instants, intruding into time, underlies the duration and continuity in the flow of experience (PH, p. 339), which are artificially constructed by vitalists and philosophers of life. However, it is not the duration, but the rupture that turns out to be primary. The truth of utopia is understood from within the discontinuity of the instant.

When Bloch lacks conceptual resources, he readily employs literary imagery. In doing so he does not simply patch the holes of his argument, but advances a utopian metaphysics. Poetic language concentrates on and realizes the very experience of the instant that philosophy tries to elaborate, while showing its inconclusiveness and relativity, allowing one to rise above raw facts without abandoning the immanence of facticity.

For instance, Bloch is fascinated by the feeling of wonder that accompanies the instant of happiness. In *Traces* there is an extensive commentary on one of the scenes from Hamsun's novel *Pan*:

> "Just think! Now and then I see the blue fly. I know, it all sounds so paltry, I don't know if you can understand." "No, no, I understand." "All right! And now and then I see the grass, and maybe the grass sees me, too; what do I know? I look at a single grass blade; maybe it trembles a little, and it seems to me, that's something; and I think to myself: here this blade of grass stands and trembles! And there's a fir I observe, and maybe there's a twig on it that makes me think. But now and again I meet people on these heights, that happens . . ." "Oh, yes," she said, and stood up. The first drops of rain began to fall. "It's raining,", I said. "Yes, just think, it's raining," she said, too, and was on her way. (Chapter 9 of Hamsun's *Pan*, cit. in: S, p. 216; T, p. 169)

The image of the world full of mysteries, obscure and unstable, transforms in a symbol of eternal youth, of detached bewilderment, reviving the true metaphysics over and over again, striving to grasp the principal mystery of the universe. To a girl surprised by such ordinary things, the 'kernel of all questioning' (S, p. 216; T, p. 169) is suddenly revealed.

Such a deferential, quivering pantheism, in which Lieutenant Glahn lives for a while, confessing his eternal love to the being – in a totally childish fashion, ingenuously and sincerely plunging into this world, partaking in its creation – is unthinkable outside of literary experience. This feeling of surprise at the world is represented in literature as a fairy tale in which the experience of a miracle is an integral, constitutive element. Bloch's technique of philosophical writing (especially in *Traces*) is close to that form of oral narrative which is a familiar characteristic of the fairy-tale poetics. Bloch seeks to preserve the *immediacy* of the message (Weissberg 1992, p. 30) and along with it the situation of both incomprehensibility and incommensurability of the narrative, in the face of any demand for ultimate clarity.

By no accident he turns to Hugo von Hofmannsthal's *The Letter of Lord Chandos*, in which the fictional lord reports that he has lost the ability for literary expression, exquisitely arguing that he needs a new language – not Latin, not English, but that language in which mute objects speak, a language he could use in the world beyond (Hofmannsthal 2008, p. 528). The things that inspire Lord Chandos are plain and mundane – a dog in the sun, a neglected cemetery, a peasant's hut. But they become, as in Van Gogh's paintings, the locus of universality, the shining of eternity in the present.

Another text exemplary for the metaphysics of the instant is a Jewish anecdote that Bloch cites in *Traces* and Benjamin – in his article on Kafka:

> In a Hasidic village, so the story goes, Jews were sitting together in a shabby inn one Sabbath evening. They were all local people, with the exception of one person no one knew, a very poor, ragged man who was squatting in a dark corner at the back of the room. All sorts of things were discussed, and then it was suggested that everyone should tell what wish he would make if one were granted him. One man wanted money; another wished for a son-in-law; a third dreamed of a new

carpenter's bench; and so everyone spoke in turn. After they had finished, only the beggar in his dark corner was left. Reluctantly and hesitantly he answered the question. "I wish I were a powerful king reigning over a big country. Then, some night while I was asleep in my palace, an enemy would invade my country, and by dawn his horsemen would penetrate to my castle and meet with no resistance. Roused from my sleep, I wouldn't have time even to dress and I would have to flee in my shirt. Rushing over hill and dale and through forests day and night, I would finally arrive safely right here at the bench in this corner. This is my wish." The others exchanged uncomprehending glances. "And what good would this wish have done you?" someone asked. "I'd have a shirt," was the answer. (IER, p. 134f.; see also GS IV, p. 758f.)

Walter Benjamin was also fond of this story; he used it to show how time is distorted in the perception of Kafka's characters, how they shake off the burden of the past and commit to the future. Bloch has a different angle. The story of the beggar begins in the subjunctive mood like in Benjamin, but then moves into *praesens historicum* and from there – suddenly, in italics – into *praesens*. 'Ten days – to the border, where no one knows me, and I get across, to other people who know nothing of me, want nothing of me; I am saved, *and since last night I've sat here*' (S, p. 98f.; T, p. 72). The story is entitled *The Fall into the Now*; Bloch tries to show how in a simple anecdote, having noted this sudden incursion of the genuinely real, not merely in dreams, we can attain enlightenment; comprehend not only the entire unimaginable, unfathomable depth of the present, but also our true destiny, having felt at least a glimpse of it. The instant gives us a chance to penetrate into the depth of time, to comprehend its essence and to grasp the unsightly truths of our social being.

Bloch also establishes another way to understand the temporality of the instant – in the moments of *déjà vu* through an analysis of Ludwig Tieck's 1796 'Blond Eckbert' (*Bilder des Déjà vu*, in LA, pp. 232–42). When we suddenly realize that we have already seen what is being experienced now, the normal flow of time is disrupted and we sense the pure form of temporality and encounter the instant of our own non-identity with this temporality; what is constituted by the ordinary state of affairs and the usual flow of time dissipates.

Bloch goes beyond simply describing these instances, not limiting himself to their contemplation, to the immersion into life like Dilthey[6]; *he seeks to derive the dynamics of the world from their unobjectifiable nature*, while always emphasizing not the feeling itself, but the very nature of the experience. Happy moments are the abode of hope, the premonition of victory over death (Lévinas 1976), and in early Bloch, the end of the world.

> We and we alone, then, carry the spark of the end through the course. Only within time, after a thousand disruptions and obstructions, does what was meant from the beginning, always, what is present without being disclosed, force its way out. (GU2, p. 285; SU, p. 227)

Bloch conceptualizes the darkness of the instant as an element of social practice, as the possibility of hope coming true, as a way to witness the inner life of history and to actively partake in it. It is important in this context that the instant marks an encounter with the other, recognizing oneself in the other.[7] This is not merely to obsess with oneself and certainly not to decay moral guidelines; on the contrary – it is the route to their absolute discovery.

Moreover, history itself is unthinkable without the hermeneutics of the dark instant; only in trying to unravel the meaning of this 'blind spot', of this quantum of time can one comprehend the nature of historical occurrences. The instant becomes the *a priori* foundation of both action and perception. It becomes a home for creative expression, a yearning for meaning from within the heart of time and longing for its own actualization. However, the instant in Bloch is never considered in the context of a hermetically sealed, decadent subjectivity (Czajka 2006, p. 322f.); it is always open, the experience of the instant is a point of genesis, of the numerous voices calling one another, of allegories, of recognizing different faces, of the world's inner restlessness.

The symbols of the instant are first revealed on the individual level only, in the ordinary, and only then do they acquire a collective significance. When a clown in a circus is asked his name, suddenly an abyss of uncertainty opens before him, the darkness of human existence that has not yet found itself. He freezes, he is paralysed, because suddenly it becomes clear to him that he *does not know* his own name (S, pp. 119–21). At this moment he has fallen out of his usual context; the force that suspends him, a sharp feeling of metaphysical instability of oneself, of society and of the whole world is followed by a conscious change of one's life, enacted from within history; this is the aim of Bloch's philosophical prose.

One cannot really discern an instant of true historical significance unless one's attitude to history remains solely contemplative and passive. Historical instants are bound to the *conscious revolutionary practice* and can only be understood as a part of it. And even though the phenomenology of the dark instant is subordinate to the individual experience, in *The Spirit of Utopia* the question of the subject that stands behind each of these experiences is posed not just in terms of the singular individual and the core of her subjectivity, but also as a problem of the coming community, the 'We-problem'. However, the correspondence between the purely inner experience and its external consequences and objectifications – in other words, between the human self and the world of intersubjectivity – was from the very beginning a point of tension and remained so in Bloch's philosophy of history, to which we shall return.

The metaphysics of the instant is a particular way to ground utopia. It is as if Bloch anticipated the critique, coming among others from Karl Popper who claimed that the utopian consciousness inevitably sacrifices the present for the sake of the future. But how can one sacrifice anything without understanding what one has, without comprehending it entirely? Bloch insists that the experience of the instant cannot be objectified, that we can only *post factum* reflect upon it, when it is no longer authentic. At the same time, how could we *feel* the unity, the completeness of the absolute in the experience of the instant, if its full realization is postponed into the future? Bloch's whole philosophy is devoted to the articulation of this paradox, it *is* this articulation. He insists that any experience is incomplete, that the absolute experience is always ahead, and all that is left to us is a hint, a trace of something that can never be registered, possessed or 'adequately' conceived as a whole. This glimmer of the apparent becomes for him a special 'technique of the self', for it gives the thought an impulse, guides us in the search for our own inner life. But where does this search lead us?

Philosophy of subjectivity and the shape of the inconstruable question

In *The Spirit of Utopia* Bloch quotes Kierkegaard, then Meister Eckhart, Böhme and Kant (GU1, pp. 368–9), finding in each an urge to turn inwards, 'to understand oneself in existence' (GU2, pp. 227, 235; SU, pp. 180, 186). This search allows us to identify a saving light within each human being, and reject the idea of human nature as inherently evil. A turn inwards is *differentia specifica* of any mystical philosophy. Looking at the world, as if in a mirror, the subject sees his own future there, and starts recognizing human features in the universe (GU2, p. 48).

Probably the most appropriate example comes from the opening of the book, where Bloch simply describes an old pitcher:

> It is hard to find out what it looks like inside the dark, spacious belly of these pitchers. One would no doubt like to occupy that space here. The endless, curious children's question arises again. For the pitcher is close kin to the child-like. . . . [W]hoever looks long enough at the pitcher soon begins to carry its colour and form with him. Not every puddle I step in makes me grey; not every railroad track bends me around a corner. But I could probably be formed like the pitcher, see myself as something brown, something peculiarly organic, some Nordic amphora, and not just mimetically or simply empathetically, but so that I thus become for my part richer, more present, cultivated further toward myself by this artefact that participates in me. . . . Everything that was ever made in this way, out of love and necessity, leads a life of its own, leads into a strange, new territory, and returns with us formed as we could not be in life, adorned with a certain, however weak sign, the seal of our self. Here, too, one feels oneself looking down a long, sunlit corridor with a door at the far end, as in a work of art. (GU2, p. 19; SU, p. 8f.)

The objects in their immanence and simplicity lead me not to the world, but to myself. They symbolize the utopian totality and the world of fulfilled dreams. Bloch's hero discerns the 'seal of our self' that marks the objects, and sets out to find one's own secret essence. In *The Spirit of Utopia*, Bloch compares this essence with a hand that guides a glove, representing empirical human existence. Bloch enigmatically adds that the glove can also be taken off (GU2, p. 310). From here stems the constant reappearance of *the self-encounter* in *The Spirit of Utopia* and the subtitle of the last part of the book (*'Karl Marx, Death and the Apocalypse'*) – *The Ways in This World by Which the Inward Can Become Outward and the Outward Like the Inward*. Invoking the inner space of the soul, Bloch seeks to open it for the encounter with itself, with one's own undisclosed contours that prefigure messianic redemption (GU1, p. 331f.). In the same fashion, an artist must transcend his enclosed and self-sufficient world through finding and expressing 'the inner image' (GU1, p. 44).

The young Bloch concentrates on this peculiar 'reality of the soul', taking the notions of subject and subjectivity seriously. The reality of the soul in *The Spirit of Utopia* possesses an absolute significance, for only through it can utopia be grasped and actualized. This reality is ethical and axiological – it is precisely within the realm of the moral that individual experience becomes clearly articulated, and in this sudden apparentness, evidence flares up illuminating the darkness of the lived instant. This turn to subjectivity was conceived as an alternative to positivism and determinism with its logic of facticity (Pauen 1992a, 1997). Whatever is really significant is significant for us, this is 'the second truth' of inwardness that has to be grasped in all its existential and political aspects.

Bloch describes the path that utopia follows as 'the preparation of the inner word, without which every gaze outward remains empty, instead of being the magnet, the force that draws forth the inner word and helps it break through the falseness of this world'. Then, supplementing this 'vertical' movement with the horizontal, he proclaims:

> Only in us does this light still burn, and we are beginning a fantastic journey toward it, a journey toward the interpretation of our waking dream, toward the implementation of the central concept of utopia. To find it, to find the right thing, for which it is worthy to live, to be organized, and to have time: that is why we go, why we cut new, metaphysically constitutive paths, summon what is not, build into the blue, and build ourselves into the blue, and there seek the true, the real, where the merely factual disappears – *incipit vita nova*. (GU2, p. 13; SU, p. 3)

The origin of the world, the first realization of a volitional impulse remains unexplained. For Bloch to ask why there is something rather than nothing is to pose an 'inconstruable question'.

> Certainly the question how one imagines bliss is so far from forbidden that it is basically the only one permitted. Meanwhile even this question, trying to brighten the twilight, already aims frivolously at something named, accustomed, already commits us to a weak, restrictive word. (GU2, p. 347; SU, p. 196)

To pose the absolute question without constructing it is, for Bloch, to utter it in its purest form, to express it.

> [O]nly one thing is ultimately left for precise, ontic discussion: to grasp the question about us, purely as question and not as the construed indication of an available solution, *the stated but unconstrued question existing in itself*, in order to grasp its pure statement in itself as the first answer to oneself, as the most faithful, undiverted fixation of the We-problem. (GU2, p. 249; SU, p. 197f.)

The problem of the origin of the world is for Bloch (especially in the later work) the most important mystery, the solution to which can only be the world itself, as well as its literary and philosophical interpretations. At the same time, in *The Spirit of Utopia*, questioning itself acquires a special existential tension, or 'existential pathos' (GU2, p. 250; SU, p. 198), and the rational construction of the question is rejected not only because it is defined as dependent on existence (like in Kierkegaard), but also because it contradicts the concealed, fluctuating nature of this questioning. Truth unfolds in a particular situation, in the experience of an existential presence. Bloch poses a question about questioning itself, to ask: where does this necessity to learn new things come from, this dissatisfaction with the known, this inescapable yearning? He postulates the feeling of wonder as its basis – 'the question which is not really posing the question and which already contains an answer' (Lévinas 1993, p. 117).

The experience of surprise helps us feel the openness, incompleteness that are the essential features of the world, while maintaining a critical, endlessly toilsome distance with respect to all possible forms of questioning and to all possible answers that can be given. It is precisely this experience that defines the image, the shape, the *Gestalt* of the inconstruable question (Schmidt 1985, p. 47). It enables us to pose this question in one way or another, even though by definition it cannot be posed. And, once again, questioning appears not as a sterile 'pure' experience, free of historical hue – it is always a questioning from inside the historical situation.

The experience of surprise and of immersion into oneself gives rise to the cultural forms that help the self to interact with the world, to plunge into a game of reflection and reconfiguration of meaning, directed towards utopian longing (Czajka 2006, pp. 330–1). The transient signs that mark the self-encounter, illuminating the darkness of the lived instant, and a hint at the unravelling of the final mystery of the utopian self, all this is qualified as 'symbolic intentions' (Wołkowicz 1985, p. 23).

But what is the subject standing behind the metaphysics of the instant? A *flaneur*, the one who hunts the present, or an extremely focused individual, who aspires – on Goethe's advice – to concentrate all of her abilities and mental capacities? The aim of Bloch's utopian subject is to develop a *sensitive intuition for the new*, the ability to become truly carried away by something that appears insignificant, making it significant for oneself and for others. It is the enthusiasm of the unknown, which finds in temporal dissonance and discord a source of inspiration, life, joy and mysterious light. In this absolute immanence, in close proximity, or, as Francis Ponge would have put it, 'siding with things', we grasp the mystery of the human.

The dynamics of the inner life – the core of the self – is 'exterritorial' to death (PH, p. 1385), for it has not yet entered into the process, it totally lacks completeness, and thus lacks the final completion, the absolute end that is associated with the fate of mortal beings. If this unclear basis within the individual is not yet involved in human becoming, then it is simply removed beyond the limits of finitude. If one assumes that it has embarked onto this path, then its end is the absence of process, and together with it – of frailty and of death. The mystery of subjectivity is beyond the ordinary logic of emergence and destruction. It is in this sense that Epicurus's analysis of death becomes relevant: when death *is*, the human being is *not*; for the subject – the true basis of its being, a certain existential 'core' – does not exist *yet* (PH, pp. 1384–91; Christen 1979, p. 168).

In later work Bloch pays tribute to the Marxist line in defining the human as a 'totality of utopian relations' (AC, p. 284). The utopian search for the self is grounded in the ontology of 'Not-Yet-Being'.

Not, Not-yet/being/conscious

Bloch's later utopian project is to build the philosophical system he envisaged in his youth, when the 'System of theoretical messianism' was being conceived. Utopian philosophy required certain simple, yet basic foundations; these are what Bloch's ontology is about.

The engagement with philosophy, following Bloch's final texts, is based on a certain lack that he calls *hunger*. It is not a feeling of devastation and absurdity (as in French existentialism), but a sense of dissatisfaction with the present. In *Traces* Bloch talks about a certain impulse of self-determination, and in *The Tübingen Introduction in Philosophy* he puts at the centre of the human world and perception – in a way similar to the German philosophical anthropology of Gehlen and Plessner – a drive forward, which Bloch calls Not (*Nicht*). Contrasted with Freud's *libido*, hunger is the fundamental instinct, 'the elemental energy of hope' (Habermas 1985, p. 61). Such bodily experience appears not just as some fundamental physical constant, but also as a spiritual hunger: the primordial impulse towards knowledge, an urge towards self-realization. Such an approach renders the abstract metaphysical notions anthropologically concrete.

Not is different from Nothing (*Nichts*) in its substantiveness and productivity, in that it is a beginning of every motion, while Nothing does not contain the negation of negation. It stays a futile, empty negativity. 'The Not is lack of Something and also escape from this lack; thus it is a driving towards what is missing. Thus the driving in living things is depicted with Not: as drive, need, striving and primarily as hunger' (PH, p. 356; PHE, p. 306. See also: SO, p. 515).

It is straightforward to see behind the formulation not only the productive Nothing (*Urgrund*) of Böhme and Schelling, who regard matter as both the 'passive recipient principle' and as an element that actively transforms and outgrows itself (Christen 1979, p. 170), but also the Hegelian dialectical scheme of being and nothingness from *The Science of Logic*. Not is an expression of lack (hunger, need) which has to be alleviated. In *Experimentum Mundi* Bloch writes that *Not* should be understood 'as a moving *That (Daß)* . . . striving towards its *What (Was)*, to utter itself and to define, predicate itself more and more' (EM, pp. 69–70). Bloch redraws any conceivable image of the world, throwing any such image into the Not-Yet-Being. Not-yet is not just a certain subjective flaw (lack of some personal qualities, knowledge or resources), but an objective property of an incomplete world, which correlates to subjective dissatisfaction. '*S* is not yet *P*' – such is the formula of Bloch's ontology and anthropological logic, irreducible to the traditional law of identity. The process of identification is described in a Hegelian fashion – as a process of constant transition, a creation of new meaning, but not a formal-logical identification.

In the '*S* is not yet *P*' formula, *S* refers to the potential – the hungry longing that simultaneously is a primordial basis of the world. But what does *P* stand for? The young Bloch answers in the spirit of eschatology and messianism: envisaged is 'the unavoidable end of this world, along with all its books, churches, and systems' (GU2, p. 249; SU, p. 197). The world is a process of redemption, a process at the end of which there is the regaining of identity, the coming of the Messiah, whom Bloch expects among the absolutely sinful, collapsing world (GU2, p. 254). The messianic kingdom is described as a community of free people, liberated from alienation and as matter – the dynamic absolute.

'Ye shall be as gods' – such is the slogan of the coming atheist kingdom of freedom. Bloch takes a radical step dating back biographically to his first clumsy act of rebellion: at his Bar Mitzvah he whispered 'I am atheist', misspelling the word that was familiar to him only from books, in a German manner (*a-tai-ist*). This later became a subversive philosophy of religion equating atheism and Christianity: 'Only a good atheist can be a good Christian, and only a Christian can be a good atheist' (AC, p. 15). And it is not just a Christian world view but also generally a messianic world view that is deemed impossible without atheism (PH, p. 1413). Interestingly, similar thoughts are now actively discussed in contemporary thought. For instance, in a recent volume Slavoj Žižek quotes Jean-Luc Nancy: 'Only an atheism which envisages the reality of its Christian provenance can be relevant today' (Žižek and Milbank 2009, p. 287). Bloch proclaims '*transcending without any heavenly transcendence*' (PH, p. 1522; PHE, p. 1288), freed from the petrifaction and fetishization of the eternal Absolute, rejecting (especially in the later writings) the postulate of God as a person (which neither Böhme nor Schelling dared),[8] but at the same time proposing to take full advantage of religious ideas and meanings. For the very notion of religion is interpreted as hope, as anticipation of unalienated being-together.

Moved by the force of existence (in the mode of *That*), the imperfect being strives to realize its essence (in the mode of *What*).

> Originating in the striving and the hunger of Not, that cannot tolerate it in itself and thus moves to its expressions, the intentions in the subject and the tendencies in the object, superordinate towards each other, may be in mutual correspondence – the utopian function in man and the latency in the world, the unexhausted Ahead (*Voraus*) in man and a utopia-containing latency in the world. (EM, p. 66f.)

Within a stream of materialism, tendency is 'the energy of matter in action', and the 'latency' is a potentiality of the matter (M, p. 469). A conjunction of subjective urges and objective tendencies occurs in the cardinal instant of correspondence (PH, p. 141), when previously unclear and immature ideas gain shape and measure.

The world is contradictory, otherwise it would have been pre-established, a view explicitly rejected by Bloch. Different tendencies grapple with one another. To embrace them means to surrender everything to chance, which can lead to a disaster. That is why Bloch insists on the significance of the *subjective* factor, human intervention into the order of the world. It is important to realize that laws are also subject to change and that this variability stems from the agent's ability to transform the world, from the inevitability and unpredictability of creative forces. The laws of the world cannot be an object of passive contemplation and compliance, they must be appropriated, used and transformed, as in an alchemical laboratory – where the spiritual mood of the alchemist determines whether he can discover the philosopher's stone, or in a monastic cell, where the inner face of the iconographer is more important than both the image and the canon of his practice.

In the apocalyptic and prophetic discourse in *The Spirit of Utopia* the anthropological factor is most forcefully proclaimed:

> Only the good, anamnestic person holding a key can draw forth the morning from this night of annihilation: if those who stayed impure do not weaken him, and if his call to the Messiah is illuminated enough to rouse the saving hands, to secure the grace of arrival for himself, to awaken the inspiring, gracious powers of the Sabbath kingdom, consequently to engulf and immediately to vanquish the brutal, satanically dispiriting flashpoint of the Apocalypse. (GU2, p. 339; SU, p. 273)

In *The Principle of Hope* the powers of redemption are assigned to nature, to matter. The Absolute is the not-yet-revealed 'core' of the matter. However, Bloch is not a pantheist, since the absolute identification of God and the world has not yet occurred; moreover – there is no anticipation of something *definite*, for Bloch's ontology is the ontology of total instability, and every utopian dream complicates this picture. The world does not move according to some pre-established idea, which has to be uncovered and revealed, and in this sense such notions as 'realization of utopian possibilities' are misleading (Zyber 2007, p. 154), since we do not yet know what exactly we need to realize. This dynamic does not allow dreams to become frozen and thus it can claim to solve the problem posed by Simmel in the beginning of the twentieth century – the problem of petrifaction and fetishization of cultural forms, of their alienation from the living creative activity that has given birth to these forms.

Thus, Bloch attempts to construct *the ontology of the Not-Yet-Being*. Its object is 'the world in which utopian imagination has a correlate' (PH, p. 224; PHE, p. 195). The will to utopia acquires its objective content in the actual tendencies of the material being, in the life of things (S, p. 175), in social struggle and revolution. The epistemological significance of such an ontology consists in the claim that the gaps, the blind spots, the questions arising in our perception are not only due to the limited nature of our abilities, they are rather an inherent feature of the world itself.

In an attempt to conceptualize this dynamic world Bloch introduces such notions as *Front, Novum* and *Ultimum. Front* is 'the most advanced segment of time, in which we exist, living and acting'; the actual *Now* of the utopian process, 'which is the Now of a certain Not that breaks free from itself and presses forward' (TE, p. 227), the edge of our actual existence. *Front* is located in the here and now, in the lived instant, it is the point at which the present meets the future; it introduces an element of *fundamental uncertainty* into the concept of human action, thus grounding 'the essence of the world' (TE, p. 275) and with it the truth of time. *Front* is also the point of decision, it has a certain affinity to *kairos* (Siebers 2012) and requires a particular intensity of attention, an active readiness and vigilance on our part.

Novum is a feature of the relationship between the present and the utopia, it refers to the radically, the truly productive new which is not, however, something entirely sudden, a culture gets prepared for it in some sense, it is embedded in tradition. Successful culture points to the future, hence Bloch calls for a project of utopian hermeneutics, proposing the *interpretation* of utopian signs of inconclusiveness.

Ultimum, All (Alles) or *homeland (Heimat)* is the aim of the utopian movement, latently contained within the present so that its glimmering can be discerned here and now. It is a kingdom, about which we can only surely say that it has not come yet and deems the world to come incomparable to our present one; for the very basis of being, the 'core' of the matter first lays this world down and then transcends it. '[I]n reality the All is itself nothing but identity of man who has come to himself with his world successfully achieved for him' (PH, p. 364; PHE, p. 313).

Bloch advances a project in natural philosophy too. The key issue here is the possibility of a subject-nature, 'the selfhood of the material' (M, p. 465). The presence of such a subject is postulated in an implicit form, existing in the germ, in unconscious subjectivity. Bloch characterizes 'the subjective factor' in dialectics:

> In the pre- or extra-human world (nature), in a less developed and conscious form it is what was thought of as *Natura naturans*. Dialectics exists only on the basis of this subjective moving force, this dominant movement with all its vicissitudes; it presents itself only as a subject-object relationship in the world, with the subject as object, with the object as subject in the end as a utopian vision. The most powerful subject and the key to the whole *Natura naturans* is – a human being. (TE, p. 266)

Like Baader, Bloch believes that the notion of freedom also has significance in terms of natural philosophy. A true transformation of the human being can only take place given the release of nature's productive forces, which is in turn impossible in the world of alienation and exploitation. Ontological as well as aesthetic constructs acquire an *ethical* dimension (Schmidt 1985, pp. 14, 101): hope obliges to transform the *status quo*, while Not-Yet-Being or Being-projected points to how and where one can go to find a new, better world. Utopian hermeneutics clearly moves beyond a humble understanding, but becomes the appropriation of meanings, their reinterpretation for purposes of utopian philosophy and practical enterprise.

Bloch's ontology also contains the notion of *possibility*, in which he distinguishes between the actual conditions of realization of utopian aspirations and these aspirations themselves (PH, p. 238). Thus, there are two aspects to the possibility:

> a reverse side as it were, on which the measures of the *respectively* Possible are written, and a front side on which the Totum of the *finally* Possible indicates that it is still open. In fact, the first side . . . teaches conduct on the path to the goal, whereas the second side . . . fundamentally prevents partial attainments on this path from being taken for the whole goal and from obscuring it. (PH, p. 237; PHE, p. 206)

The two sides of 'possibility' correspond to the 'warm' and 'cold' currents of Marxism, which will be elaborated upon later.

The ontology of the *Not-Yet-Being* is augmented by the theory of the *Not-Yet-Consciously-Known/Realized* (*das Noch-Nicht-Bewusste*). Bloch argues contra Freud that the dark, the opaque domain of consciousness, is not the sphere of the repressed and forgotten past, but, on the contrary, of hopes and dreams, of the not-yet-realized future (Gekle 1986; Wurth 1986).[9] This idea occurred to Bloch, as he himself recounted, when he was 22; a sudden revelation that subsequently became a fundamental intuition. In fact, he viewed his entire project as directed at the explication of this thought and at opening the *Not-Yet-Conscious*. As opposed to Freud's subjectivism and his unconditional acceptance of the reality principle, Bloch links the *Not-Yet-Conscious* to the *Not-Yet-Come-to-Be*, to coming reality – whether natural or social.

Not every dream or fantasy, however, is a productive anticipation of the future. Dreams can be arbitrary, banal or plain destructive, sitting outside the utopian prefiguring of the good. It is, however, crucial to realize that at some point the subjective and the objective may coincide, that my lonely voice may suddenly be streamed with utopian sentiments. When this community might come is not yet known – it depends both on our actions and on the evolution of the material world.

The *Not-Yet-Conscious* finds its authentic expression in art, which is always ahead of its time pointing at the utopian horizons. Daydreams of the *Not-Yet-Come-to-Be*, fantasies, premonitions comprise for Bloch the starting point, the first and the simplest form of creativity.

> Not everything that helps develop the object remains idealistic, in the sense of unreal. Rather, the most important element of reality might comply with it – the not yet lived possibility. In such a manner meaningful poetry makes the world become aware of an accelerated flow of action, an elucidated waking dream of the essential. . . . Therefore, the correlate of the world to the poetically appropriate action is precisely the tendency. To the poetically appropriate waking dream it is precisely the latency of existence. (*Marxism and Poetry*. In: LE, p. 117)

Western Marxism (originating, roughly, with Lukács) became the system of thought that provided utopian philosophy with its language and method, something Bloch willingly accepted and self-consciously advanced.

Re-energizing Marx: Bloch's social philosophy

Bloch not only favoured Marxism, but perceived himself as a Marxist (Fahrenbach 1986). Whether his texts conform to the classic Marxist canon is a separate question and will not be discussed here at length. One issue, however, is obvious: Bloch was engaged in leftist movements and social-democratic political projects, but he was not really a successor or an interpreter of Marxist philosophy. His primary motive was undoubtedly ethical, combining Marxist revolutionary pathos with a utopian appeal for renewal, for a rejection of eternal recurrence, tautologies of bourgeois life, the mythical nature of positivist rationality (that which Adorno and Horkheimer attempted to unmask) and naïve scientism.

Bloch regards the 'utopian function' of being as a product of social relations. Any dream, any project, any outline of the future is conditioned by the objective tendencies of the epoch, is embedded in social history. Bloch would never give up his Marxism as articulated in *The Principle of Hope* (PH, pp. 555–6). For instance, arguing against George Sorel's activism and virtually in unison with Marx in the latter's attitude towards French socialism, Bloch writes ironically that the author of *Reflections on Violence* needs a storm, needs thunder and lightning, not electricity or power lines; he needs a spontaneous impulse, not a bureau or political programme (PH, pp. 1108–9). This later view reveals a contradiction of utopian thinking, present as early as *The Spirit of Utopia*, in its ambiguous relation towards science and technology. A German conservative sociologist Helmut Schelsky (1979, p. 69ff.) in his extensive critique turns these reproaches of Sorel into arguments against Bloch himself, claiming that, first, Bloch did not understand the strict distinction between the ethical domain of values and the domain of economic and social technology in Sorel; and, second, that what Bloch himself proposed was an unmediated, arbitrary and subjective vision. Schelsky based his critique almost exclusively on *The Principle of Hope*. However, what deserves attention in his otherwise politically charged and grouchy discussion is that he excludes (although admitting the importance of) Bloch's existentialist and aesthetic views, and the contradiction between Bloch's later Marxism and his early subjective, anti-dialectical pathos – a contradiction to which I shall return elsewhere.

Bloch had already become known as a political essayist by the end of the 1910s. But his main work in social philosophy (if one could apply that term to a collection of notes and essays) is *Heritage of Our Times* (1935), a book in which he introduces the notion of *non-contemporaneity*.

The immediate context for this was formed by the success of Nazi ideology, which attracted not only Bloch's attention but was also of primary concern for Benjamin, Lukács, George Bataille and subsequently Hannah Arendt, Adorno and many others. Like Benjamin, Bloch clearly understood the danger of fascism as early as 1924, at the time of Hitler's trial, and its ability to rouse passions among the youth (Vogt 1985). Bloch employs a Marxist approach to the concept of non-contemporaneity (sometimes translated as non-synchronicity) as the unevenness of social-historical evolution, showing that social contradictions are not necessarily of class origin, not necessarily tied to economic class antagonism. He analyses the lives of social strata that seemingly live in the present, but in reality inhabit the past. Examples of these include romantically minded daydreaming youth, the people who want nothing to do with the present; peasantry, immersed in its traditional lifestyle that has not changed for decades; petty bourgeoisie, office clerks, disappointed with their everyday lives, who while having lost immediate contact with the production process, strive to return to the past and yearn for legend.

Through all of these holes and gaps of desire bursts the energy of mass myths. Unlike France and England, Germany had failed to completely adopt the new capitalist forms of social life. Non-contemporaneous elements of this life conflict with the dominant form of production. They, however, cannot be homogenized just by 'elevating' them into a 'simultaneous', 'progressive' culture – they are in principle 'heterogeneous', to use Bataille's (1985) dichotomy. Despite being contemporaries, bumping into each other on their everyday journey to work, people live in different temporal modes.

The so-called non-contemporaneous contradictions in capitalist society are accompanied by and interact with the 'contemporaneous' – objective contradictions, immanent to these formations. And capitalism deploys non-simultaneous elements to nip in the bud the upcoming sprouts of the future. Moreover, fascists use them, to gain popularity by means of nationalist rhetoric and appeal to the archetypes of the past. 'Both hell and heaven, berserkers and theology, have been surrendered without a fight to the forces of reaction' (EZ, p. 66f., HT, p. 60). Ideas of the *Third Reich*, of blood, soil, *Volk, Führer* and the like must be *integrated into the socialist ideology*, they should not be rejected out of hand (as many communists did). On the contrary, they must be reconquered from the hands of fascists, 'to win the energies of intoxication for the revolution' (OWS, p. 236). Peasants, craftsmen, workers and the dissatisfied petty bourgeoisie must enter into an alliance to overcome rightist radicalism. Anti-bourgeois, mythical energy can form the basis of a new bright world, or it can (as had actually happened) degenerate into barbarism. However, one should not surrender Marxism to a false sobriety, depriving it of fantasy, myth and the elemental force of imagination. Bloch relates this tendency to a young romantic who dreams of becoming a poet but is forced by an uncompromising father to go into commerce (LA, p. 130).

Bloch himself tried to instil this active, romantic, mythical principle in socialism, ending up in an inevitably paradoxical situation, quite accurately described by Adorno (1991): while criticising the entanglement of the natural order, eternal recurrence and the inescapable captivity of the mythological consciousness, Bloch himself *depends upon this consciousness*, for precisely this myth, this natural yearning, the dark Dionysian force and the Will are constitutive for his project of utopian philosophy.

Note that in 1935, Bloch looked with hope to the East, believing, with a mixture of naivety and misjudged strategy, that the Bolshevik cultural policy was going in the right direction and that the organic, chthonic elements of the social community were aligned to *the correct* ideological course.

Bloch's ideological credentials clearly served as one of the inspirations for Adorno and Horkheimer's *Dialectic of Enlightenment*. Thomas Mann (1968), another of Bloch's active supporters, in the article entitled *Culture and Socialism* contended that the ideological task was to unite Marx and Hölderlin. The theory of non-contemporaneity became employed in numerous unusual forms. In particular, Reinhart Koselleck (1979) adopted it in his project of conceptual history. For Koselleck, a concept is the simultaneity of the non-simultaneous, a sublimated merging of different practices, both the ones that the concept refers to here and now, and the obsolete, the archaic. This undifferentiated whole is precisely what enables the concept to be what it is.

A characteristic feature of Bloch's political philosophy, which became apparent in the debates with Lukács on Expressionism, was the imperative to study and to include into the ideological construction elements of the archaic doctrines, but also of modernist aesthetics and the avant-garde.[10] This imperative is partly responsible for Bloch's tendency towards a philosophical synthesis as well as his passion for Jewish messianism. Moreover, both rhetorically and intellectually Bloch's pre-1914 views, his attempts to contact the circle of Stefan George, could be reconciled quite well with right-wing conservatism. In an interview quoted by Pauen (1992, p. 44) he admits that before 1911 he was trying to bring together Marx and Nietzsche in a vision of a spiritual aristocracy. In a 1915 letter to Lukács, who inspired him with his early notion of castes so pathetically invoked in his dialogue *On Poverty of Spirit* (1912), Bloch recalls his previous Prussian ideals (Br I, p. 164), and in the first edition of *The Spirit of Utopia* talks about the genius of the German nation (GU1, p. 303). Thus, it is possible to see the later Bloch criticizing what he knew well, his own aristocratic impulses. However,

Bloch soon realized that the 'conservative revolution' is a dead end and that romantic ideals without any social critique, lacking the vaccine of heterodoxy, can easily be reformulated to serve the *status quo,* that the erratically transformative, diffusive logic of myth puts an unsuspecting, blissfully ignorant humanity to sleep.

Another factor that played an important role in Bloch's shift to the left was Lukács's enthusiasm with and finally initiation into Marxism. Of course, Bloch did not conduct an economic analysis in the manner of Marx and Rosa Luxemburg (to whose memory he devoted his last book). For him it was, again, crucial to not lose spontaneity in reacting to the current political situation; a profound and a repeatedly mediated economic analysis would be a serious distraction. Bloch particularly underscores a genuine influence that the key elements of the 'superstructure' exert on the 'base'. In *The Spirit of Utopia* he notes that Marxism as a critique of political economy moves towards a critique of pure reason, for which the critique of practical reason has not yet been written (GU1, p. 407f.).

Marxism was initially seen by Bloch as a programme of human liberation from the bondage of material production, a liberation that prepares one for a higher goal. Later Bloch regarded his philosophy of the future as a complement to the critique of the present. Along with the question 'What can I know?' one must also ask oneself 'What must I do?'. Not that Marxism was a theory and now must be supplemented with practice. What is relevant is a dialectical interaction between the moral postulates regulating the aims or projects of the future, and the critique of the actual conditions of social action constraining it here and now. Such visions of the world to come are experimental prototypes, and not pre-established recipes or static pictures of future life; and the realization of these prototypes, of course, has an impact on the prototypes themselves.

It is precisely in this context that the difference between the 'warm' and the 'cold' streams of Marxism is introduced (PH, p. 235). The qualification of 'warmness' may seem strange, but in fact it is a recurring trope in Bloch's writings (cf. S, p. 65). 'Warm' is vivid, unalienated, flexible and in a sense unfinished, amenable to transformation. While the 'cold stream' is primarily preoccupied with the objective tendencies of social development, 'warm' dreams of its *aims.* Bloch resonates with the Russian religious thinker Sergei Bulgakov who claimed in 1910:

> In socialism one should distinguish between the "aim", or the ideal, and the movement, the practice. The latter is the subject of the scientific political economy and of realistic social policy; the former belongs to the sphere of beliefs and hopes of religious character (in a broad sense). (1993, p. 423f.)

As a matter of fact, 'cold stream' Marxism is historical materialism, that is, a scientific analysis of historically specific forms of production and culture or ideology. Bloch wanted to be a 'warm' Marxist and proposed to reverse the famous scheme of Engels in *The Development of Socialism from Utopia to Science,* posing a question in a different manner: from science to utopia, to the naturalization of the human and humanization of nature. This amounted to the discovery of a practical and ethical dimension in Marxism (see for example: AC, pp. 349–50), while turning the rationalization and disenchantment, described by Weber, into *prophecy* (Bolz 1984). First we are led by an affect – surprise, shock, hope – and without this Marxism is unthinkable, but then we mediate our utopian search by the analysis of particular situations. Bloch's social and political thought is formulated like a reproach to the guilty conscience of pragmatically minded engineers, engaged in the current social planning and *Realpolitik*, while having long lost the ability to 'shift gears', to abstract themselves from everyday tasks.

Of course, Bloch's Marxism evolved significantly. The main reason for these changes was the impression that *History and Class Consciousness* made on him, to which I shall return. In *The Spirit of Utopia* Bloch treats Marxism with restraint: a communist state for him is something at best preliminary, a step on the way to a complete overcoming of the external organization and regulation of life, on the way to the liberation of souls and to the new congregation. Marx himself was just one of the prophets, whose teaching must be thoroughly revised, disregarding the orthodox bureaucratic rhetoric and remembering that Marxism is and remains a theology, and only in the second place – an economic theory (DW, p. 35). Lacking theology, like lacking a dwarf hidden behind the chess-playing puppet, historical materialism cannot win its most important game – this metaphor borrowed from Benjamin can be used *mutatis mutandis* to describe Bloch's philosophical situation. Capitalist hell, soul, sin, Messiah, redemption – only this conceptual imagery makes a true revolution possible.

In *The Spirit of Utopia,* a way outside is a way inside, while banal Marxist atheism has nothing to offer to a human soul (GU2, pp. 303–7), and thus the socialist project becomes subordinate to a gnostic one (Lellouche 2008, p. 41f.). Later his position becomes quite different:

> Marxism, above all, was first to bring a concept of knowledge into the world which no longer essentially refers to Becomeness, but to the tendency of what is coming up; thus for the first time it brings future within our theoretical and practical grasp. (PH, p. 160; PHE, p. 141. On the humanistic meaning of Marxism, see: PH, p. 1607.)

Marxism thus stands for the philosophy of the future of action and the constitution of a new subjectivity. George Steiner (1978) is exactly right when he writes that Bloch gives Marxism a new style, combining the will to liberation with the symbolism of a literary tradition, in which Odysseus, Prometheus or Faust become no less important than proletariat and bourgeoisie.

Marxist politics had to be mediated by theology *and* by aesthetic reflection. For Bloch politics and art always stayed so tightly interdependent that he saw no point in separating them. Moreover, an aesthetic gesture helped one take a punch in politics – in a literary image the whole metaphysics of the instant was concentrated, conferring a sensory appearance and a certain ostensiveness to political principles. Bloch's philosophical effort could even be described as a political articulation of aesthetic intensity, of a creative search for oneself. This moved him when he was writing the anti-war *Spirit of Utopia,* in which art (painting, architecture) goes beyond purely technical goals, encapsulating the world and amending or even overcoming it (GU1, p. 49). Brecht's criticism that *Heritage of Our Time* has an essayistic, liberal style was refuted by Bloch, who claimed that no scientific treatise would define contemporaneity (Wizisla 1990, quoted in: Czajka 2006, p. 56). Still, this combination in later, systematic works was subordinated to an even more general synthesis, having become a part of a giant manuscript, in which the author depicted (or found) the writings of utopia.

A brief excursus: Bloch and Heidegger

The existential pathos of Bloch's early texts, his sensitivity towards the everyday, the 'ready-to-hand' (*Zuhandenheit*), allow one to draw parallels with the work of Martin Heidegger.

According to Gert Ueding's (2009, p. 19) recollection, after the war Bloch met Heidegger only once in Tübingen, but there was no philosophical discussion. They talked about Johann Peter Hebel (an Alemannic writer, whom they both held in high regard) and Hölderlin (on Bloch and Hebel see a recent illuminating analysis in Siebers 2011).

The intellectual points of contact are evident: both were concerned with the experience of authenticity, with the phenomenology of the intimate (Riedel 1997). Both regarded the reflection on the instant and surprise as central to the process of philosophy (Safranski 1999). Bloch's critique of the alienated technical civilization could be taken to be in accord with Heidegger's philosophy of history from the 1940s to the 1960s.

However, Bloch has always been critical (even if, at times, quite unjustly) of his younger contemporary, only to prove how important Marxism was to his doctrine of utopia. Bloch considered the being of the 'fundamental ontology' to be static and devoid of historical change, of the dynamic of Not-Yet-Being; and existentialism as a whole as being divorced from social praxis, degenerative and obsessed with its own morbid, gloomy subjectivity. He saw in Heidegger a certain strange desperation, a monotonous and narrow preoccupation and an unequivocal critique of the everyday, an inability from within the desperation and the thrownness to find one's own place in history and the audacity to act (PH, p. 118f.; EZ, pp. 302–11; Becker 2003, pp. 207–11). Bloch always contrasted the pessimism of existential thrownness with the optimism of being in the mode of awaiting and anticipation; the fear, the *Sorge*, the despair, the 'survival' (Schmidt 1985, p. 26) are counterposed to the active transformation of the world; the forgetfulness of being is opposed to its lack of accomplishment.

For the sake of justice one has to admit that there is a place for existential horror in 'the unbearable moment' (PH, p. 350ff., PHE, p. 301ff.) in Bloch's writings, although he does not ascribe to these affects a special significance.

While Heidegger, following Novalis, conceived of philosophy as a perpetual urge to be at home everywhere, for Bloch the true aim of metaphysics is not going home, but a movement towards that home, which we have never seen and never tasted, towards the promised land. The unfrocked Marxist Nikolai Berdyaev closely followed the new tendencies in European philosophy – both the right and the left – and wrote, in agreement with Bloch: 'The atheism . . . of Heidegger's philosophy consists in that, for it the *care* and the modernity of being are insurmountable' (1995, p. 266).

Bloch does not think of history, of thrownness, of *Sorge* as something that has befallen and forever accompanied us. One has to find the way out in a particular historical situation, *hic et nunc*, with the understanding that we are the ones who hold the keys to the future. As Heidegger writes in *Being and Time*:

> In the wish Dasein projects its Being upon possibilities which not only have not been taken hold of in concern, but whose fulfilment has not even been pondered over and expected. On the contrary, in the mode of mere wishing, the ascendancy of Being-ahead-of-oneself brings with it a lack of understanding for the factical possibilities. . . . Wishing is an existential modification of projecting oneself understandingly, when such self-projection has fallen forfeit to thrownness and just keeps *hankering* after possibilities. (1962, p. 239f.)[11]

– Bloch sarcastically notes that this critique of immature anticipating sounds like a eunuch accusing the infant Hercules of impotence! (PH, p. 164f.; PHE, p. 145)

Similarly Bloch rejects Heidegger's tendency to 'mystify' Hegel and Hölderlin (Fetscher 1965). Heidegger regards Hegel's thought as an unsuccessful attempt to 'question Being', while Bloch sees in Hegel a bourgeois enthusiasm, anticipation of the world, to which human history, at the risk of losing it, aspires. He accuses Heidegger of failing to grasp dialectics and historicity. Unsurprisingly, Bloch stresses the significance of the French revolution for Hölderlin, which is suppressed in Heidegger (PA, p. 307), just as Rousseau's influence is concealed (Lacoue-Labarthe 2002). Bloch's half-words correspond to those of Heidegger.

In general Heidegger's philosophy is appraised only as an evidence of universal alienation, which permeated the life of the bourgeoisie of the 1920s (cf. Lukács 1973; Goldmann 1973; Münster 1986). Likewise, Bloch could not agree with the interpretation of historical materialism in the *Letter on 'Humanism'* ('The essence of materialism is concealed in the essence of technology. . . . Technology is in its essence a destiny within the history of being and of the truth of being, a truth that lies in oblivion' (Heidegger 1998, p. 259)). Bloch was a proponent of technology, unalienated from true human needs, based on the harmonic coexistence of man and nature, on the overcoming of the abstract attitude of man and technology (PH, pp. 807–17). A contemporary Marxist view on the problem of technology (alluding unambiguously to Heidegger) is well expressed in Badiou:

> The meditations, calculations and diatribes about technology, widespread though they are, are nonetheless uniformly ridiculous . . . all this pathos . . . [is] spun only from reactionary nostalgia. . . . Not enough technology, technology that is still very rudimentary – that is the real situation: the reign of Capital bridles and simplifies technology whose "virtualities" are infinite. (Badiou 1999, p. 53f.)

Badiou almost verbatim repeats Bloch's ideas, that technology will only then uncover its true potential when the society liberates it from coercion and exploitation (PH, p. 770ff.).

Again, this simple landscape should be relativized since, first, Heidegger himself in *The Question Concerning Technology* left room for the potentiality of technology; and, second, what Heidegger criticized was in fact the exploitation of nature, which makes him much closer to Marxists than it could at first appear. Interestingly, Heidegger in this text is driven by Hölderlin's famous dictum that 'where danger grows/the saving power also'. His point is that technology puts us on the brink of our being, with its enhancement we run the risk of total annihilation, but that is what gives us a historical chance. This way of dealing with the philosophy of history will be discussed below, suffice to say that the Heideggerian vigilance comes unusually close to the form of life advocated by Bloch.

Today it is clear that Bloch and Heidegger represented different moments in more or less the same philosophical movement. Some interesting parallels between the two can be found in Becker (2003, pp. 295, 306) who shows that Husserl, Heidegger and Bloch saw time as the form of constituting meaning, and the essence of time as enabling self-disclosure, the 'performance' of being. But whereas Husserl concentrated on the constitution of meaning through intentionality, the working of consciousness, and Heidegger deprived the disclosure of being of any anthropological or social and historical specificity, considering time as a condition of the openness of *Dasein* and being towards each other, Bloch becomes, for Becker, an intermediary between the two – a philosopher of culture, who specifies the existence of meaning, always evasive and requiring clarification, unfolding it while recognizing the temporal element of its constitution.

On the (im)possibilities of utopian philosophy

Who was Bloch? Today Bloch scholars include not only philosophers, cultural theorists, sociologists, political scientists, but also literary critics. Any utopian discourse needs a literary effort to depict and grasp it as an open and dynamic universe and to connect this quivering whole with the world of ordinary things and meanings. Their movement illuminates the darkness and the unclarity of *That*, the dynamic basis of the world. Philosophy becomes not simply a reflection of the world, but a *praxis* of liberation; its medium is a prophetic discourse of a philosopher uncovering the cosmic 'latencies'. Bloch goes so far as to say that Marxist anthropology is impossible without Marxist cosmology.

Marxism as a movement towards socialism and humanization of nature, together with dialectics as an 'algebra of revolution' (Herzen), became a part of an overwhelming utopian project. Its final aim being the creation of the communist 'kingdom of freedom' where no alienation is possible, and where nature and technology are humanized (nature, as in Schelling, becoming more and more 'conscious'), freed from the rigid capitalist forms and violence. This movement is aided by *hope* (the positive affect of the anticipation of new possibilities), which, like utopia itself is grounded on the ontology of the *Not-Yet-Being* and interpreted as the ultimate foundation of cultural change and the driving force of all world religions.

Why does hope turn out to be the central affect, the locus of utopian truth? Bloch is hostile towards 'subjectivist' theories, he takes hope to be the very affect that links subjective aspirations with objective tendencies, directing a human being not just to his future psychological state, but to a future world as well. Moreover, hope is important not only in the mode of dreaming, but in the realm of active revolutionary transformations, which are impossible without hope.

The essence of *homo sperans* is inherently incomplete, it is always in the process of becoming, conditioned by the future that is never fully predictable. While a mere illusion would just strengthen the *status quo*, the more conscious the hope the more powerful it is. In hope, intuition and reason recognize each other, and all the conflicts between the individual and the social vanish. What distinguishes Bloch from many other subjectivist, spiritualist ontologies is that hope focuses on progressive self-consciousness and revolutionary social practice. All the incredible complexity of the world, its enigmatic shape, does not stop Bloch's hero; rather, it provokes his activity. In the philosophy of hope, ideas and meanings – like rhythm, colour or taste – permeate the world, and their influence is real, however mediated. The world itself hopes, it lacks certainty (complete certainty, like complete mistrust, excludes the possibility of hope). It is in the essence of hope that one can fail, like Christ failed – a rebel who tried to oppose the stable, complacent and self-sufficient world with love and to suggest a new way (PH, p. 1490). This uncertainty, the possibility that we all cheerfully and joyfully advance towards an abyss, 'saves' Bloch's doctrine from a straightforward and a primitive interpretation, in which subject and object would schematically move to the absolute aim, exchanging tendencies and expectations.

Critical thinking is embedded in the very core of Bloch's utopian construction, which at the same time does not pretend to know the future or to normatively judge it – it merely uncovers it as Not-Yet-Being. Crucially, the realization of possibilities in Bloch is by no means a teleological process, it is not a germination of seeds that already contain the project of the future – if only in a contracted form. *The project itself has not yet taken shape, the structural logic of becoming has not been revealed, is not ready yet, that is why the development can end nowhere, and can fail.* Indeed, in history we move between an absolute 'In Vain' and an absolute Absolute (*Überhaupt*, GU2, p. 338; SU, p. 272). In other words, the system has no plan, no invariant whole, no centre, from which it would unfold and to which this unfolding would be reducible.

The very possibility of a certain moral affecting, discussed in Bloch's early *oeuvre*, of understatements and loose ends of reality, which we must feel from within the present, – all this is conditioned by something external, *objective*: the future world of our premonitions and aspirations glimmering in their apparent being and thus giving life to utopian consciousness. Therefore Bloch's later evolution towards a philosophy of nature is not accidental. However, his early texts contain a convincing idea of delving into oneself and of self-encounter, an idea of self-determining subjectivity. Later this instant of free self-determination becomes muffled, dissolves in speculation and is only preserved by the references to the Shellingian notion of nature-subject and to Hegelian dialectics, without, however, reproducing the systemic ambitions and constructs of German idealism. We can only confront these inconsistencies by appealing to the 'third realm' of culture and social institutions where human creativity and hope are effective and at the same time wholly objective, where the subject-object distinction is never absolute.

The end, the highest good, the *All*, the Whole, *Ultimum*, Identity, Omega, Kingdom, homeland, that is the aim; the future which is in focus of utopian consciousness can be conceived only as something perfect, but Bloch insists that the global process is incessantly moving forward. But what will this utopian goal actually be – the eternal now or the same state of insatiable utopian longing? Some interpreters

(Holz 1975, p. 24) believe that the final state which we are all waiting for will have nothing in common with tranquillity and 'nirvana'. On the contrary, the aim of the utopian movement represents its maximum intensity. But what might this end look like, a land where only the new, only the everlasting spring is permitted, free from alienation, dismal statics and dark myths? Would this absolute aim of utopian longing perhaps be an absolute stasis, shrivelling up time to snap historical narrative? After all, this is what Bloch envisages when talking of the absolute presence where all contradictions have faded away (SO, p. 453). The symbol of utopian homeland remains ambivalent, it invariably escapes the final fixation.

How can one combine the openness of historical process and the rejection of teleology with the notion of the end of history? How can one explain that the ultimate state cannot be conceived as a *state*? And how can one conceive it at all, if we consider it essential for the thought process to fix certain definitions, ensuring at least a logical non-contradiction? Even the language itself, based on a variety of conceptual *distinctions*, can hardly digest the complete *identity* defended by Bloch. Hence, there is not much to say about this identity, it has not yet acquired its complete definition. Bloch's thinking is constantly glimmering, dashing around – as though recalling Friedrich Schlegel's philosophical *esprit* – between denying the system altogether and realizing that the system is indispensable, between the necessity and the impossibility of the absolute utterance. Adorno (1991) once gave a succinct account of Bloch's philosophical style; he described it as groping, alien to conceptual grasping, as an experimental exegesis of the world, which emerges only on the borders of a rational, systematic thinking in its traditional sense. Such thinking is fragile, for its object is unstable and uncertain.

The criteria that Bloch deploys to judge various philosophical systems, religious and ethical notions of the past, politics and art, could be perhaps applied to his own philosophy. What would be left resembles something unaccomplished and inconclusive, a kind of draft that longs for a whole. Stuttering, its irregular rhythm reveals the attempt to uncover the images of utopia, but not utopia itself, for the whole evades us, it has not yet come about for itself as well (Jameson 1974, p. 158f.).

Utopia only specifies the direction, there is no detailed account of the utopian aim in Bloch. Thus, Michael Löwy (2008) points out that *The Principle of Hope*, a book devoted entirely to the future and written in an anticipatory mood, contains very little material on the future itself. The future is not addressed in any precise way, we hardly learn anything about it. Indeed, what Bloch deals with is rather the past (see also Marzocchi 2008), and even in what has already happened, we look for what is not yet.

However, the exhibits in the collection of hopes and aspirations must be described in a certain way, even if the only things left are their openness and incompleteness. Only this can historicize the utopian and mediate it with our reality. One cannot literally enter the picture, merge with an image, like characters of *Traces* do (S, p. 155), but this does not mean that the image does not affect our real existence. We must observe, anticipate and listen to the life of the future. On the other hand, this anticipation is not reduced and cannot be reduced to an objective positive knowledge, it cannot correspond to the known only. The epistemological status of Bloch's categories prompts one to treat them as hypotheses, for which only the future can show whether they were really fruitful.

In his youth Bloch was fascinated by the mystical experience of the instant and has built his philosophy of utopia on the basis of the self's urge to illuminate the darkness of this subjective mystery. His epistemological strategy in *The Spirit of Utopia* is oriented towards an expressive knowledge of a communicative-practical kind, towards a revelation that unfastens subjectivity into the world and enables one to recognize oneself in others, to grasp the ethical clarity inherent in the emotion of community (Simons 1983, p. 80). The existential pathos of *The Spirit of Utopia* and the perpetual inconclusiveness of *Traces* are complemented by broad historical material and acquire new dialectical foundations in Bloch's social philosophy, with utopia as a centre of historical dynamics, as an essence of the revolutionary practice and of the movement towards socialism. Hence, the perpetual movement can be interpreted not as a vicious infinity, but as a presence of multiple possibilities of social development at any instant, as a productive indeterminacy. Bloch embarks on a risky venture, trying to complement the experience of the avant-garde with a system of categories that simultaneously revolve around the humanistic ideals of socialism and Marxism.

On the one hand, Bloch rejected the authority of the transcendent, unable to accept a notion of a petrified, static Absolute – his work strives with heretical revolutionary spirit, to pull the heavens down to earth. On the other hand (in his debates with Lukács) he criticized the immanent nature of art, demonstrating that 'aesthetic' fetishism also leads to a mortal rigidity and tautology, but this time in a stagnancy of the mundane. This critique was based, of course, on a kind of synthetic world view, and Bloch placed it above the distinct forms of intellectual efforts – be it art, religion or philosophy. However, his dependence on the artistic, religious and philosophical traditions – both stylistic and substantial – is clear, and below we shall try to describe it in more detail. Moreover, this feature will play a crucial role hereafter.

The Principle of Hope ends with an open statement:

> *True genesis is not at the beginning, but at the end,* and it starts to begin only when society and existence become radical, i.e. grasp their roots. But the root of history is the working, creating human being who reshapes and overhauls the given facts. Once he has grasped himself and established what is his, without expropriation and alienation, in real democracy, there arises in the world something which shines into the childhood of all and in which no one has yet been: homeland. (PH, p. 1628; PHE, p. 1375f.)

This text, among other things, reveals a genuine Blochian gesture I have discussed above: to become the leftist Heidegger; to return home, but without, as Novalis had it in *Faith and Love*, conservative elitism and uniforms. It is, however, not a simple reversal, and the problems associated with it, especially those arising in the philosophy of history, will be dealt with below.

How was the utopian philosophy constructed? Bloch was constantly searching for new plots and characters to assemble and cut together various situations and meanings; to have argued, persuaded, becoming disappointed, being remarkably sensitive to history, to the new styles in art and to emerging cultural forms. But amidst all the heroes of this utopian narrative, the ones who played the main part were his friends. It was their questions, their admiration and contempt, their indifference and delight, and finally, their thought that defined the fate of his philosophy, and it is this that can inspire something new and give meaning to its – at times dusty, rumpled, thumbed – metaphorics.

Notes

1. Moreover, at times he appeared to his contemporaries as too stubborn and uncompromising. See for example: Scholem 1975b, p. 103.
2. Jürgen Habermas (1971, p. 164) also maintained that Bloch's philosophy borders on totalitarian thinking.
3. As it is put by Theodor Adorno, 'Giving primacy to expression rather than signification, concerned not only that words interpret concepts but also that concepts reveal the meanings of words, Bloch's philosophy is the philosophy of Expressionism'. (1991, p. 210). However, in an earlier work, Adorno asserts that Expressionism is a rejection of going deeper into oneself, a pure outcry, directed from within oneself, against the world (1992, pp. 257–9). Such a characteristic is not particularly congenial to the tone and mood of Bloch's main expressionist book – *The Spirit of Utopia* – which is centred on the encounter with oneself. And in general Adorno's evaluative statement, which neither takes account of Bloch's context nor makes any more precise qualifications, as was later shown by Ujma (1995, pp. 234–5) and Czajka (2006, p. 101ff.), has simply led to confusion, and the subject of stylistic relation between Bloch and the Expressionists has not yet been sufficiently illuminated.
4. Bloch, however, did not accept Hartmann's pessimism and irrationalism (Eduard von Hartmanns Weltprozeß, in PA, pp. 197–203).
5. This is the label coined by Negt in his afterword to the volume of Bloch's political writings *Vom Hasard zur Katastrophe* (1972). However, Bloch's attitude towards this revolution was by no means simple or straightforward, especially in the light of his almost anarchical views, proclaimed in *The Spirit of Utopia* (GU2, pp. 299–302), and political articles of those years, where Lenin appears as 'the red tsar' and 'the new Genghis Khan' (Franz 1985, pp. 239–73).
6. '[T]he stream of time in the strict sense cannot be experienced. The presence of the past replaces for us the immediate experience. Wishing to observe the time, we destroy it by this observation, for in the observation time is fixed, grasped by attention; the observation freezes the current, the becoming. We only experience the changes of what has just been, while also experiencing the fact that these changes of the just-have-been continue. But we do not experience the stream as such. We experience a state, coming back to what we have just seen or heard' (Dilthey 1992, p. 195) See also: Schiller 1991, p. 57. Similar ideas can be found in James, in descriptive psychology of the Würzburg (Külpe) and Munich (Lipps) schools, they also play a certain role in Husserl (Pelletier 2009, p. 256).
7. Anna Czajka, pointing to the important aesthetical tradition of understanding *anagnorisis*, discovery (in Aristotle's *Poetics*, 1452a–55a), writes of the musical examples of such instances in Bloch (2006, pp. 238–40).
8. See Christen 1979, p. 169f. Christen notes that the rejection of personal will of God, who decides to create the world (as in Böhme), and of a certain divine incarnation prior to the creation of the world (as in Schelling), forces Bloch to ascribe anthropomorphic characters to the impersonal, super-personal matter.

9 Wurth convincingly shows that Bloch's accusations against Freud are not sound, for not every gaze directed towards the past is reactionary.
10 Bloch was not the only one who tried to save the philosophical heritage of the nineteenth century from the appropriation by Nazi ideology. Herbert Marcuse (1934, 1941), for instance, defended Hegel and warned against the inadequate Nazi interpretation of the philosophy of life.
11 Bloch for rhetorical reasons omits an important passage: 'When the world has been primarily projected as a wish-world, Being-in-the-world has lost itself inertly in what is at its disposal; but it has done so in such a way that, in the light of what is wished for, that which is at its disposal . . . is never enough' (Heidegger 1962, p. 239).

2
Heidelberg's Apostles: Bloch Reading Lukács Reading Bloch

For several years, Bloch was a close friend of György Lukács (1885–1971), a Hungarian-German philosopher and politically engaged literary critic, one of the towering figures in the history of Western Marxism. Their mutual influence was, intellectually and existentially, enormous. They met in 1910 in Berlin at Simmel's colloquium (according to other sources in Budapest), and in 1911 they were already plotting a joint philosophical system (Münster 1982, pp. 63–5, 75–8) in which Bloch was to be responsible for music, and Lukács for the fine arts. It was a project that never materialized (according to Bloch's recollection, it was him and not Lukács who initiated this project (TL, p. 373)).

Bloch had an important part in Lukács's break with Neo-Kantianism, drawing his attention to Hegel. Lukács later recalled that before he met Bloch he could never understand how one could do philosophy in the 'classical' sense while remaining contemporary. Perhaps it was this encounter that finally persuaded Lukács to become a philosopher.

Jewish messianism and gnosticism, Dostoyevsky and Kierkegaard – subjects of which Bloch, avowedly, learnt from Lukács (Tagträume, pp. 104–6; Interview, p. 37) – were arousing their common fascination. We shall discuss Dostoyevsky later, but Kierkegaard brought out the central issue that defined the philosophical agenda in the 1910s and 1920s, not only for Lukács and Bloch. The German-Jewish religious thinker Franz Rosenzweig (1887–1929) developed his philosophy arguing against the Hegelian system, opposing to it an experience of finite existence absorbed by the desperate search for ultimate meanings. Theodor Adorno devoted his first major work to Kierkegaard, despite substituting critique for admiration. Lukács wrote an essay on Kierkegaard that was included in the collection *Soul and Form* (1911). Undoubtedly, Karl Barth's dialectical theology also originates in Kierkegaard. In 1930, Benjamin wrote in his notes on the philosophy of history and the work of the historian: 'Such mindfulness (*Eingedenken*, also translated as remembrance – I. B.) can make the incomplete (happiness) into something complete, and the complete (suffering) into something incomplete' (GS V, 1. p. 589; AP, p. 471); a Kierkegaardian gesture, that might disrupt and turn back time. Kierkegaard's sensitivity for the uniqueness of the stubborn, wilful self, for the experience of finitude and solitude which did not fit into positivist or dialectical constructs, his disposition towards an essayistic, fragmented, literary-philosophical style, and his idea of an existentially saturated instant – all this was crucial for Bloch as well.

Both Bloch and Lukács – in contrast to most German intellectuals of the time – hated war, and in their pacifist hubris found themselves as outcasts. Even though Bloch's father was a railway employee, while Lukács was an aristocrat and an aesthete, a son of a Budapest banker, these class differences did not hinder their friendship.

Having come to Heidelberg to obtain an habilitation (Harth 1986), Lukács and Bloch became frequenters of Max Weber's circle. Weber favoured them both, but especially the gifted Lukács, finding Bloch at times somewhat arrogant. The latter imagined himself to be a new prophet: 'This man is possessed by his God,' Weber said, 'and I am just a scholar' (Karadi 1986, p. 73). Lukács saw the coming of World War I as the new apocalypse, which drew him towards Bloch and away from Weber.

However, Weber himself did not exclude the possibility of the new prophets coming. *The Protestant Ethic* diagnosed modernity in a way quite compatible with utopian messianism:

> [I]n the United States, the pursuit of wealth, stripped of its religious and ethical meaning, tends to become associated with purely mundane passions, which often actually give it the character of sport. No one knows who will live in this cage in the future, or whether at the end of this tremendous development entirely new prophets will arise, or there will be a great rebirth of old ideas and ideals, or, if neither, mechanized petrification, embellished with a sort of convulsive self-importance. (Weber 2005, p. 124; see also Lellouche 2008, p. 20f.)

Bloch and Lukács were looking for a new philosophical style, in which their epoch could express itself, to unite a new aesthetic experience with a new politics. This implied, however, that they had to give up on their desire to build systems. Although they both attempted to do that (*Heidelberg Aesthetics* and *Philosophy of Art* by Lukács and Bloch's *Summa of Axiomatic Philosophy*) these projects remained unfinished. It was only with time that they were able to find suitable forms beyond the systematic.

After 1918 their friendship declined. To a large extent this was due to Lukács's rebuttal of avant-garde art and Expressionism that Bloch defended in *The Spirit of Utopia* and in his numerous essays in the 1920s and 1930s. For a long time (except for a brief meeting in Vienna in 1929) they did not communicate with each other. This chapter will explore some of the topics that were important for both of them and that became the subject of their explicit and implicit polemics. 'The polemic totality' of their relationship, as Friedrich Schlegel would put it, was of decisive significance for utopian philosophy, compelling Bloch to extend, modify and sometimes even alter his views. A significant part of Bloch's *oeuvre* can be read as a reaction to Lukács's particular works. Therefore the chapter is arranged as a journey around the traces of these works and this largely invisible dialogue.

Episode One: Metaphysics of Tragedy

In order to provide a rough outline of the philosophical and aesthetic discussions around the nature of the tragic and the peculiarity of tragedy as a genre, one would have to pay tribute to a variety of different intellectual traditions. This subject is hard to approach without touching upon Aristotle's *Poetics*, Hegel's *Aesthetics* or Nietzsche's *The Birth of Tragedy*. Furthermore, it seems inadequate to discuss tragedy as such, without considering the ideas and the theatrical practice of one or another specific epoch. Anybody who writes on the subject will have to find an appropriate solution.

However, we shall make a more modest attempt, namely to trace the fate of Lukács's famous essay, *The Metaphysics of Tragedy* (1910), and to show the life of some of his ideas in post-war philosophical aesthetics, and particularly Bloch's reaction to them. And though their common ground extends far beyond the metaphysics of tragedy, it makes sense to discuss this particular subject in detail. This is especially imperative, given that Bloch's *Spirit of Utopia* and Benjamin's *Origin of German Tragic Drama* contain explicit reactions to Lukács's essay – the landmarks of aesthetic reflections between 1910 and 1930, when not only Bloch and Lukács but also Benjamin underwent a period of rapid intellectual transformation, with breaks and reversals along the way.

The essay *Metaphysics of Tragedy*[1] is dedicated to the work of Paul Ernst (1866–1933), a German author and playwright, who then maintained an intensive correspondence with Lukács. It is clearly written under the impression of Ernst's theoretical writings. Lukács discusses both the metaphysical ideal of the tragic drama *and* the particular tragedies of Ernst, thus complicating the matter.

He follows Ernst in maintaining that tragedy should be purged of halftones and the incompleteness of real life, 'the anarchy of light and dark' (SF, p. 152), sheltering in its folds base and profane consciousness. Lukács's position is not all that far from the aesthetic values of symbolists and decadents – he is explicitly anti-realistic: 'Realism is bound to destroy all the form-creating and life-maintaining values of tragic drama' (SF, p. 159). In less than ten years Lukács moved away from such aesthetics, to brand Ernst a fascist literary theorist – not without reason.

Similarly repulsive for the later Lukács is the proclaimed elitism of the younger Lukács: 'In vain has our democratic age claimed an equal right for all to be tragic; all attempts to open this kingdom of heaven to the poor in spirit have proved fruitless' (SF, p. 173, translation slightly altered). Tragedy is the lot of the privileged, those capable of letting the form (as the sovereign authority decreeing the highest ethical and aesthetic judgement) prevail over their lives. The idea of his own chosenness and of creating an invisible church persisted in Lukács's thought, as his attention shifted from aesthetics to ethics.

Interestingly, Benjamin, invoking both the decadent views of early Lukács and Nietzsche's book,[2] would later criticize the contemporary views on Greek tragedy as 'cultural arrogance' – above all from an ethical point of view (OD, p. 101ff.). Benjamin believed that the ancient tragedy should not be compared to contemporary drama (contrasting the emancipated and 'free' bourgeois with the dying antique hero crushed by his fate) and that it should not be subjected to a conclusive judgement on moral grounds. Ethics is only valid in matters of life; judging or praising the tragic hero is pointless (Benjamin wrote about this more extensively also in his essay on Goethe's *Elective Affinities*). The proper place of ethics *sensu stricto* is in life, and not in art, where we are always dealing with a complete, self-sufficient, invented world. And though the ethical principles of this world are not abolished, they cannot be absolutized. The ancient tragedy cannot be brought back anymore (as is also maintained by Lukács in the *Theory of the Novel*); the dramatic potential should be found in the present.

But let us go back to Lukács. He considered the metaphysical basis of tragedy to be a longing of the human existence for identity, for genuine life. Tragedy is based precisely on the life's most important instant of essentiality, on the self-revelation of the essence, which powerfully asserts itself, denying all that is incomplete, all hesitations, all external ornamentation. In tragedy a new space is created, without any external reasons, 'the clear, harsh mountain air of ultimate questions and ultimate answers' (SF, p. 155). A new ethics is established, according to which all that is uncertain, including the past, is rejected in favour of pure essentiality (Lukács thought that Ernst succeeded exactly in this regard). Tragedy violently establishes a new existence opposed to ordinary life.

Even though this critique of the ordinary life and the longing for authenticity is similar to the aspirations of German romanticism, this is not acknowledged by the author of *Soul and Form*. In the essay on Novalis, Lukács criticizes the romanticists for a passive, overly contemplative and subjectivist attitude to life and to the aesthetic ideal, and for a metaphysical 'pantophagy' of their aesthetic and practical commitments. In this sense, Lukács maintained that the romantic ideal is opposed to the tragic one, in that it smooths the edges of tragic oppositions.

The life of a tragic hero is the life brought to the maximum capacity, brought to its limit, it is an existentially meaningful life. The tragic in Lukács lies not only on the other side of the ordinary life, but also *beyond the limits of culture* (Lukács 1982, p. 233, in a letter to L. Ziegler July 1911). The soul discards the vestments of its spiritual conditions, it has nothing else to rely on.

Tragedy erases the distinction between the world of ideas and the world of things. '… [E]very true tragedy is a mystery play', and its genuine purpose is to awaken to life the transcendental God, who lies hidden within the human (SF, p. 154). This awakening is not mediated by anything, it happens abruptly and without any preparation, the latter is left to propaedeutics. Any gradual development, upbringing, the becoming of a hero, is meaningless in tragedy.

A violent compulsion to the form[3] that Lukács suggests is a consequence of any artistic act and of any consistent *point of view*, linked to the violent rejection of compromises, a refusal to take account of the alternatives. This violence is inherent to creativity. Aesthetic tyranny of form can take the shape of a religious conversion, of a political practice or simply an existential sensitivity, but its violent nature remains. The question is to what extent we can allow such absolutization, what is the threshold of toleration and how productive can democratic, postmodern pluralism be in art and philosophy?

Thus, Lyotard (1993) talks about the unrepresentable and the striving for wholeness as a syndrome of the twentieth century, unmasking beneath these phenomena the source of the will to terror. But tragedy, according to the early Lukács, is precisely the art of the impossible, and formalistic terrorism, attained through disposing of any compromises, is thus self-defeating. Lukács does not see a dialectical solution, but neither does Lyotard who identifies Hegelian dialectic with totalization.

An anti-Hegelian stance is quite visible in Lukács, something of which he may not have been fully aware. In a letter to Leopold Ziegler, the author of *Metaphysics of the Tragic* (1902),[4] looking back at the text that quickly became alien to him, Lukács explains that Ziegler's concept of tragedy is based on classical (and in this sense also Hegelian) notions of guilt and conflict, while he (Lukács) draws on the notions of essence and boundary. Conflict and guilt, retribution and death are the only manifestations of the tragic as becoming-substantial (Lukács 1982, p. 232). The higher metaphysical meaning of tragedy lies beyond the issue of conflict and the ethics of duty – a tragic hero is not affected by these notions (Fehér 1985a, p. 418).

Here metaphysical problems are discussed in their most canonical forms. Lukács draws on the example of tragedy to ask anew whether the world of ideas exists, to discuss the status of ideal essences and – most importantly – their *sensuously apprehended existence*. The liveliness of essentiality, and its capacity to be embodied in sensuous being, is the main philosophical and aesthetic paradox of tragedy, the paradox of the 'great moments' (SF, p. 156f.). These are anticipated in the 'moments of destiny' for a critic –

> at which things become forms – the moment when all feelings and experiences on the near or the far side of form receive form, are melted down and condensed into form. It is the mystical moment of union between the outer and the inner, between soul and form. It is as mystical as the moment of destiny in tragedy when the hero meets his destiny. (SF, p. 8)

The metaphysics of tragedy gives the answer to 'the most delicate question of platonism: the question whether individual things can have idea or essence'. The answer is: 'only something whose individuality is carried to the uttermost limit, is adequate to its idea – i. e. is really existent' (SF, p. 162). Benjamin's formulation is quite similar:

> The concept has its roots in the extreme. Just as a mother is seen to begin to live in the fullness of her power only when the circle of her children, inspired by the feeling of her proximity, closes around her, so do ideas come to life only when extremes are assembled around them (OD, p. 35).

But the Lukácsean world of tragedy is not the world of universals (they are too perfect to live an actual life) nor is it the totality of Spinozist substance. It is more intriguing, does not rule out a chance; the latter does not merely supplement it as an external factor, but is integrated into the tragedy. Bloch notes, commenting on Lukács, that if one simply excludes chance from tragedy the result then would be 'the shallowest and most listless kind of life' (GU2, p. 276; SU, p. 220). Chance is, as Lukács puts it, everywhere and nowhere. In other words, the world of essential life is beyond the opposition of necessity and chance.

It appears *in a single instant*, which is both the beginning and the end. Lukács interprets it as the metaphysical basis of the unity of time in tragedy. He apparently took the notion of the instant from Kierkegaard (Fehér 1980) who saw in it the touch of time and eternity. The author of tragedy, amidst the temporality of language, struggles in vain to express the mystical experience of the self through a consecutive unfolding of events in time. Instant as something extra-temporal can be represented in tragedy only in an inadequate fashion. Of course, Lukács contested the normative demands of classicists as a shallow parody of mystical extra-temporality, an attempt to smuggle the unity and wholeness of the instant into time, whereas in genuine essentiality, temporal relations are altogether reversed and transposed, and the sequence of times is irrelevant. This is exactly the reason why for Lukács the heroes of tragedy going to their doom have been long dead[5]; the relations of 'before' and 'after' are incompatible with the instant.

This deliberate sharpness, lack of mediation and transition is a significant characteristic of Benjamin's *Theological-political Fragment*. Neither Lukács and Benjamin nor Bloch made any considerable distinctions between tragedy and messianism. The logic of messianic time and utopian temporality were also the major theme of Franz Rosenzweig's *The Star of Redemption* (1921) – a paradigmatic text of German-Jewish messianic philosophy. (Benjamin was among the first to recognize its importance.) Rosenzweig describes the fundamental metaphysical stance of the tragic hero as the obstinacy of silence, which enables him to affirm his identity. The genuine language of tragedy is silence. The self is the main and only hero of tragedy, who silently encounters death as his greatest solitude and triumph. Rosenzweig's hero at once both *is* and *is not* dying, because a character as a heroic self is immortal (Rosenzweig 1988, pp. 83–6).

Turning back to the tragic instant, one could suspect that it is mystical by nature. But Lukács opposes the tragic and the mystical. While the former is the path of struggle and of the triumph of the self in the instant of its highest manifestation, the latter is the path of self-repudiation, of the self's dissolution within the Absolute. In the tragic world view the self preserves itself, but, paradoxically, only to become the witness to its own destruction. The tragic consciousness fully accommodates and interiorizes death; in tragedy death is 'an always immanent reality, inseparably connected with every tragic event' (SF, p. 161); 'Tragedy is only possible when the world in which death as it is, regardless the connection to transcendent reality ... becomes the only thinkable, solemnly affirmed climax of life' (Lukács 1974, p. 126).

The mystic, on the contrary, abrogates the real (as well as the aesthetic) significance of death, thereby making redundant the form of tragedy. Taking up this line of thought and comparing it to Rosenzweig's 'metaethics', Benjamin shows that the silent stubborn persistence of the tragic hero is superseded in the history of drama by *the speech* of Socrates and readiness for death, which is peculiar to him inasmuch as it represents Christian martyrdom. Death for Socrates is meaningless; Benjamin, however, places the spirit of dialogue above the rational Socratic propaedeutics: 'This purely dramatic quality [of the dialogue. – I. B.] restores the mystery which had gradually become secularized in the forms of Greek drama: its language, the language of the new drama, is, in particular, the language of the *Trauerspiel*' (OD, p. 118). And while the tragic hero always faces towards his death, for his life is built upon death, new literary forms are organized around the new hero, who despises death. Benjamin's treatment of the tragic hero is also linked with messianism and is thus close to Bloch's concerns.

Lukács considers another difficulty, that of the historical tragedy, or, more precisely, the relation of the tragic and the historical. (This is particularly important because *The Metaphysics of Tragedy* was preceded by the book *The History of the Development of Modern Drama*, where a sociological analysis of the evolution of drama was attempted.) The summits of the tragic in their universality are confronted by historical universality and necessity. Lukács's tragedy grapples with the ordinary life, and the object of the dispute of tragedy and the ordinary life is history. But the uniqueness of historical facts, the eternal mismatch of the original ideas and intentions and the actual historical deeds always provoke 'metaphysical dissonance' (SF, p. 172) in tragedy. However, the form acts as its categorical imperative, which remains unchanged and independent of the real manifestations of the tragic; an eternally unattainable ideal of purity and clarity, which Ernst's grandiloquent tragedies attempted to realize (as well as certain dramatic works of Friedrich Hebbel[6] and Paul Claudel). The form, as Lukács writes to a philosopher and writer, Salomo Friedlaender, is the embodied paradox, the coexistence of mutually exclusive and irreconcilable principles. This struggle is not present in ordinary life; principles pass over each other, without recognizing their counterparts, for they are 'non-homogenous' (Lukács 1982, p. 230). But in Ernst's historical dramas behind the heavy gait of historical necessity, Lukács beheld the high spirit and blinding light of the form.

Since a tragedy is an experience of negating ordinary life and exists beyond the realm of culture, the emphases are somewhat shifted, and the aesthetic value of particular tragedies becomes secondary. In order to establish the hero's identity, Lukács needs a form, while readily neglecting any particular form in its historical uniqueness. This tension between Lukács-the-philosopher and Lukács-the-literary-critic becomes apparent in the excessive abstractness of his concepts. Hebbel and Ernst were both playwrights *and* theorists, whereas Lukács, who never composed any dramatic work, was, fortunately, insightful enough as theorist to move away from the narrow and rigorous interpretation of tragedy towards the investigation of other literary forms – particularly, the novel.

Lukács's aesthetics was a central reference point and a major inspiration for Bloch, whose interest in *The Metaphysics of Tragedy* was evident, given that his early philosophy reproduced the same constellation of thought-images: the essential life; the self spontaneously attaining its identity; the awakening of an internal God. Bloch's polemic with Lukács highlights the earliest differences between their perspectives, despite the frequently mentioned fact that they were in general surprisingly unanimous, completed each other's thoughts, exchanged newly finished manuscripts and entered intellectual differences into 'the red list'.

Their similarities are manifest almost everywhere: for instance, in the introduction to *Soul and Form*, Lukács interprets the essay as an intermediate, transitional genre; a precursor imbued with longing for a new philosophical synthesis, that might appear in the form of a new grand system. This is also how Bloch thought of his philosophy. Bloch's theory of utopia ultimately boils down to the anticipation of a future total synthesis, and the genre most common to him was undoubtedly that of the essay, similar to the poetics of a Lukácsean essay, that speaks of 'the ultimate problems of life, but in a tone which implies that he is only discussing pictures and books, only the inessential and pretty ornaments of real life' (SF, p. 9; cf.: PA, p. 258). In fact, all the books Bloch has written are collections of essays composed at different times and assembled together (although, for example, Czajka (2006, p. 71) discusses different genres of different books). This stylistic unity only reinforced the similarity of their perspectives – both of them tried to construct a philosophical system and both, having failed to produce one, switched to other genres.

Metaphysics of the instant as an intrusion of eternity into time is another common theme. 'The darkness of the lived instant' that reinstates the mystical experience in terms of everyday life is discussed extensively in *The Spirit of Utopia*. Lukács argues that any essay must be based on an experience of the instant, but also places the instant itself at the top of tragic aesthetics. In *Soul and Form* the instant acquires a revolutionary character through the experience of an aesthete. Obsessed by the idea of the tragic, Bloch's radical determination came out of the revolutionary struggles of 1917 and 1918. But both of them despised the dreary landscape of the bourgeois world and considered art the main alternative in the epoch of 'absolute sinfulness'. Lukács searched for this alternative primarily in literature, while Bloch was exploring the spaces of music.

A text, which is basically a review of *The Metaphysics of Tragedy*, in the final version entitled 'Excursus: obstruction and tragedy on the way towards real self-invention'[7] is a part of all editions of *The Spirit of Utopia* (1918, 1923 and 1964).[8] As everywhere in this work, the style is vague and obscure, the implicit references are hard to reconstruct (an authoritative commented edition is still lacking); however, Lukács's essay is among the most obvious sources.

Bloch notes approvingly that tragic death is a privilege of the chosen, inseparable from their lives. It 'can be defined only as something that happens absolutely from here, a recursive, immanent, unmystical compulsion to form, to *horos*, to shape and the definite terminus of the self' (GU2, p. 274f.; SU, p. 218).

Like Lukács (and Benjamin), Bloch omits the Aristotelian motives of fear and compassion; he is not so much interested in the poetics of tragedy, but rather in the philosophy of the tragic. It is important to him that tragedy (in the ideal form invoked by Lukács) is a product of a world that lost its God or fate as *external* necessity that governs characters like puppets. The fact that God leaves the stage but remains a spectator is 'the only kind of piety still possible, it is also the historical, the utopian possibility for tragic ages, epochs without a heaven' (GU2, p. 275; SU, p. 219). Tragedy for Bloch, as for Lukács, is possible only in the disenchanted world – this is exactly how they saw their own epoch and how their aesthetics and philosophy of history differed from the mythological prophetism of the Nietzschean theory of tragedy. God has forsaken this world, but remains a spectator – an ambiguous situation that is open to different interpretations, but certainly not to a Nietzschean one. This particular idea could be interpreted as a substitution of the divine principle by the supra-individual form, which serves as a model for the individual, both as a means and as an end of the radical transformation of life.

A tragic hero, having appropriated his own death, being open to fate, overcomes his guilt and his sin. But Bloch posits that if we were to regard this immanence of death from an exclusively historical and religious point of view, then in order to make sense of it, one would have to assume some sort of karmic theory that would link fate to something more fundamental, preceding the life of the hero. The issue of utmost interest for Bloch in tragedy, something Lukács ignores, is the problem of the *external world*, forsaken by God and imbued with evil. Only when this world is completely indifferent to Lukács's tragic hero does he become capable of liberation through separating himself from the world. But the world is not just a passive background for tragedy; Bloch cannot give up the problem of the world as a process and of attaining 'the apocalyptic kernel' (GU2, p. 278; SU, p. 221, cf. GU1, p. 71). In such a dynamic and unstable environment, Lukács's symbolism (in the spirit of Stefan George) becomes meaningless – one cannot complete oneself without completing the rest of the world. This forgetfulness and neglect of the world – conceived as dark, yielding neither to rationalization nor to mystical insight – is an important point of departure not only for Lukács but also for Meister Eckhart (Pelletier 2008, p. 208), which relativizes Lukács's alleged departure from mysticism.

Bloch believes that tragedy as an element in the universal process depicts not the encounter with oneself (as all other arts do), but with Satan, with an obstacle, with an obstruction (*Hemmnis*) of the world. But this meeting should be followed by a different, more fundamental experience – the 'real', that is, grounded in the world, absolute encounter with oneself – perhaps still in Hegelian parlance. The tragic hero is not a cold-blooded terminator, long dead and indifferent to his own pain (possibly even deriving some sort of masochistic pleasure from it). Bloch accuses Lukács of idealizing insensitivity, of forgetting 'murder, death, and tragic darkness' (GU2, p. 276; SU, p. 220), effectively rendering the ideal of the tragic form deficient and irrelevant. Later Bloch would argue that 'in Lukács' still neo-classical theory of tragedy, dying, indeed destruction itself, is omitted . . . both are the same atmospheric chiaroscuro as the life of experienced reality, are verbs and not essentialities' (PH, p. 1376; PHE, p. 1170), retreating before the instant of decision, which is even more important than the Promethean *hybris* of the tragic hero. Otherwise it would turn out that Shakespeare's *Richard III* is a tragic hero. It is also Bloch who asks the question of where the hero is heading, and whose flag has he raised on the mast of his sinking ship.

In *The Spirit of Utopia* Bloch makes another move, attempting to distance himself from the tragic narcissism of Lukácsean aesthetics. In fact, he declares that a more substantial, more fundamental stance to the world, which is closer to the apocalyptic and utopian attitude, is the comic. Recognition of the tragic foundation of reality is undoubtedly meaningful, but comedy (Bloch recalls Dante here) and the comical novel (in the first edition of *The Spirit of Utopia* a comic hero was illustrated by Don Quixote (GU1, pp. 74–6), who is pejoratively described in *The Theory of the Novel*) reveals deeper mysteries, showing us that something is wrong with this world. Spontaneous joy, a sudden feeling of easiness and humour as a very human while creative force of the soul, refusing to back down before the given, raises US above the crude facts of life and tragic fate, enabling, as though from within, the destruction of the dull flow of life (also cf. PH, pp. 1031–9, where Bloch brings Hegel to his cause).

The tragedy and its heroes are beyond history, they are the figures of utopia. Their path always appears to be half-completed, like that of Christ's, who overcame fate and at the same time surrendered to it. The historicity of drama is accompanied by its religious reinterpretation.

> The hero thus does not die because he has become essential; rather, because he has become essential, he dies. Only this turns a serious having-become oneself into heroism, into a category of tremendous destiny and of tragedy, which raises the man up whom it crushes, by crushing him, and only this supra-subjective

correlation places the tragic into an unconsummated-consummated context, into the self-consummation, self-invention destroyed midway; into the pitiless old conflict of Prometheus, of Christ, with the upholder of this world and the guilty conscience of its end. (GU2, p. 282f.; SU, p. 225)

Tragedy cannot occur only in the hidden realms of inner life, it does not belong to a solipsist, for redemption is a cosmic event (Christen 1979, p. 78). The tragic hero is a suffering Messiah, a revolutionary figure, but deep down in the genuine revolutionary aesthetics persists *laughter* – a powerful creative element that might engender indeterminacy; not having ultimately occurred to enter the world, to institute its own hitherto unknown laws. The long and pompous speeches are alien to revolutionaries, however full they may be of dignity and self-assertion.

One should not also forget about the general meaning of Christianity here. A Christian hero is not a knight, rattling his armour, his image is not royal, he is poor, the son of man, and only in this inconspicuousness can his deeds occur (S, p. 53).

The early aesthetics of Bloch was especially pronounced in his rejection of accomplished and self-sufficient architectural forms, of dead architectural rationality, which he saw embodied in the Egyptian pyramids. The tragedies of Ernst, apparently, represented to him the crystals of death, absent in the utopian architecture of the Gothic and Baroque.

Of course, the differences between Bloch and Lukács are not only aesthetic (even though their debate around tragedy unfolded in this sphere), but primarily ontological. Lukács's tyranny of form was unacceptable to Bloch (Münster 1982, pp. 61–9). It is no accident that in *The Spirit of Utopia* Bloch criticizes the formalistic musical aesthetics of Eduard Hanslick and understands the form as a kind of internal, rather preliminary, connection within the material (Czajka 2006, p. 199), as a colourful *carpet* – a notion used by Lukács's early deceased friend Leo Popper (Münster 1982, p. 171; Korstvedt 2010) – that is a vague interweaving of lines, an undeciphered expression of *unio mystica* (Lehmann 1985).[9]

Bloch does not accept the abstract sublimity and sterility of the tragic; he never understood how one can declare the work of art to be complete in itself as a self-sufficient whole, why the form cannot be historical[10] and why it should be so strictly separated from life. Blochian forms have to serve the purpose of elevating, or deepening life, not judging it. In other words, Bloch's critique reveals his implicit Hegelianism, sometimes reinterpreted along the lines of the subject-object opposition. While for Lukács the analysis of *objectivations* is key to philosophy and aesthetic inquiry, for Bloch the major significance is attached to the subject (Radnóti 1975). A form should thus be given up if it becomes merely external and alien to the expression of subjectivity (Pauen 1992a).

In the domain of ethics, ontological disagreements focus around Bloch's rejection of Lukács's 'moral demonism': one cannot impose one's vision of the good on another person, however confident one may be, for the human heart is a mystery, and in the new world to come heroes of today can fade and turn out to be worthless (S, p. 54). The spiritual '*führership*', to which Lukács was inclined, is in principle rejected by Bloch, for the moral absolute does not live among us, and nobody can lay claim to be *the* immutable example: any virtue is transient, relative. 'Till we have faces', till our innermost essence is manifest, we may not impinge upon spiritual power (PA, pp. 204-10). Only in the dianoetic sphere – where the creative element rules over itself, where the Aristotelian *poiesis* occurs, a spiritual leadership of the creator is possible, but only with respect to the kingdom of absolute virtue, which has not yet come (Riedel 1994). In Bloch's 'mystical democracy' the leader is the community itself, the invisible church of the future (Bolz 1987). His talk of the *Führer* is marked by an anarchistic paradox: The *Führer* demands total obedience, allows no discussion, but only to destroy any hierarchies and thus to negate his own authority (Pauen 1992). This strange perspective was explicable, first, on the ground of Bloch's apocalyptic vision and, second, in view of his praise for a utopian subjectivity that becomes the measure of all things. This framework would surely deny any rights of the transcendent forms defended by Lukács that were for Bloch, even in the years of friendship, unwarranted anticipation that distorted the genuine morality of the human soul.

This implicit debate was revived under new circumstances and on a different occasion in the 1930s in the debates around Expressionism (that became for Bloch the genuine art of the future), when Lukács's position became uncompromisingly classicist. Bloch became an avant-gardist, while Lukács advocated the purity of forms and, similarly to Carl Schmitt's *Political Romanticism*, the suitability and orderliness of art. Ujma (1995, p. 174ff.) maintains that Lukács and Schmitt were unanimous in rejecting the merger of the political and the aesthetic (which was quite typical for Bloch) and in their propensity towards order and hierarchy. However, it should be clear that Lukács the Marxist never denied the link between literature and society. On the contrary, he emphasized it. Just that in social relations the practice of art occupied a subordinate position, whereas in Bloch, on the contrary, social thought had to follow art. Neither Lukács nor Schmitt could accept this. (Interestingly, when Schelsky (1979) attacked Bloch, he also involuntarily reproduced Schmitt's arguments against romantics who allegedly overemphasized the subjective reaction of individuality and neglected the political realism that was, for Schmitt – and for Schelsky suggesting a 'principle of experience' – actually relevant. But Schmitt was at least sensitive to the existential dimension and to the aesthetic figurations of subjectivity, whereas Schelsky's conservatism degenerated into a stubborn clinging to the given sanctified by a dubious tradition.)

Bloch on the contrary defended the artist's right to self-expression and the right of the spectator to the freedom of interpretation, insisting that a genuine realist sees in reality not only complete, total forms, but also the disjunctions, the ruptures, the non-contemporaneities. The work of art for Bloch is not something solid and eternal, it is part of the utopian process, constantly redefining itself and transcending its own limits. An affinity one cannot neglect is associated with Sergei Eisenstein and his montage theory:

> The work of art, as conceived dynamically, is the process of images emerging in the feelings and the reason of a spectator (... the same dynamic principle underlies the genuinely living images in the seemingly motionless and static art as painting). This is the particular feature of the genuinely living work of art and its difference from the dead one, in which one reports to the spectator the already depicted

results of some elapsed creative process instead of involving him in a process that is ongoing. (Eisenstein 1998, p. 70; See also: Kessler 2006, pp. 198–207)

No book and no picture can *ever be completed*, any completeness is only something preliminary (EZ, p. 250),[11] this utopian excess points at the hidden potentialities of every creative effort. 'Raphael without hands would never have become a great artist but, since he was nonetheless Raphael, perhaps an even more faithful remembrance of ourselves' (S, p. 93; T, p. 68).

While Lukács saw the anarchy of life as simply useless wandering, a collision of heterogeneous and mutually indifferent elements, which he opposed to immutable forms – realized utopias – Bloch saw in it the anticipation of the apocalyptic future.[12] Life, even being meaningless and hostile, must become an element of play, must enter the tragic. The artist, who created such drama and who in *The Spirit of Utopia* is ranked among the seers, the harbinger, was not Paul Ernst, but another, and admittedly a more significant author – August Strindberg (GU1, p. 238; Jung 1988).

Bloch and Lukács created neither a common philosophical system nor a unified theory of tragedy. Their polemic is not to categorize some minor disagreements of allegiances; ultimately it dealt with fundamental ontological and ideological preferences. Philosophically Bloch was always a rebel, whereas Lukács rather quickly reconciled himself with reality, both on political and aesthetic grounds. As Bloch accurately put it, his friend was obsessed with a passion for order, for straight lines that made him accept not only Ernst's neoclassicism, but also Stalinist aesthetics (Interview 1976, p. 39). Totalitarian thinking, unwillingness to compromise in the defence of classicism and a critique of modernism – all of these features of Lukács's intellectual attitude prevented him from making peace not only with Bloch but also with the main tendencies of the philosophical aesthetics of the twentieth century. The immanence of form in early Lukács was in a perfect accord to what Nancy (1991) would later call 'immanentism' of communal life.

At the same time, in 1910 Bloch and Lukács were able to considerably transform the theoretical discourse that was dominant in Europe at the time, thus becoming precursors to the aesthetics of a completely different kind. Lukács's and Nietzsche's metaphysics of tragedy became one of the starting points for Benjamin's theory of German tragic drama. Not without Bloch's influence, Benjamin focused on the contemporary theatre (apart from the seventeenth century), drawing analogies between the Baroque epoch and Expressionism. Later Benjamin commented on Brechtian Epic Theatre and tried to show, using the notion of 'dialectics at a standstill', the extreme tension of the dialectical opposition that breaks the solid mechanism of historical development. What becomes the subject of Benjamin's aesthetic reflections is the new theatre, alien both to Aristotle's moralism and Ernst's aristocratism. It is the theatre of estrangement and shock where the gesture rules, and the attainment of identity does not throw one into total solitude, but, by involving the spectator, makes her take part in the fate of the collective revolutionary subject.

While Bloch's and Benjamin's elective affinity in the 1920s and 1930s was obvious, Lukács, who in the 1930s had almost no 'stylistic disagreements' with the Soviet government, chose a completely different path. Benjamin writes to Scholem in 1930: 'Are you interested in hearing that Ernst Bloch is in Vienna visiting Lukács and is trying to renew old, seemingly rather fruitless debates with him under very different circumstances?' (CWB, p. 362). Bloch never joined the party, which for Lukács was the desired instance of unity between theory and practice, 'the form taken by the class consciousness of the proletariat' (HCC, p. 41).

Episode Two: Theory of the Novel

The writers of Russia, whose work is of world-historic significance, were seeking to rise above 'European' individualism (and anarchy, despair, and godforsakenness), overcome it in the deepest depth of the soul and to place into the reclaimed realm the new man, and the new world with him.

(Lukács 1916–17)

In the preface to the republication of *The Theory of The Novel* (1962), Lukács characterizes Bloch's philosophy (and his own thinking in the 1910s) as a synthesis of 'left' ethics and 'right' epistemology. He uses this rather questionable formula[13] – indeed, was it not the case that all the 'right' in Lukács's thought followed from his ethical considerations (Löwy 1986)? And, on the other hand, was the proletarian activism of the early 1920s not, after all, a product of unconscious Nietzscheanism?[14] – to compare his former work, of which he spoke with deliberate detachment, to Bloch's philosophy, and to criticize the latter for being unable to move away from this strange synthesis.

The Theory of the Novel – which marked a new stage of Lukács's literary and philosophical work – was written in the winter of 1914–15 as an introduction to the planned but never completed book on Dostoyevsky (see the materials in Lukács 1985). *The Spirit of Utopia* was written, according to Bloch's recollection, towards the end of 1915 and the beginning of 1916. Bloch undoubtedly knew of Lukács's text, even though, judging by his correspondence, he read it only after publication, when most of *The Spirit of Utopia* had already been completed.

Two points are important in this respect. Lukács's aesthetic and philosophical stance in *The Theory of the Novel*, and particularly his notions of 'historical-philosophical' determination of literary forms can be considered as an answer to Bloch's criticism, an attempt to correlate the novel and the time corresponding to it; to regard the epoch as a mould of its philosophical achievements and intellectual dead-ends. However, this is not the only text in which Lukács proposes an alternative to his extra-temporal metaphysics of tragedy. In an essay on the 'non-tragic drama' he finds another dramatic form which does not end with the classic tragic finale – death (Indian plays, Euripides, Calderón, some of the plays by Shakespeare, Corneille, Racine, Goethe's *Faust*, Ibsen's *Peer Gynt*. See the new edition: Lukács 1998).

In the *Theory of the Novel* Lukács makes a Hegelian move, claiming that philosophy and literature cannot be reduced to their historical context: the historico-philosophical conditioning of a novel is described as a dependence of the form on the philosophical age, on the degree of philosophical maturity of each epoch ('historical-philosophical situation', TN, p. 139). And while in his analysis of the tragedy Lukács gravitates towards the static nature of the genre itself, towards fixing the forms of art so that they are exempt from the dictates of time, the novel in this new interpretation is an evolving whole that breaths in unison with its intellectual environment, remakes itself all over, conforming to 'the historico-philosophical position of the world's clock' (TN, p. 91). The feeling of history, a conscious position from within one's own epoch, shows the affinity between *The Theory of the Novel* and *The Spirit of Utopia*.

Secondly, admitting that the empirical immanence of meaning and homogeneity of individual and the world are totally lost, Lukács sees the possibility of a new *epos*, based on the work of Dostoyevsky. Dostoyevsky's heroes are 'gnostics of deed' (Lukács 1912, p. 74), prophets of 'the second ethics' of brotherhood, dictated by the goodness of souls, which for Lukács is akin to the inner obsession (called to replace 'the first ethics' of duty, dictated by social arrangements). They are the saviours of mankind, ready to sacrifice their souls, but save the world, the ones who overcame the gap between the idea and the action.

Such interpretation of Dostoyevsky's work is justifiable. For instance, in the drafts of *The Devils*, Dostoevsky constantly returns to the coming of God's kingdom and deification of human kind, referring to the experience of Russian mystical sects (*Khlysts*, Dostoyevsky 1974, pp. 182–93). Religious searches of Dostoyevsky's heroes, these spiritual revolutionaries, striving to find faith while overturning the world, fit perfectly into the mood of Lukács and Bloch and the restless times of the 1910s and 1920s. It would suffice to look at the biography of Elena Grabenko, who was then Lukács's wife – a Russian revolutionary, to whom *The Theory of the Novel* is dedicated – in order to expose the ideological and existential background of the book.

At the time Lukács liked to recite the frenzied cry of Judith from Hebbel's drama with the same title: 'If you place a sin between me and my deed, who am I that I should wrangle with you over it, withdraw from you?' (cited in Shaffer 1987, p. 200). It is precisely the revolutionaries, the heroes of Boris Savinkov's *The Pale Horse*, who are ready to kill, being fully aware that they commit a horrible sin, for *murder cannot under no circumstances be sanctioned* (Lukács 1972), who are needed when the world is falling into sin, enveloped by the madness of war and longings for redemption. Interestingly, the same figure of thought is present in the Jewish messianism with its idea of the 'sacred sin' and with its ethics of the transitory messianic time, to which I shall return.

This messianism, the notion of the new God who 'appears not in a flash but warm and nearby, as our guest' (GU2, p. 244; SU, p. 193), is characteristic both of Lukács, with his gnostic passages about God the creator and God the redeemer (TN, p. 92 f.), and of Bloch (GU2, p. 335f.). Calling Lukács 'a Franciscan father' (S, p. 37; T, p. 23)[15] and 'the absolute genius of morality' (GU1, p. 347), Bloch interprets his 'second ethics', communication of souls above and apart from social obligations, as metaphysics of the inner life, inner speech, directed at the I. 'The humility should overcome the shame of vanity to see our vile, cankered I as it is . . . naked; piety has to overcome the shame of the coldness . . . to let us endure the overthrowing shine of [our aim's] glory' (GU1, p. 348f.).

One of the main tenets of the apocalyptic prophecy in *The Spirit of Utopia* is precisely establishing this community of souls, laying completely bare before each other, whose conversation is neither bound nor limited by anything and is a conversation of those who completely give themselves to others as servants (GU1, p. 332) and who are ultimately responsible for the God of the utopian kingdom to come (GU1, p. 445).

Lukács and Bloch found such a stream in Russian literature. In the 1940s Erich Auerbach, Bloch's good acquaintance, remarked:

> ... the effect of Tolstoy and still more of Dostoevsky in Europe was very great, and if, in many domains ... the moral crisis became increasingly keen from the last decade before the first World War, and something like a premonition of the impending catastrophe was observable, the influence of the Russian realists was an essential contributing factor. (2003, p. 524)[16]

Lukács was especially fond of Dostoyevsky. He wrote a dialogue, very characteristic of his mood at the time, *On Poverty of Spirit* – a radical manifesto of the new hero, who rebels against the logic of 'ordinary life'. Apparently, this is where Bloch takes the idea of castes and social hierarchy, which appears several times in the first edition of *The Spirit of Utopia* (See: GU1, p. 410f.). Dostoyevsky's heroes are present there – on the last pages Bloch extensively quotes *The Brothers Karamazov* and discusses Ivan's famous words about the tear of a child. They are represented as the figures of the apocalypse, particularly Ivan, who does not accept 'God's world'. 'Russia will rekindle the heart, and Germany – the fire in the depths of the rejuvenated mankind' (GU1, pp. 302–3). This messianic drive is presented in *The Theory of the Novel* as a search for a new form, able 'to uncover and construct the *concealed* totality of life' (TN, p. 60. Emphasis mine. – I. B.). The ones who can see, who can suddenly realize this lack, are the demonic personalities, capable of renouncing 'all the psychological or sociological foundations of their existence' (TN, p. 90), going beyond the limits of everyday experience and taking upon themselves the great sins of the world, having renounced the second ethics for the sake of the first.

'Heidelberg's apostles' were obsessed by such a straightforward and uncompromising attitude towards life. Lukács associated Dostoyevsky's characters with Russian terrorists and anarchists and Bloch associated the same with the members of medieval religious sects. Both did not avoid merging these historical associations into a single *Gestalt* – that is why Thomas Müntzer 'integrated and embodied a Russian, an inner human being' (TM, p. 110). The spirit of the Russian revolution was for Lukács and Bloch more immediate than the French revolution, which they considered too reasonable, too close to Western rational culture. Moreover, both of them might have been influenced by Vladimir Soloviev, whose works were then being translated into German and popularized in Heidelberg by Fyodor Stepun and other Russian philosophers. The reception of Russian philosophy in the work of Lukács and Bloch still awaits examination. In 1918 Bloch did not doubt that

> Jews and Germans have to once more, through the optics of the new proclaiming, measured by the thousand fold energies, *aions*, once more designate the last, the Gothic, the Baroque, in order to prepare the absolute time – united with Russia, this third bosom of waiting, bringing the new God into the world, and messianism. (GU1, p. 332)

The traces of Soloviev can be found not only in Lukács, but also – even if rather hypothetically – in Bloch: '[T]he final thing that absolutely awaits man [beyond any possible worldly realm and in the eternal life] *is woman in form and essence*' (GU2, p. 266; SU, p. 212).[17]

Lukács's attitude towards Bloch's conceptual apparatus was ambivalent. On the one hand, he admitted the presence of utopian aspirations as an integral part of any philosophy. The opening pages of *The Theory of the Novel* contain a description of the 'enclosed cultures':

> ... the happy ages have no philosophy, or ... (it comes to the same thing) all men in such ages are philosophers, sharing the Utopian aim of every philosophy. For what ... is the problem of the transcendental *locus* if not to determine how every impulse which springs from the innermost depths is coordinated with a form that it is ignorant of, but that has been assigned to it from eternity and that must envelop it in liberating symbols? (TN, p. 29)

The novel itself always contains movement, the will to overcome oppositions, and in this sense it works within utopian dynamics: 'The inner form of the novel has been understood as the process of the problematic individual's journeying towards himself' (TN, p. 80). Moreover, in his early *Aesthetics* Lukács – obviously under Bloch's influence – described the perfect work of art as realized utopia (Cf. Riedel 1993, p. 428).

On the other hand, Lukács constantly attacked abstract philosophical utopianism, which he would later also identify with his friend's philosophy. But what kind of thinking did he have in mind? In his theory of utopia, Bloch emphasizes the opaqueness of the soul:

> [H]uman strength even *in hoc statu nascendi* still has its particular spiritual shadow, its unknowing of the deepest depth as such, and the centre in itself is still night, incognito, ferment, around which everyone, everything, and every work is still built. (GU2, p. 218; SU, p. 173)

In putting together the structure of the genre and the philosophical context, Lukács also describes the process of going deeper into oneself in terms of the hero of a novel. Thomas Mann, following Schopenhauer (but possibly also referring to Lukács) defended a similar stance: 'When the prosaic novel differentiated itself from the *epos*, the narrative entered the path of deepening into the inner life and the subtleties of the human psychological experience' (1955, p. 466).

Lukács generally does not accept this subjectivist turn, considering it to be futile, solipsistically passive and overly romantic (a critique that goes back to *Soul and Form*). It is no accident, then, that discussing the turn to the inner life in the 'novel of disillusion', he touches upon 'the problem of utopia':

> [C]an this rounded correction of reality be translated into actions which, regardless of outward failure or success, prove the individual's right to self-sufficiency – actions which do not compromise the mental attitude from which they sprang? To create, by purely artistic means, a reality which corresponds to this dream world ... is only an illusory solution. (TN, p. 115)

Of all the novels of disillusion, Lukács marks out Gustave Flaubert's *Sentimental Education*, praising it as a model of epic concreteness unique to this literary form, attained by virtue of the *active experience of time (dureé)*. Time, in *The Theory of the Novel*, expresses the resistance of life and meaning to the merciless machine of finitude. The fate of the novel as a genre of the godless world is linked to this resistance. Time as such never acts in drama, nor in epic, it appears only as an objectivation of the eternal past or the eternal present. Only in the novel the resistance of 'organic life' turns decline and decay into the source of epic poetry, capable of grasping the reality of this decay and not just withdrawing into subjectivity, but courageously recognizing and accepting this suffocative and sorrowful world. Moreover, in Flaubert, Lukács sees motives quite similar to those of Bloch: the affective reconstruction of totality, hope and recollection (in the 1962 introduction, Lukács also mentions Proust) that help one overcome the illusions of lyrical subjectivity; time is appropriated by the hero and enriches his soul, the subject returns to itself (cf. Bloch's discussion of the self-encounter in *The Spirit of Utopia*), and the novel thus establishes its own temporality. The experience of time in general becomes a constitutive moment of the novel's form. At the same time, Flaubert manages to avoid the dead ends of subjectivist illusions and destruction: 'The lyrical character of moods is transcended in the mood of experiencing this homecoming because it is related to the outside world, to the totality of life.' (TN, p. 128f).

And while hitherto the characters of the novel, like Don Quixote, travelled in space, now they make themselves at home in time, projecting their thoughts and feelings into the past and the future. But time does not become analogous to space, as it does in an epic; it undergoes a qualitative transformation, it becomes linked to 'the unique and unrepeatable stream of life' (TN, p. 125).

Fredric Jameson showed that the ideal paradigm for Bloch's utopian hermeneutics could be found in the novels of Proust – in those exquisite protocols of emotional experiences (1971, pp. 151–6): an acute sense of time, universalization of emotions; subordination of the whole surrounding world to the affective intensity; an inevitable deviation of the real future from the expected. 'Hopes are always disappointed' – said Bloch once, for the intrusion of utopia in reality radically changes the world, and we are unable to experience or to analyse the radically new before it occurs. Viewing the present as raw material, as a collection of fragments, from which only the subjective effort can 'put together' a genuine experience; a special role of art and language in this process, in the genuine experience of time (including the past) are all the themes common to Proust and Bloch.[18] In this sense, the 'romanticism of disillusionment' as it is discussed in *The Theory of the Novel* is surprisingly illustrative of such a mindset:

> [H]ope ... is not an abstract artefact, isolated from life, spoilt and shop-worn as the result of its defeat by life: it is a part of life; it tries to conquer life by embracing and adorning it, yet is repulsed by life again and again. ... And so, by a strange and melancholy paradox, the moment of failure is the moment of value; the comprehending and experiencing of life's refusals is the source from which the fullness of life seems to flow. What is depicted is the total absence of any fulfilment of meaning, yet the work attains the rich and rounded fullness of a true totality of life. (TN, p. 126)

It might seem that Bloch should not be interested in recollection, since hope is a more fundamental affect for him. However, both of them have their place in utopian philosophy, for they manifest something unforeseen, linking the affective centre of our present life-situation with recollection and, in general, with the essence of time, which neither Lukács nor Bloch conceived merely as a force of destruction and decay.

Reading Tolstoy's novels through the Lukácsean lens can provide a further illustration of Bloch's thought – this concerns an immediate unity with nature, the return to materiality, ensuring the epic integrity of the novel, which, however, is revealed to Tolstoy's characters only at 'very rare, great moments' – Lukács remembers the field of Austerlitz. The same examples from *War and Peace* and from the ill Anna Karenina's bedside would later appear in *The Principle of Hope* (PH, pp. 1389f.).

> This world is the sphere of pure soul-reality in which man exists as man *(in Tolstoy – I. B.)*. . . . If ever this world should come into being as something natural and simply experienced, as the only true reality, a new complete totality could be built out of all its substances and relationships. It would be a world . . . which would have outstripped our dual world of social reality by as much as we have outstripped the world of nature. But art can never be the agent of such a transformation: the great epic is a form bound to the historical moment, and any attempt to depict the Utopian as existent can only end in destroying the form, not in creating reality. (TN, p. 152)

Anticipation of the new in this case does not go beyond the examination of literature. In *The Spirit of Utopia* such an approach is put into question, and not as a metaphysical, but as an aesthetic programme. Criticizing in general the interpretation of art in the formal-technical sense, Bloch asserts that such an approach necessarily leads to arbitrariness and superficiality. He touches upon Lukács as well:

> One should . . . not believe that one can give each particular mode of presentation its respective, self-evident background by serving it up historically; by regarding the forms of the novel, the dialogue or the other expedients of talent as fixed onto a revolving firmament of intelligence within the philosophy of history; where particular forms of expression then just come and go; in sum, by reinterpreting the history of the artistic *whos* and their *whats* into a history of medieval-realist hows. (GU2, p. 147; SU, p. 113)

The target of this critique is obvious. Bloch opposes the transcendence of religion, the tendency to illuminate the mystery of the inner world and the hermeneutics of the not-yet revealed meanings in the open and dynamic universe (but first and foremost – in music, 'the only subjective theurgy' (GU2, p. 208; SU, p. 163), not nearly as helpless as art for Lukács) to the immanence of art and the analysis of aesthetic objectivations. In other words, we are talking about a different aesthetic programme in which, for instance, the Greek world is inferior to the Gothic style, as it better reflects utopian imperatives.

There are other, more obvious differences. *The Theory of the Novel* begins like this: 'Happy are those ages when the starry sky is the map of all possible paths – ages whose paths are illuminated by the light of the stars' (TN, p. 29). This utopia belongs to the past that is forever gone. Bloch has a completely different opening: the first edition of *The Spirit of Utopia* begins with the words: *'Wie nun?'* (What, then? or How?) (GU1, p. 9). How can one continue living, what future to look for? And although Bloch sometimes also speaks of the times 'when gods were close' (GU1, p.183),[19] he immediately shifts his emphasis to art as a herald of the new time; bravely stepping over the abyss, on the one side of which is the soul, and on the other, the action; without staring, like Lukács, into this chasm, and without admitting the irreconcilable differences between the great moments in literature and the arrival at another reality (Harth 1985).

The comparison of Bloch's and Lukács's approaches to another genre – the *fairy tale* –helps to give a more precise characteristic of the difference in their aesthetic views at that time (Czajka 2006, p. 201ff.). For Lukács, the fairy tale is a symbol of a past, prehistoric epoch; he deems the return of the fairy tale as the possibility of a new reality commensurate to the infinity of genuine life. Because fairy tales are absolutely heterogeneous with the rational, 'the actual' arrangement of things, they create different worlds. Bloch, on the other hand, places them into time and contests their immutability, their stillness and fixation, insisting on the possibility of their constant reinterpretation, while paying almost no attention to the novel in his aesthetics.

It would be wrong to say that Lukács did not understand the risk of fetishization of form, on the contrary, he admitted that

> The longing for the dissonance to be resolved, affirmed and absorbed into the form may be so great that it will lead to a premature closing of the circle of the novel's world, causing the form to disintegrate into disparate, heterogeneous parts. The fragility of the world may be superficially disguised but it cannot be abolished; consequently this fragility will appear in the novel as unprocessed raw material. (TN, p. 72, translation slightly altered)

Lukács overcomes this formalism rather quickly, cf. a passage from a letter to Paul Ernst from 14 April 1915, written in absolutely Blochean style and, possibly, evoked by conversations with Bloch, where he says that genuine existence is only we *ourselves*, our soul, and not the artistic image. He realized that the world is incomplete, vulnerable, that the purely aesthetic solution is inappropriate, but as long as the socially acceptable solution is not found, one can only overcome the abstractions through the revealing, the description, the narrative. One should *report* about the decline of the integral self-same world, trace the fate of this universal dissonance narratively, in order to somehow survive the 'epoch of absolute sinfulness'. And so the author's only lot is irony – 'negative mysticism to be found in times without a god', 'freedom of the writer in his relationship to God' (TN, pp. 90, 92).

A little later than Lukács and Bloch, in a different intellectual context – however one still determined by neo-Kantianism and the philosophy of life – *Mikhail Bakhtin* underwent the same development. Here we can only roughly outline the significant points of correspondence between the aesthetic polemic of Lukács and Bloch, on the one hand, and Bakhtin's development of aesthetics of verbal creation, on the other (See the most detailed analysis available, where, however, Bloch is not discussed, in: Tihanov 2000.) In *Author and Hero in Aesthetic Activity*, Bakhtin constructs the conception of *outsideness* (*vnenakhodimost'*) and opposes the aesthetic *givenness* with ethical or religious *positedness*, the complete being of the hero to the 'not-yet-being' of the human, who contemplates his own life from within himself:

> My determination of myself is given to me (given as a task – as something yet to be achieved) not in the categories of temporal being, but in the categories of *not-yet-being*, in the categories of purpose and meaning – in the meaning-governed future. (Bakhtin 1990, p. 123)

What is interesting, of course, is not the coincidence of words (*Author and Hero* was not published in Bakhtin's lifetime, and Bloch, undoubtedly, did not know it), but the consonance of ideas. The intellectual strategy in the metaphysics of the dark instant, the theory of subjectivity, unclear to itself, carrying in itself a non-rationalizable utopian 'excess', is performed by Bakhtin in the guise of a purely aesthetic problematization, and is described as an incompatibility of the hero from within herself, and the possibility of such grace through her consummation by the author. Bloch discusses this possibility – both epistemologically and ontologically – in *The Spirit of Utopia* only in the light of the apocalypse, and in later works renouncing it altogether. But Bloch's aesthetics turn out to be essentially extra-aesthetic, or more precisely, if we rely on the principles of *Author and Hero*, Bloch develops not *the aesthetics of form* (for any form is complete and lives within the organic rhythm), but *the aesthetics of the creative act*, of realizing the essential incommensurability of the *ought* and the *is*, of audacity and living into the

> absolute future . . . not into the future which will leave everything in its place, but into the future which must finally fulfill, accomplish everything, the future which we *oppose* to the present and the past as a salvation, transfiguration, and redemption. That is, the future . . . as that which axiologically does not yet exist, that which is still unpredetermined . . . not yet *discredited* by existence, not sullied by existence-as-given, free from it; that which is incorruptible and unrestrictedly ideal – not epistemologically and theoretically, however, but practically, i.e., as an ought or obligation. (Bakhtin 1990, p. 118)

Lukács somehow depicted in the *Theory of the Novel* all the moments of the crisis experienced by his times: disintegration of unity, the loss of subject, the collapse of traditional literary forms. He associated this homogeneity with the 'enclosed cultures' of Antiquity and the Middle Ages, thus recurring to the pattern of thought typical for German aesthetics beginning from the eighteenth century, and, among others, evident in young Hegel. Opposing the immanence, the stasis of the self-sufficient world of Antiquity to the dynamism of modernity, linked to the Christian outlook, is also quite strong in Heidegger, as well as in twentieth-century literary criticism (see, e.g. the discussion of Homer in Auerbach 2003). Lukácsean aesthetics could then be readily reformulated as a philosophy of history, and the form that was opposed to life, was thereby conceived as an unambiguous indication of how to change this life (even if such change turned out to be impossible within the novel). But having recognized, in the shadow of Hegel, all the ultimate importance of the precise and rigorous attunement towards the epoch, Lukács was able to complete this transition from aesthetics to history – via *History and Class Consciousness*.

Episode Three: Grappling with Totality

History and Class Consciousness was published in 1923 and remains to a large extent the definitive book for left-wing radical thought. This is the last of Lukács's works in which Bloch's influence can be accurately traced. Although they continued to read each other's work after 1923, the period of common intellectual concerns was largely over (some common themes persisted though, of Hegel and Goethe, to which we shall return).

The complex intellectual formation of the young Lukács could be, to put it basically, delineated as a search for the absolute, a wholly immanent constellation of meaning. Lukács went from *Soul and Form* with its intentionally ahistorical ethics and aesthetics to *The Theory of the Novel*, showing the way to the totality that had been lost, the experience of which becoming the constitutive principle of the novel's form; and from *The Theory of the Novel* to *History and Class Consciousness*, outlining fairly straightforward ways of reconciling the subject and the object, of overcoming alien, reified forms, weighing upon the human, in order to reclaim a previous, 'organic' culture (see a characteristic article *The Old Culture and the New Culture* (Lukács 1970) written at the same time as *The History and Class Consciousness*). The dissociation between the individual and the reality, or, more precisely, the discrepancy between the subjective ethical ideals and the realities of bourgeois life, is no longer metaphysically self-evident. It is redefined as a unity of historically determined social circumstances (Jameson 1971, p. 182), which, as Lukács claims directly, is relative and can be overcome.

The change brought by *History and Class Consciousness*, as perceived by the European intellectuals in the 1920s or, especially, in the 1960s, boils down to a new understanding of Marxism and the dialectical method. A comprehensive account of these issues cannot be given here. However, it is absolutely indispensable to show affinities and tensions between the ideas in the book, for without it, Bloch's philosophical project would have undoubtedly been different.

Lukács considered his work to be Hegelian and it was in this that Bloch saw its merit. He noted, however, that Lukács, though in some way more Hegelian than Hegel himself, explained the Hegelian origin of Marxist thought and reconsidered the very notion of dialectics. What is the kernel of this reconsideration?

In his review of *History and Class Consciousness* (entitled *Actuality and Utopia*), Bloch discovers the instant that 'is sublimated [while] becoming the moment of decision, of an insight into the totality' (PA, p. 600). Bloch's Lukács manifests a tension between Hegel's political philosophy and a new version of Hegelianism; between the regularity of a progressive movement in the spirit of historical materialism and the messianism of the proletariat. But both Lukács and Bloch perceived Hegelianism and the revolutionary conception of totality as a remedy against positivism and vulgar-rational thought with its schematics. Apart from this, Lukács also saw in the category of totality a potential to radically renew Marxist theory (Jay 1986), while Bloch sees in it his own motives: the darkness of the lived instant, 'the Now', the idea of mutual permeation of subject and object in 'the secret face of the human' (PA, p. 600). But of course, the revolutionary subject, apostle of history, still plays the key role in overcoming the social conventions and structures hostile to inner life.

Lukács quickly lost interest in *History and Class Consciousness* explaining this in the introduction to the 1967 edition, in which he asserted that the notion of *praxis*, so important for the new conception of history and revolution, lacked a sufficient material foundation. The coming of totality, as in previous work by Lukács, remained purely *conscious*: the proletariat, that destitute Messiah, had to see its own marginal position, *to understand* that it had become absolutely central to the production and reproduction of capitalist relations, as the fate of capitalism defining the limits of this social formation that had to be transcended.

> [T]he coercive measures taken by society in individual cases are often hard and brutally materialistic, but *the strength of every society is in the last resort a spiritual strength*. And from this we can only be liberated by knowledge. This knowledge cannot be of the abstract kind that remains in one's head – many "socialists" have possessed that sort of knowledge. It must be knowledge that has become flesh of one's flesh and blood of one's blood; to use Marx's phrase, it must be "practical critical activity." (HCC, p. 262)

Proletarians thus had to recollect themselves, to look at society from the outside, realizing that it is historically relative and transient. Only the proletariat's 'quest for a democratic world order' makes it 'the agent of the social salvation of mankind, the messianic class of world history. Without the fervor of this messianism, the victorious path of social democracy would have been impossible' (Lukács 1977, p. 420f.). Following Hegel, Lukács sees in the historical process a realization of certain ideas, or, better still, a metamorphosis of particular social classes into ideas. For both the proletariat and the bourgeoisie are moments in the historically unfolding social totality. See, for instance, the following characteristic Hegelian passage:

> [A]s the mere contradiction is raised to a consciously dialectical contradiction, as the act of becoming conscious turns into *a point of transition in practice*, we see ... the character of proletarian dialectics ... since consciousness here is not the knowledge of the opposed object but is the self-consciousness of the object *the act of consciousness overthrows the objective form of its object*. (HCC, p. 178)

But the very attainment of this totality seemed to Lukács a spontaneous and, generally speaking, accidental process. '[I]n my presentation it would indeed be a miracle if this "imputed" consciousness could turn into revolutionary praxis' (HCC, p. xix) – he writes in 1967 looking back, trying in vain to separate the wheat from the chaff. But today this past appears in an entirely different light.

> Jünger and Bloch, Lukács and Schmitt – they all realized that the crisis of modernity should come to an end. They all think of the finality of the modern society in the unsurpassed puissance in which the original experience and the keenest scent for governing modernity – in Jünger; in the illuminated We of the community that breaks the logic of the state based on need – in Bloch; in the real aesthetics of the collective subject discovering its total form – in Lukács; in the finally secured homogeneity of concrete state order – in Schmitt (Eßbach 1994, p. 232).

The proletariat in Lukács recalls Münchhausen, who pulls himself out of a swamp by his own hair (Dmitriev 2004, p. 172). The self-enclosed structure of this argument could be associated with the logic of Fichte's doctrine of science, in which intellectual activism is preoccupied by the process of self-grounding. If we ask the Lukács of *History and Class Consciousness* – 'What is the proletariat?' – the answer would be: 'The identical subject-object of the historical process that gains consciousness'. 'What is the consciousness of the proletariat?'– 'This consciousness is visibly manifest in the party, a consciously organised unity of theory and practice'. – 'What should the proletariat be guided by?' – 'The world-historical interest of the social totality, which it alone can discover, by piercing through to a new, post-revolutionary epoch.' – 'How can one see this new epoch?' – 'By establishing it through action, for the reality of history "is not, it becomes" (HCC, p. 203)'.[20] This circle of concepts referring to one another designates a space occupied by the thought of the Hungarian revolutionary.

Maintaining that history can, in fact, change its direction and that everything depends on the consciousness and will of the proletariat, Lukács sternly criticizes all the opponents of revolutionary violence (which in 1923 was blatantly anachronistic) and anyone who subordinated the political element to the economic one (cf., for instance, his critique of a rather sober position by Rosa Luxemburg). Curiously, Lukács's activism was formulated in the best traditions of the Expressionists' political rhetoric of the time (and earlier), which later he would subject to such a merciless critique (Ujma 1995).

Bloch, of course, also interprets the revolutionary event as an instantaneous apocalyptic illumination, and shares with Lukács the voluntaristic and activistic notion of the revolution and the revolutionary subject.

> Marx, no doubt, relied to a great extent on Hegel's *List der Idee* ("Cunning of Idea") in the construction of his historico-philosophical process that claims the proletariat, while fighting for its immediate class interests, will also free the world of tyranny forever. In the moment of decision that has now arrived, one cannot overlook the dualistic separation of the soulless empirical reality and the human – that is, the Utopian, the ethical, the objective. (Lukács 1977, p. 421)

Clearly, Bloch's later distinction between the 'Warm' and the 'Cold' streams of Marxism originates in *History and Class Consciousness*: 'While the unsatisfied need is the drive and impulse of the dialectic-material movement, the totality of the not-yet-existent All – basing on the same, not yet appeared content – is its tightening and unifying goal' (SO, p. 512).

The idea of reification and Marxist motifs in general are present everywhere in Bloch's texts from then on. In particular, he agreed with the dichotomy of the quantitatively cognizable, accomplished world of reification, in which positive science dwells; and the realm of history, where the qualitative appears. In their project of conceptualizing these dynamic forms of history, Bloch and Lukács drew heavily on Simmel's *Philosophy of Money* and Weber's theory of rationalization. (They both distanced themselves from their teachers, and both came to Hegel and Marx albeit in different ways and with different results.)

For instance, Bloch argues that even though one could conceive of the bourgeoisie as *active*, this does not mean that their action embodies any truth, for their activity is provoked by a calculated interest which motivates the bourgeois entrepreneur or worker *within* a giant capitalist machine (PA, p. 602). The qualitative peculiarity of the non-reified world is not only a mystery and a limit for bourgeois thinking – it is a limit of capitalism as such. Science in the reified world (Lukács refers, in particular, to the social-economic theories), due to its methodological limitations (studying only the given, complete forms, ignoring the interdependence of understanding and transforming the social world), is unable to rise above 'the facts, to see the tendency or the objective possibility', the link between tendency and practice. Lukács discusses in detail the propensity of bourgeois science to classify, to formalize, to order the given and – as a reflection of the division of labour – to analytically dissect the social whole (totality) and specialize.

For bourgeois science, therefore, the world of matter is impenetrable, irrational; somewhere on the surface of the matter, on the borders of this chaos it constructs its phantom worlds. Despite the fact that at times, in the moments of crisis, the fragility of the system becomes evident, the bourgeois has no other way of understanding. The philosophical reflection of this situation is characterized by Lukács as the problem of the thing-in-itself, which in fact implies the problem of totality, of grasping reality as a whole. And if Kant postpones this problem into eternity, here its solution is associated with the revolutionary overturn as the only means to adequately understand society. The epistemological problem transforms into the problem of the 'processual sublimation of facts' (PA, p. 611) and of transforming the reality, for which finally a suitable subject is found.

In a later interview Bloch said that a substantial part of their common philosophy – the ideas of 'the darkness of the lived instant', unconscious knowledge, objective possibility, utopia – was taken up by Lukács.

> [T]he concrete here and now dissolves into a process ... is no longer a continuous, intangible moment, immediacy slipping away; it is the focus of the deepest ... mediation, the focus of decision and the birth of the new. As long as man concentrates his interest contemplatively upon the past *or* future, both ossify into an alien existence. And between the subject and the object lies the unbridgeable "pernicious chasm" of the present. Man must be able to comprehend the present as a becoming. He can do this by seeing in it the tendencies out of whose dialectical opposition he can *make* the future. Only when he does this will the present be a process of becoming, that belongs to *him*. Only he who is willing and whose mission it is to create the future can see the present in its concrete truth. As Hegel says: "Truth is not to treat objects as alien" (HCC, p. 203f.)

In this extensive quote where Lukács accounts for the arrival of the proletariat at the point of view of totality we find the common ground for Bloch and Lukács, in their *attention to modernity*, the need to affirm actual political decisions. Perhaps, owing to these notions, Marxism became an indispensable methodological reference point not only for Bloch (for whom in 1914–15, when *The Spirit of Utopia* was being written, Marx remained just another apocalyptic figure), but also for Benjamin who wrote to Scholem from Capri in 1924: 'Bloch reviewed Lukacs's *History and Class Consciousness* in the March issue of the *Neue Merkur*. The review seems to be by far the best thing he has done in a long time and the book itself is very important, especially for me'

(WCB, p. 244). The historical moment here is not accidental, but it is grasped with all the universality that is appropriate for historical totality.

Bloch, after summarizing the thesis of the book in his review, claims that Lukács was able to discover the problem of the subject's proximity to itself in all its historical dimensionality. He argues that the book unpacks the understanding and recognition of oneself as existing, and opposes the concept of the 'Now' as used by Hegel in the *Phenomenology*, in which the 'Now' appears only as a first step in a process. Lukács, as Bloch contends, speaks from within the core of historical temporality; and staying at the centre of this process, grasping its tendencies, the proletariat is capable of creating, and thereby appropriating the future. This historical subject is described by Bloch in terms of the 'We-problem' (GU2, p. 249; SU, p. 187ff.) – the soul, discovering in itself a God-given spark, is driven to reveal the mysteries of the world, to attain the not-yet-realized utopian unity, in which the subject and the object turn towards each other. Lukács is treated as one of the prophets of modernity and is placed together with Chagall, Schoenberg and Döblin – new names in painting, music and literature (PA, p. 600).

Of course, it was necessary for Bloch to make certain reservations. Here, like in the case of *The Metaphysics of Tragedy*, Bloch found an odious strand of over-totalization. He could not exclude nature from the utopian horizon, that which gives rise to uncertainty and dynamics; he thus renders the need to transform theory into practice by force (or by miracle) unnecessary. The pressure of an expansive sociological 'homogenization' destroys life, nature and the elements of 'dianoethical comprehension, which are mostly eccentric' (PA, p. 618). Bloch mentions specific spheres of historical being, like, for example, the system of natural rights or classical art that became a problem in each epoch, and therefore resist historical-materialist schematism. Here Bloch writes for the first time that subjectivity, not yet fully manifested, is also present in nature (analogously to the working subject of history). This speculation in the spirit of natural philosophy is hardly compatible with the Marxism of *History and Class Consciousness*.

Interestingly, in the first edition of *The Spirit of Utopia* and in *Thomas Müntzer*, Bloch understands nature, rather, in the spirit of gnosticism, as an alien shell that has to be overcome by the utopian consciousness (GU2, p. 13),[21] while Lukács in *The Theory of the Novel* opposes 'the first' and 'the second' nature (i.e. the world of spiritual objectivations that has become alien to the soul):

> Estrangement from nature (the first nature), the modern sentimental attitude to nature, is only a projection of man's experience of his self-made environment as a prison instead of as a parental home. When the structures made by man for man are really adequate to man, they are his necessary and native home; and he does not know the nostalgia that posits and experiences nature as the object of its own seeking and finding. The first nature, nature as a set of laws for pure cognition, nature as the bringer of comfort to pure feeling, is nothing other than the historico-philosophical objectivation of man's alienation from his own constructs. (TN, p. 64)

But now Bloch expresses interest in nature, revealing a contradiction: in *History and Class Consciousness* Lukács criticized Engels's view that dialectics is applicable to nature, writing that nature is a social category. (The same idea will be later held by Lukács's opponent Sartre.)

The misunderstandings that arise from Engels's account of dialectics can in the main be put down to the fact that Engels – following Hegel's mistaken lead – extended the method to apply also to nature. However, the crucial determinants of dialectics – the interaction of subject and object, the unity of theory and practice, the historical changes in the reality underlying the categories as the root cause of changes in thought, etc. – are absent from our knowledge of nature (HCC, p. 24).

Here, the figure of Vico plays a special role. Vico's idea that only something created by the human being can be cognized led Lukács to the conclusion: the dialectic makes sense only with reference to historical reality (see also: EM, p. 62). Precisely the ability to change the world, to guide its laws in the right direction was the heritage of that very 'clever idealism', which was so importantly engaged in the formulation of relevant Marxist doctrines, although it sometimes leaves one wondering whether such 'sociologisation' of nature contradicts the rejection of dialectics in the natural realm (Schiller 1991).

Bloch believed that excessive totalization ossifies Marxism and deprives it of utopian obstinacy, resulting in a new mythology:

> [T]he same man who drove the fetish character out of production, who believed he had analyzed, exorcized every irrationality from history as merely unexamined, uncomprehended and therefore operatively fateful obscurities of the class situation, who had banished every dream, every operative utopia, every *telos* circulating in religion from history, plays with his "forces of production," with the calculus of the "process of production" the same all too constitutive game, the same pantheism, mythicism, upholds for it the same ultimately utilizing, guiding power which Hegel upheld for the "Idea", indeed which Schopenhauer upheld for his alogical "Will." (GU2, p. 301; SU, p. 241)

Bloch talks of Marxism, while referring to Lukácsean Marxism. He proposes to supplement Lukács's concept of totality with that of a sphere, which is 'a representation of the different levels of the subject-object posited in the process itself' (PA, p. 619). Bloch's Marxism is sensitive to non-contemporaneity, the ruptures and sudden changes in the homogeneous flow of history; it is eventually a search of certain broader ontological grounds, a protest against the univocal emphasis on the indeterminacy and openness of the historical process, and possibly a hint at Hegelian ideas or at the notion of Weberian 'value spheres'.[22]

Bloch could agree that the proletariat's highest goal is to grasp modernity, that actuality and utopia are not contradictory but, on the contrary, the mystery of utopia is in its actuality. It is in the instantaneous Now that this mystery must be illuminated, so that the subject of history can ground itself, thus solving the mystery of the future. But this solution is largely affective, intuitive, subconscious, it is precisely in this way that we can become imbued with the 'syncopated rhythm' (EZ, p. 395; HT, p. 358) of history. At the same time Lukács, even at the beginning of his 'journey towards Marx', was an apologist of the rational and the epistemic, already shunning the apocalyptic fantasies and religious overtones so characteristic of Bloch. And while Bloch insists that 'the Soul, the Messiah, and the Apocalypse, which represents the act of awakening in totality, provide the final impulses to do and to know, form the *a priori* of all politics and culture' (GU2, p. 346; SU, p. 278; cf. also: Jay 1984, pp. 174–95), Lukács, criticizing Bloch's book on Müntzer, writes:

> Real actions . . . appear – precisely in their objective, revolutionary sense – wholly independent of the religious utopia: the latter can neither lead them in any real sense, nor can it offer concrete objectives or concrete proposals for their realisation. When Ernst Bloch claims that this union of religion with socio-economic revolution points the way to a deepening of the "merely economic" outlook of historical materialism, he fails to notice that his deepening simply by-passes the real depth of historical materialism. When he then conceives of economics as a concern with objective things to which soul and inwardness are to be opposed, he overlooks the fact that the real social revolution can only mean restructuring the real and concrete life of man. He does not see that what is known as economics is nothing but the system of forms objectively defining this real life. The revolutionary sects were forced to evade this problem because in their historical situation such a restructuring of life and even of the definition of the problem was objectively impossible. (HCC, p. 193)[23]

This is followed by the famous words that it is not the individual, but only the class as totality that can ascend the summit of history. Class consciousness 'is identical with neither the psychological consciousness of individual members of the proletariat, nor with the (mass-psychological) consciousness of the proletariat as a whole; it is, on the contrary, *the sense, conscious of the historical role of the class*' (HCC, p. 73); a unity that lies above the mere givenness of a fact. However, it is also hard to reconcile with real historical and social circumstances, with the actual condition of the proletariat and 'the system of forms objectively defining' its real life, demonstrating how it could achieve class consciousness. It is precisely this transition from the normative order to the real being that is still irrational and arbitrary in Lukács's work, precisely in the respect that he is similar to Bloch, except that the latter never excluded from his analysis the affective element and, in general, forms of the everyday. On the contrary, Bloch tried to give them meaning within his philosophy of history.

After *History and Class Consciousness* Bloch's philosophy gets much closer to Marxism.[24] The dialectics and historical concretization of utopia now form the basis of his thinking, and the critique of shallow positivism – clinging to 'facts' – acquires a new dimension. An individual who refuses to submit to the rigid, fetishized forms of social being, revolutionizes his life, turns this being into 'Not-Yet-Being', into prehistory. Bloch, following Lukács, redefines this revolutionary overcoming and therefore an elevation of the human as a Marxist project. Lukács taught Bloch to discern the social totality, to envisage its total transformation, and to note down the distortions resulting from the betrayal of this all-embracing perspective.

But still, the alternative to Lukács's radical immanentism remained problematic, especially because Bloch proposed to look for the traces of the future in the present, thus partly affirming the given reality and hardly providing any clues to distinguish the 'bad' from the productive presence. Furthermore, Bloch himself had a tendency towards excessive totalization. What proved more important, however, was the idea of the performative *self-assertion of utopian* inherited from Lukács. How can one measure the concreteness of the utopia? How do we know if it can be realized? The answer suggested by *History and Class Consciousness,* that from then on became a part of Bloch's intellectual arsenal, looks roughly like this: one can know only by doing, by asserting the utopian, by mediating theory with practice. The truth of the utopian movement is born in this self-establishing praxis, in the political struggle that does not unfold according to a predefined plan, but emerges from the logic of the historical situation and concrete decisions here and now. However, in practicing such an attitude, Lukács gravitated towards the totality of party forms, while Bloch tended, rather, to creative restlessness and eternal wandering; a significant feature of which was the permanent refusal to accept the reality of the present.

The concept of totality no longer functioned for Bloch as an instrument for the analysis of contemporary culture. While in *Actuality and Utopia* he talks of the spheres, in the 1930s he begins to characterize the contemporaneity as a hollow space (*Hohlraum*)[25] – that, which remained after the destruction of organic culture, the space of possibilities, which came in place of monumental projects and *Gesamtkunstwerks*, the world of the new art, consisting entirely of debris and fragments; projects of the future that resist unilateral organization.

Bloch recollects how once (it is unclear when exactly) he approached Lukács, sitting in a café in Berlin, and in his passionate manner said to him: 'Listen, Djuri, just imagine that the world spirit opens its gigantic chops, stretching from Lisbon to Moscow, and promises to give you an outspoken answer to any of your questions. What would you ask?' Lukács replied: 'Knock it off with these silly things. I would not ask anything. The world spirit is unable to answer any questions. It is stupid. We, and we alone have to summon up, and act, and think' (Benseler 2002, p. 489).[26] The previous idealistic passion had clearly disappeared. Bloch never accepted Lukács's partisanship, a virtual invitation to join him in the grand ideological project, tacitly aspiring to realize his old dream – to retire into a monastery and to devote himself to ascetic practice within a religious community (Interview 1976, p. 40; Ujma 1995, p. 197).[27] Bloch continued to believe in the power of the words; Lukács, as the debates around Expressionism show, became more and more absorbed in concrete affairs while mastering a new, imperial style in philosophy, in literary and political journalism. We shall not discuss these debates separately here – they already were subject to a number of detailed studies. However, it is worth mentioning that in this dispute, which played a key role in Marxist aesthetics, both Benjamin and Brecht together with Hanns Eisler and Anna Seghers were on Bloch's side. They refused to accept Lukács's critique of expressionist and avant-garde art in general. (See Schmitt (1978). A detailed account of Bloch's position is given in Ujma (1995), among others).

For justice's sake, it should be noted that, in this, Bloch also followed his friend, having paid homage to both authoritarianism and the ideology behind it, though in his own peculiar, passionate, but no less repugnant form. He ardently supported the Soviet show trials of 1937,[28] and was accused for extensively editing his political texts when he republished them in 1972. Heidegger, on the contrary, surprised everyone by defiantly leaving his works of the Nazi period unchanged, putting them into print word for word after the war. European intellectuals have never fully forgiven these political errors – neither to the former, nor to the latter philosopher.

Episode Four: The Instant (*Faust* and *The Phenomenology of Spirit*)

The journey is out of the inadequate, which is eternally thirsting, to the event, which ends disposal.

(PH, p. 1196; PHE, p. 1018)

The paths of Lukács and Bloch crossed several times more, as they both returned to the origins, interpreting the classics. Among them were the two central texts of German modernity – *Faust* and *The Phenomenology of Spirit*.

The notion of totality, the desire for the authentic fullness and wholeness of life – all of these figures turn out to be features of the Faustian personality. Lukács's and Bloch's interest in Goethe is therefore a reflection, albeit not fully conscious, of their own early predilections. Jameson (1971, p. 140) argues that Bloch's philosophy as a whole may be regarded as an extended commentary on *Faust*. In an early letter to Lukács, Bloch notices that the destiny of his philosophy as a whole is an interplay between Don Quixote and Faust (Br I, p. 114).

Indeed, the multitude of images in Goethe – not only in *Faust* – seems to illustrate ideas of the discovery of the new, the Not-Yet-Being, the conquest of unexplored worlds, and the 'restlessness of the negative': a homunculus striving to overcome the obstacles that separate him from the real world, Mignon or Euphorion – children as yet unformed as personalities, images of movement and transition, inhabitants of the future, nomads, subjects of utopian languor (Wieland 1992, p. 158f.).

One of the ways in which *The Phenomenology of Spirit* departs from 'scientific' philosophical discourse (both in Hegel's sense and in the sense of contemporary historical-philosophical discipline) and enters the broader, more familiar space of culture, must be the exchange of meanings between philosophy and literature. Hegel's work is itself full of literary allusions: Sophocles, Diderot, Goethe, Schiller, Lichtenberg, Jacobi. Hegel's words are fully applicable to his own work: 'Every philosophy is complete in itself, and like an authentic work of art, carries the totality within itself' (Hegel 1968, p. 12).

Parallels between Goethe and Hegel have been drawn more than once. For instance, Hegel's first biographer Karl Rosenkranz (1844, p. 340) mentioned that the right Hegelians perceived their works as a single whole (Göschel 1832). The similarity of philosophical and literary intentions of Goethe and Hegel has been discussed by, among others, Rudolf Honneger (1925), Karl Löwith (1941), Paul Tillich (1932) and Hans Mayer (1959). But it was Lukács and Bloch who gave philosophical content to these parallels. And again – one can see that this follows from their own experience, their urge to give meaning to the subjective dialectics of *The Phenomenology of Spirit*, to the notion of thought mediated by being. Bloch writes: 'We – Lukács and I – were ourselves both still young, and this work excited us to the verge of insanity' (cit. in: Horster 1987, p. 13). Lukács called Bloch's thinking 'a mixture of Hebel's jewel casket (*Schatzkästlein*) with Hegel's *Phenomenology of Spirit*' (Gespräche, p. 34).

Before it can be understood in what sense it is possible to draw parallels between *Faust* and *The Phenomenology of Spirit*, the story of their authors' relations must be at least briefly recounted. Goethe and Hegel met in 1801, when Hegel arrived in Jena. During the first years of the nineteenth century, Goethe was an attentive reader of the *Critical Journal of Philosophy*, brought out by Hegel and Schelling. From the letters of those years, it is clear that they carefully read each other's works and were in quite close communication. Goethe's library contained Hegel's *The Difference Between the Philosophical Systems of Fichte and Schelling*; for his part, Hegel, in addition to the majority of the books of Goethe that came out at this time, read *Faust: A Fragment*, and possibly heard the author recite an extract from the first part of *Faust*.

These contacts continued until Hegel moved to Bamberg in 1806. Subsequently they met much less frequently; sometimes they exchanged letters in which they discussed mainly Goethe's theory of colour (Hegel was one of its few influential supporters); and they sent each other books.[29] The famous encounter between Goethe and Hegel and their conversation on dialectics took place in October 1827. After this they met one more time in 1829. It is well known that Goethe sometimes spoke harshly about Hegelian philosophy. This, however, did not prevent him from holding Hegel in esteem while preserving a respectful distance from the dialectical investigations of the Berlin professor (Sandkaulen 2004).

Did Goethe understand the Hegelian dialectic? It is possible to give a number of quick answers to this question, but they will not be complete and exhaustive, so without denying the importance of Goethe's attitude towards classical German idealism and Hegel in particular, I shall follow Lukács and Bloch in their comparative enterprise.

The problem here is not only that *The Phenomenology of Spirit* is a work in which the movement of the forms of consciousness correlates with the dialectic of literary images, while *Faust* is a tragedy that embodies Goethe's broad philosophical concerns. One needs to go beyond the analysis of correlations, beyond the essential difference of the two texts, trying to discern a common experience that was decisive for Lukács and Bloch and eventually shaped their utopian philosophy. But to give a full picture, it is necessary first to show how Goethe's tragedy figures explicitly in *The Phenomenology of Spirit*.

Hegel uses Goethe's text *Faust: a Fragment* in his section on 'the actualization of rational self-consciousness by way of itself'. He quotes the words of Mephistopheles in the scene 'Faust's Workroom', which was included in the final text of the tragedy; moreover, he quotes from memory, abridging and altering the text. In Goethe Mephistopheles says the following:

> Verachte nur Vernunft und Wissenschaft,
> Des Menschen allerhöchste Kraft,
> Laß nur in Blend- und Zauberwerken
> Dich von dem Lügengeist bestärken,
> So hab' ich dich schön unbedingt –
>
> ...

Und seiner Unersättlichkeit
Soll Speis' und Trank vor gier' gen Lippen schweben;
Er wird Erquickung sich umsonst erflehn,
Und hätt' er sich auch nicht dem Teufel übergeben,
Er müßte doch zu Grunde gehn!

Reason and Science only thou despise,
The highest strength in man that lies!
Let but the Lying Spirit bind thee
With magic works and shows that blind thee,
And I shall have thee fast and sure!

...

The dream of drink shall mock, but never lave him:
Refreshment shall his lips in vain implore –
Had he not made himself the Devil's, naught could save him,
Still were he lost forevermore!
(Faust I, 1851–67, transl. by Barnard Taylor)

In Hegel, however, this quotation is given as:

Es verachtet Verstand und Wissenschaft
des Menschen allerhöchste Gaben –
es hat dem Teufel sich ergeben
und muss zu Grunde gehn.

It despises intellect and science,
Man's highest gifts –
It has given himself over the devil
And must fall into ruin.[30]

It is well known that in the *Phenomenology* Hegel uses literary imagery to describe the phases of the historical development of spirit. After the stage of 'observing reason', self-consciousness wishes 'as an individual spirit' to be 'in its own eyes the essence' (358); in historical terms, the epoch of Modernity begins. 'With its destiny that of being in its own eyes the essence as existing-for-itself, self-consciousness is the negativity of the other.' Self-consciousness appears here as 'an individuality immediately articulating itself' (359).

> Insofar as it has elevated itself to its being-for-itself from out of the ethical substance and from out of the motionless being of thought, the law of ethos and existence, together with the knowledge related to observation and theory, only lay behind it as a gray and immediately vanishing shadow (360, Pinkard's translation of this passage is slightly altered)

Here too we encounter a hidden quotation from Faust. The mere observation and theory are not relevant any more, the action comes to the forefront.

On the whole, Hegel tries to reconstruct the image of early modern man, whose attitude towards the world leads him along the path of self-destruction (and this is fully in the spirit of the deviltempter whose words are used by Hegel). 'Its experience [the experience of self-consciousness – I. B.] enters its consciousness as a contradiction in which the attained actuality of its individuality sees itself destroyed by the negative essence' (363). Hegel has in mind that a purely singular individuality is unable to affirm itself in the world because it is abstract, and 'instead of having plunged from dead theory into life . . . [it] has now to an even greater degree merely plunged into the consciousness of its own lifelessness, and the cards it is dealt are merely those of an empty and alien necessity, a dead actuality' (363). Moreover, at this stage of the development of consciousness, the unrestrained lust and self-affirmation of those who are in love with each other in defiance of social conventions run up against the might of the law.

> The individual has been led to his ruin, and the absolute intractability of individuality is by the same token pulverized on that hard but uninterrupted actuality. Since, as consciousness, it is the unity of itself and its opposite, this transition is still something for it. It is its purpose, and its actualization as well as the contradiction of what *to it* was the essence and what *in itself* is the essence. It experiences the twofold meaning which lies in what it did. It *helped itself* to *life*, but in doing so, it to an even greater degree laid hold of death (364).[31]

Hegel hints at the murder of Valentin and the tragedy of Gretchen. And although the law here appears as something alien to the lovers (Gretchen and Faust), they experience the absolute alienation from their own selves. 'The final moment of [this form's] existence is the thought of its loss within necessity, that is, the thought of itself as an essence absolutely alien to itself' (366). In the final reckoning, it becomes clear that the truth of self-consciousness is this alien necessity – that is, social conventions. However, consciousness still has to traverse a long road to absolute knowing, a road full of setbacks, in order to finally come to this conclusion.[32]

It has been established in the literature, however, that Hegel was inspired less by Goethe's fragment than by the review of F. M. Klinger's novel, *Faust's Life, Deeds, and Journey to Hell*, written by J. G. Gruber and published in 1805 (see Falke 1996; Speight 2001). Speight particularly showed that what interested Hegel in this context was primarily the idea of the blind necessity that confronts the individual and makes the actions she considered to be her own result in something fully alien, something she cannot subscribe to anymore. It is astonishing that here Hegel takes up a genuinely Blochian theme. In his review Gruber quotes Klinger's text excerpted by Hegel: 'Everything is dark for the spirit of man; he is to himself a riddle' (see Speight 2001, p. 26). Here the Blochian lack of completeness and transparency and his general idea of the Not-yet, correspond to the Hegelian notion of inferiority and flawedness of this form of spirit, of the inevitable deadlocks that drive the dialectic forwards. Curiously, even this historiographical evidence supports this speculation.

Coming back to Goethe – we find references to him in other works of Hegel as well. In the *Aesthetics*, Hegel calls *Faust* an 'absolutely philosophical tragedy' that presents 'on the one side, dissatisfaction with learning, and, on the other, the freshness of life and enjoyment in the world, in general the tragic quest for harmony between the

Absolute in its essence and appearance and the individual's knowledge and will' (Hegel 1975, Vol. II. p. 122).[33]

Here, evidently, Hegel refers to the first part of the tragedy, which came out as a separate publication in 1808. The very issue of *Faust* as a philosophical work was not an original one: thus, Schelling stated in his *Philosophy of Art* – that is, in lectures delivered even before the first part of *Faust* was published – that if any poetical work at all deserved to be called philosophical then that work was *Faust*.

Now, we can state that Hegel's real interest to Goethe's *Faust* should not be overestimated. His Faust is a more generalized metaphysical and practical attitude that clearly never can fully coincide with Goethe's literary universe. However, at the time of the *Phenomenology*, the second part of *Faust* was not known to Hegel, and he was not able to appraise the whole scope of Goethe's literary task – this task by no means being contrary to his philosophical project and, above all, to the project he tried to realize in the *Phenomenology of Spirit*. It was to this circumstance that Lukács and Bloch turned their attention.

Lukács on Hegel and Goethe, or What humanity can accomplish

Lukács mentions the kinship between *Phenomenology* and *Faust* in his book *The Young Hegel*. However, a much more detailed analysis is provided in *Faust Studies,* where he interprets Goethe's work as 'the drama of humankind' (Lukács 1968). Lukács argues that Goethe proceeded from a recognition of the insoluble conflicts and contradictions of human life to their (dialectical) resolution at the level of humankind, Faust being its embodiment.[34] Already in his *Fragment* of 1790, Goethe makes Faust say what later became programmatic for Lukács and Bloch:

> ... Und was der ganzen Menschheit zugeteilt ist,
> Will ich in meinem inner Selbst geniessen ...
> ... Und so mein eigen Selbst zu ihrem Selbst erweitern,
> Und, wie sie selbst, am End auch ich zerscheitern
> (Faust I, 1770–71; 1774–75)

The meaning of the verse is understandable from a literal translation:

> All that has fallen to the lot of mankind,
> I wish to take into my inner self ...
> ... And so expand my own self to its self,
> And together with it rush down into the abyss.

This idea of humanity is present also in *The Phenomenology of Spirit*, where the individual carries the torch of humankind, renouncing his own self:

> If therefore this spirit begins its cultural maturation all over again and seems to start merely from itself, at the same time it is nonetheless making its beginning at a higher level. The realm of spirits, having formed itself in this way within existence, constitutes a sequence in which one spirit replaced the other, and each succeeding spirit took over from the previous spirit the realm of that spirit's world (808).

Lukács is interested above all in the literary problems of identifying the individual with humankind. Above all, he is concerned with the creation of literary types and with the problem of the 'lifelikeness' of those types in an artistic universe in which the attempt has been undertaken to portray the process of world history as a whole. And while comprehension of the fate of mankind is for Lukács the key to the success of a literary work, simply copying the universe is, according to him, a dead end (he points to Milton and Klopstock as those who chose this path). Although the fate of Faust in Goethe represents a pan-human tragedy, his image and his historical and personal individuality do not suffer from the vast scale of Goethe's presentation. Goethe does not hypostasize the principle of humanity and does not suppress individuality.

In the spirit of traditional Marxism, Lukács asserts that the historical development of the individual through various forms of labour lies at the foundation both of *Faust* and of the *Phenomenology of Spirit*. The latter is interpreted as a truly democratic educational project, in the sense that any consciousness is capable of pursuing the path to the supreme.

> For its part, science requires that self-consciousness shall have elevated itself into this ether in order to be able to live with science and to live in science, and, for that matter, to be able to live at all. Conversely, the individual has the right to demand that science provide him at least with the ladder to reach this standpoint (26).

Intellectual and literary collisions in *Faust* are connected with how the powers of humankind arise, how they develop within the individual and what obstacles they encounter. If the fate of humankind becomes manifest in a person in 'abridged' form, then the mental series of categories and stages of personality development must not be subordinated to objective dialectical logic. The sequence of stages must be dictated by the specific characteristics of the individual consciousness. It is a matter not of an arbitrary ordering of events, but of a special *logic of the individual*. In *Faust*, Lukács observes that the individual and humankind are intertwined: when the development of humanity stagnates, the action in *Faust* almost ceases; when it takes an abrupt progressive 'leap', the dramatic events acquire additional dynamics. For this reason, Lukács refers to a spasmodic, rapid, uneven, subjective-objective temporality and succession of time. In his letter to Wilhelm von Humboldt, Goethe wrote of the 'fullness of times' in *Faust*, meaning that the action encompasses several historical periods. This is held in common with the *Phenomenology of Spirit*, a work that is marked by the irregularity of conceptual movement, above all, at the level of composition: unevenness of the presentation, disproportion among key sections of the book, etc. Hegel understands dialectics as 'the immanent rhythm of the concept' (58), but how volatile and unpredictable this rhythm sometimes is!

Lukács discovers in *Faust* an 'unevenness' in an element of fancy, which he immediately associates with Goethe's realism. This special 'concrete-historical' fantasy creates 'a real environment – but one free of any naturalistic triviality – such that from the imaginary situation and from the individual characters ennobled thanks to this situation problems raise themselves to the height and typicality of the human' (Lukács 1968, p. 147). Fantastic imagery is the most adequate literary means for expressing the contradictory unity of the individual and humankind. In the constructions of Lukács, who at that time was at great pains to uphold the principles of realistic literature, this unity is of extreme significance. This does not imply that he reduces the true meaning of literary realism to the dialectic of the fantastic and the socio-historical principles, but in the case of *Faust* it is precisely this idea that guides his reasoning.

Of course, Lukács is quite orthodox and dogmatic here, without, alas, being always adequate. The dialectic of the individual and humankind is a fine explanatory device, but it is not clear why, for example, this particular intellectual strategy has to be used to interpret one of the initial scenes – when the memory of childhood and the mystical recollection of past religious experience return Faust to life and save him from suicide.

Lukács maintains that in Goethe's tragedy one can observe both the emergence and the overcoming of the tragic principle. All the *personal* dramas of Faust (the scenes with the spirit of the earth, Gretchen, Helena, the finale of the tragedy) become intermediate stages in the development of humankind. Lukács quotes later correspondence with Zelter in which Goethe insisted that for him irresolvable tragedy was an absurdity; pure tragedy did not interest him. Goethe thus carefully masquerades as a dialectician. In Lukács's opinion, Goethe and Hegel share the view that the path of humanity is not tragic as such but consists of innumerable objectively necessary individual tragedies. The reversals of man's personal fate are described without any sentimentality, and when an individual has performed his historical role he must leave the scene. Hegel defends the same idea in terms of the limited and finite nature of the individual human being as contrasted to the Absolute. Thus Lukács finds the common philosophical ground between the *Phenomenology of Spirit* and *Faust* in the idea that tragedies in the micro-cosmos of the individual manifest ceaseless progress in the macro-cosmos of humanity as a whole. For example, the tragedy of Gretchen is merely a necessary stage in Faust's life – a stage to be overcome. It is in the same spirit that Lukács interprets Goethe's statement to Eckermann that the first part of the tragedy is subjective and the second part – objective. The naive historicism of the first part passes into the reflective historicism of the second part, direct history into experienced philosophy of history. (In *The Young Hegel,* Lukács frames the relationship between the second and third parts of the *Phenomenology* in exactly the same way.) While the first part of *Faust* is a drama in terms of style, the second part is not an epic but a description of the past from the perspective of the present. Thus, the 'Classical Walpurgis Night' expresses the 'phenomenological' history of the development of humankind. Subjectively this is Faust's path to Helena, but objectively it is the development of Greek beauty, starting from its primitive, natural forms. Hegel, as is well known, also arranged the objective-historical development of the spirit starting from the classical ideal.

In the *Phenomenology* the single path of the individual and humankind is traversed by consciousness with the aid of numerous dialectical transitions. But what about *Faust*? What kind of dialectic, if any, guides him? One could immediately reply: he is on a journey, guided by the spirit of negativity, and through this journey he rids himself of the inert, fossilized forms of thought that once constrained him (Marotzki 1987; Wieland 1992).

Dialectical journey

Why was it precisely the motif of the journey that for Bloch became the point of contact between *Faust* and *The Phenomenology of Spirit*? Faust's journey is a model of the utopian attitude towards the world. The Faustian motif is the active need to go beyond the bounds of the known and established, to venture upon an experiment (Bloch 1961),[35] to depart on a pilgrimage.

This interpretation of the Faustian motif can also be found in German philosophical anthropology. For example, Max Scheler pictures a human being as 'an eternal "Faust" ... always avid for breaking through the confines of its now-and-here-so-being, always striving to *transcend* the reality surrounding him, including the corresponding actual reality of his own self' (Scheler 1991, p. 56).

Nor did Bloch ignore the theme of cultural formation (*Bildung*) in *Faust* and in the *Phenomenology*. *Bildung* as general elevation of the individual is a key concept in German culture, and if we refer to Faust's dramatic path along with the peripeteia of subject–object mediations in Hegel's *Phenomenology*, we reach the very essence of the German spirit. The travelling hero does not just symbolize the spirit's lack of spatial attachment, he also puts time to the test, living in a world that is not closed to the future. He crafts this future, enacting it in and through his own life.

Faust's self-perfection is not mere subjectivism, not the desire to go with the flow, simply indulging in the present, nor is it a futile self-admiration but 'an eye-opening of the world he has thoroughly experienced' (PH, p. 1191; PHE, p. 1014) – it is fully consistent with Enlightenment ideology. Bloch and Lukács argue that both Hegel and Goethe share the faith of the Enlightenment in man's capacity for endless self-improvement. Bloch depicts Goethe turning from the early images of Faust as rebel, Werther and Götz to the 'grownup' Wilhelm Meister, but in mediated fashion – via the *Phenomenology of Spirit* (which, however, Goethe probably never read). Faust is the moving principle of the whole world (that is why he seeks intimacy with the spirit of the earth). For both the Hegelian subject and Faust, the outward gaze, into the world, becomes inward, directed into their inner being. Bloch calls this journey dialectical because Faust sublates each level he has reached out of newly awakened curiosity and yearning for the new and unexplored (PH, p. 1192).

Until the splendid instant is achieved, Faust will find no peace of mind. Nor will it be found by the Hegelian consciousness, which

> suffers this violence at its own hands and brings to ruin its own restricted satisfaction. Feeling this violence, anxiety about the truth might well retreat and strive to hold onto what it is in danger of losing. But it can find no peace; even if it wants to remain in an unthinking lethargy, thought spoils thoughtlessness, and its unrest disturbs that lethargy. Even if it fortifies itself with a sentimentality which assures it that it will find that everything *is good in its own way*, this assurance likewise suffers violence by the rationality that straightaway finds out that precisely because it is just "that way," it is thus not good (80).

Bloch conceives of this becoming in a special fashion: consciousness (or Faust) uncovers within itself new possibilities and feels its otherness as its own not-yet-being, which it might become, and this compels it to wander eternally. Faust and the world over which he travels – the social '*topos*' – undergoes transformation, and depends on their mutual changes within one another. Bloch calls the self (the subject) a question and the world an answer, and vice versa (TE, p. 54).

Historical becoming appears in the *Phenomenology of Spirit* as the development of forms of consciousness, which, as it were, puts on a succession of historical masks, one after the other. Bloch argues that the same sort of historical progression involving the structural similarity of various stages is present in *Faust* as well as in the *Divine Comedy* (TE, p. 69ff.). However, while in Dante we see static constructions by which the heroes descend into hell and ascend to the heavens, in Hegel and in Goethe, the being is plastic: subject and object are interwoven in the fullness of historical and substantial life.

Excursus: Bloch's Hegel

The time has come to clarify the essence of Bloch's very ambivalent and contradictory attitude towards the Hegelian dialectic. Was dialectic meaningful for him, and what was this meaning?

Hegelian Marxism, adopted by Bloch primarily under Lukács's influence, was Bloch's way to concrete thinking, both in metaphysics and in the philosophy of history. Utopian thought would have remained a mere slogan, a phrase without consequences, if it was devoid of the revolutionary ferment allegedly provided by dialectics.

Bloch's principal problem with Hegel lies in the figure of *Er-innerung* or recollection – the consciousness's 'gathering in' its preceding forms and their sublation into absolute knowing. To this effort of remembering and subordination of the individual to the entirety of spirit, in which each form of consciousness 'bestows on itself the status of being a moment, and . . . gives itself a place in the whole' (53), Bloch, summoning Goethe as an ally, counterposes the subjective, emotional, utopian principle and an open, incomplete system.[36] He misses fundamental novelty and uncertainty in Hegel's system (SO, p. 125), insisting that even the effort of recollection becomes meaningless, if it is abstract, if remembering is not followed by anticipation and hope (TE, p. 280f.). Furthermore, the Bloch of the 1920–30s, a defender of the avant-garde, an opponent of Lukács and of his stubbornly orthodox view of literature, did not accept, as we have already seen, the notion of completeness and 'roundness' of literary forms. Lukács gravitated towards a rather monstrous oxymoron, which his epoch was preparing for him: he reconciled dialectics and Stalinism, trying to find a convincing way of putting literature at the service of society (Ujma 1995, p. 38ff.). For Bloch, on the other hand, the Hegelian reconciliation with reality (however superficial such interpretation of dialectics might be) was denounced as treachery in *The Spirit of Utopia*, as a justification of a universal lie and an abandonment of revolution. Bloch's aim here is to radicalize the contradictions rather than to neutralize them (Pauen 1997).

The 'openness' of dialectics, according to the later Bloch, is achieved through a special understanding of its materialist version – the essence of phenomena lies in their materiality, exempt from the realm of any external logic. It is precisely this circumstance that makes materialist dialectics more 'realistic', and connects it with multiplicity, discontinuity and incompleteness. '[W]hen observed from a Marxist perspective, reality is more coherent than ever, but only as *mediated interruption,* and the process of reality as such, traced by Marxism, is still open, therefore objectively fragmentary' (Bloch 1988, p. 161).

For the utopian philosophy, the uniformity and logical transparency of the Absolute are unacceptable, just as the attempts to dissolve 'natural being' within the medium of logic are inadequate (and on this point Schelling becomes Bloch's ally). 'Reality is *nominalism and not conceptual realism* – nominalism, however, of such a kind that all its moments and details are gathered together *by the unity of objectively-real intention* and its foundation is *the utopian unity of a goal*' (SO, p. 508, compare: p. 398).

Logic without instinct, without an affective tension remains for Bloch a herbarium of dried-out words or tautologies. 'The truly dialectical motif is need: only need, as an insatiable feeling not realized through the world, which each time becomes need, is a constantly arising, slipping, and explosive contradiction' (SO, p. 137f.).

It is the intervention of the subject that is only capable of giving objective contradictions a historically progressive character, that orientation towards the future which may be considered the true power of dialectics – the power to overcome a plain negativity and to embrace a productive one. Subjective contradictions make it possible to grasp objective ones.[37] The operation of the subjective factor makes the being more concrete and mediated, more intense and thus contributes decisively to its beingness (cf. Holz 1975, p. 98ff.).

In the later work Bloch seems to replace the methodically constructed attainment of totality in Hegelian dialectics with anthropology and natural philosophy, invoking a drive to achieve this totality, which takes loose, dynamic and discursive forms. Bloch denounces any philosophical system for having a static, pre-established foundation – something that should not exist in the world of philosophy, which is fundamentally uncertain and unstable. This dynamics shared by Hegel and Bloch was sensed even by Heidegger, who actually never referred to Bloch, but described the movement of Hegel's *Phenomenology* in Blochian parlance as the movement of knowing that was not yet true and of a subject that had not yet found itself (Heidegger 1977, pp. 150, 154).

Bloch, unlike Marx, never consistently employed the dialectical methodology, and there is much evidence of his hostility towards the idea of dialectical mediation. Despite constant references to dialectics and rationality he was inclined, rather, to adopt a mystical view of final identity as the end of the historical process. 'That reaches its What and the last What reaches the first That (and this is identity, the goal of the utopian process – I. B.) not as the closing of a circle, but rather as a sheer bolt of lightning that at some time will transfix its surroundings' (TE, p. 277). However, here, again, Bloch remained faithful to the general orientation of Hegelian Marxism as formulated by Lukács in *History and Class Consciousness*.

In the 1950s Bloch has given his dues to Hegelian-Marxist philosophy and even accomplished with its help several modest feats of civil duty: giving a lecture in 1956 when the Soviet troops invaded Hungary entitled *Hegel and the Violence of the System* (*Hegel und die Gewalt das Systems*), a dangerous title for the moment; as well as criticizing the distinction between Hegel's 'progressive' method and 'mystifying' system canonized by Engels.

The task was a rejection of positivism and mechanistic materialism as well as extreme subjective irrationalism, while the tendency to mediate them would be impossible without the Hegelian legacy. For Bloch, the stasis of mythological thinking, which tries to 'return to the origin', is no better than the inertia of vulgar materialism. 'Revolutionary gnosis' is impossible without a revolutionary dialectic, which revives past ideas, giving them a chance to take part in history, charging them with *hope*.

Negativity

Faust's journey has an important feature that brings Goethe close to Hegel: Faust negates reality. But the world is inhabited by 'a sort of objective Mephistopheles, an objective Negation' (TE, p. 75). Both Lukács and Bloch emphasize the positivity of Mephistopheles and his creative role despite the evil he embodies. He is reinterpreted as the motor of history referring to the Hegelian 'cunning of reason'. And of course his celebrated self-description is recalled: 'Part of that Power, not understood,/Which always wills the Bad, and always works the Good.'

Mephistopheles is indeed immanent to the world; he is not only a moment in Faust's mental history (like the devil in Dostoevsky's *The Brothers Karamazov* or Don Quixote as a devil that has taken possession of Sancho in Kafka's fragment *The Truth about Sancho Panza*). He is also a moment in a general historical development, a part of the divine order. He calmly comes to be received by the Lord and asks permission to seduce Faust from the true path. Were Mephistopheles not an integral part of the world, God would not say to him: 'Of the spirits of negation, you least of all/Have been onerous to me, a rogue and merry fellow.' Mephistopheles's thoughts are seditious; they do not fit into the harmony of the spheres – but this does not prevent him from remaining a part of this harmony.

The positive meaning of Mephistopheles has long been recognized by literary critics. He is often smarter than Faust; he utters generally known truths, never loses a sober common-sense perspective and often prevails in arguments with Faust, as was already noted by Schiller (Schiller and Goethe 1845, p. 271). Thus the individual (be it Goethe's Faust or Hegel's 'consciousness') is interpreted as a dialectical unity of the positive and negative principles. By reaching an agreement with Mephistopheles, Faust posits his 'other' as the will and potentiality to change.

In Hegelian dialectics the negative is a means for the self-revelation of the Absolute; it is sublated in the course of development while remaining an integral part of the whole process. Hegel introduced the concept of negativity in order to fight the philosophy of understanding and common sense and transform it into higher forms of reason. The philosophical cognition is

> the process which creates its own moments and passes through them all; it is the whole movement that constitutes the positive and its truth. This movement equally includes within itself the negative, or what would be called "the false" if it were to be taken as something from which one might abstract (47).

It is in the unfolding of those forms that evil may contribute to the course of history. Even self-seeking as an immediately abstract desire may prove necessary in a dialectical context:

> In this dependence and reciprocity of work and the satisfaction of needs, subjective selfishness turns into a contribution towards the satisfaction of the

needs of everyone else. By a dialectical movement, the particular is mediated by the universal so that each individual, in earning, producing, and enjoying on his own account [*für sich*], thereby earns and produces for the enjoyment of others. (Hegel 1991, p. 233)

Mephistopheles is a spirit who 'has always been accustomed to negate'. But what kind of negation is it?

> Part of the Part am I, once All, in primal Night, –
> Part of the Darkness which brought forth the Light,
> The haughty Light, which now disputes the space,
> And claims of Mother Night her ancient place.
>
> (Faust I, 1349–52, trans. B. Taylor)

Here we no longer have a dialectical interpretation of the devil, but rather an argument in the spirit of German mysticism (a tradition continued in Goethe's time by Baader and Schelling) and the Manichean dualism of good and evil. Bloch, too, points to the Schellingian roots of Goethe's theories and concedes that under Schelling's influence Goethe saw as the main natural forces polarity and intensification (*Steigerung*), adhering to the 'old' pantheistic views associated with the coincidence of opposites in a universal harmony. Bloch therefore acknowledges that it is difficult to combine Faust's insatiable passion (interpreting him in the Hegelian spirit) with such a Spinozian ideology of harmony.[38] Here is a characteristic example from Goethe (Bloch does not mention this poem, but it is clearly among those which he has in mind):

> Wenn im Unendlichen dasselbe
> Sich wiederholend ewig fließt,
> Das tausendfältige Gewölbe
>
> Sich kräftig in einander schließt;
> Strömt Lebenslust aus allen Dingen,
> Dem kleinsten wie dem größten Stern,
> Und alles Drängen, alles Ringen
> Ist ewige Ruh' in Gott dem Herrn.

Lukács and Bloch were surely concerned with the moral implications of negativity. Did Goethe go so far as to 'dialectically' recognize *the positive role of evil in history* and, in general, did he adopt the idea of a 'constructive' negativity?

Goethe was hardly interested in the subtleties of speculative thought; this is also shown by his famous conversation with Hegel as recorded by Eckermann, in which Goethe sarcastically touched upon the art of dialectics. An attentive reading of the dialogue reported by Eckermann makes it clear that Goethe adhered, rather, to a Kantian interpretation of dialectics as the logic of illusion. However, this does not mean that Eckermann's notes should be directly compared with the philosophy of *Faust*; it is important only to show various dimensions of Goethe's thought.

Bloch, unlike Lukács, thinks that if there was a 'dialectics' in Goethe at all then it was a dialectics in the spirit of Spinoza and the early Schelling – a sort of 'old' dialectics attacked by Hegel both in the *Logic* and in the *Phenomenology*:[39]

Although the life of God and divine cognition might thus be articulated as a game love plays with itself, this Idea will be downgraded into edification, even into triteness, if it lacks the seriousness, the suffering, the patience, and the labour of the negative (19).

Such a revolutionary mood was in many respects alien to the 'Olympian' Goethe with his often contemplative political position and his striving to stand above the fray. While Bloch asserts that Goethe simply failed to comprehend Hegel, for Lukács Goethe's philosophical thought embodies the evolution of Enlightenment rationalism into dialectics.

Let us note in passing that the crucial idea of Goethe's natural philosophy is the direct contemplation of a proto-phenomenon, the intuitive grasping or glimpsing of essence, a common basis of natural phenomena that cannot be captured in scientific abstraction. 'It is not easy to express in words that which should be presented to the gaze' – Goethe writes to Hegel on 7 October 1820, sending him the fruits of his natural-scientific searchings (Hegel 1969, p. 236). And this idea is congenial to Bloch. From the outset he was fascinated by the notion of the pure phenomenological experience: in a letter to Ernst Mach, the 18-year-old philosopher qualifies 'the principle of phenomenality' (that reality is visibility) as the 'golden rule' of philosophy (Br I, p. 20). However, in Hegel's system this principle was not of crucial importance.

But what do we make of Mephistopheles and his ambiguous negativity? It might be considered, for example, that Goethe's God is the wholly positive God of Spinoza, who tolerates no negativity of any kind within himself and for whom Mephistopheles is merely a curious incident. In a conversation with Eckermann on 2 March 1831, Goethe remarked that Mephistopheles should not be regarded as a demonic image because he is too *negative* for this, while the demonic often appears attractive. Indeed, it was attractive in Hoffmann, Kleist, Jean Paul and then, after Nerval (the translator of *Faust* into French) would become – in Baudelaire and Lautréamont – the leading motif in French literature.

From this point of view, Goethe's Mephistopheles has nothing to do with the 'cunning of reason' or the Smithian 'invisible hand'; he is rather something barren and empty, like the devil in Spinoza, who consists of undiluted negativity. (Spinoza (2002, p. 98f.) was surprised how such a repulsive creature could have existed even for an instant.)

Another interpretation of *Faust* would imply that the hero is spared punishment and sent to heaven not because he is a sinner and the negative principle within him is a moving force of world history, but because he has *good will* (a Kantian[40] notion!) and this is the fundamental feature of his personality.[41] At this point, the Hegelian interpretation of *Faust* based on the economy of sin becomes problematic.

Pertaining to this context is Bloch's distinction between vain ('Mephistopheles without Faust') and creative negativity. Evil can thus be both productive and destructive. Bloch associates a hypertrophic, 'abstract', and sterile negativity with fascist (but not communist) terror. However, the consequences of this distinction are not clearly appreciated.

The critique of Hegel's philosophy often emerged in periods when fruitless, absurd negativity was experienced in reality, giving rise to universal horror.

The outstanding Hegel scholar Rosenzweig acquired this experience in the trenches of World War I – meaningless and hence especially terrifying, bloody massacre – facing death every day. For Adorno, it was Auschwitz that was the image of irreducible, 'un-sublatable' negativity not to be explained by any immanent historical logic.

But is the *composition* of *Faust* really arranged in accordance with Hegelian laws? Is it possible to subordinate it to the dialectical teleology in treating Faust's unexpected insights as merely a necessary stage in the world-historical development of mankind? Does Faust learn, does he become wiser, having forgotten the fate of Gretchen, about Helen, about Euphorion (Lacoste 2008, p. 93)? The German literary critic W. Voßkamp recalls an episode in Goethe's conversations with Eckermann, in which the latter addresses the structure of *Faust* and refers to certain layers of the world that influence one another but are not closely interconnected (Voßkamp 1985). The poet (i.e., Goethe himself) must express this variety of meaning to reflect in one another, this diverse and multivalent world, and he uses the famous legend as a connecting thread to string together whatever he thinks fit. Goethe confirms Eckermann's words adding that in a composition of this kind, each individual section must remain clearly distinct and significant: the whole cannot be reduced to any one of them. Vosskamp argues that the realization of the subject in the world, according to Goethe, never ends with reconciliation and dialectical identity and is not directed towards any sort of a consciously set goal, that as soon as Faust's titanic and unrestrained passion comes into contact with rational/teleological calculation this leads to tragedy (referring to the episode with Philemon and Baucis). The position of Faust as a person who has acquired power is ethically indifferent; his life-force borders on an evil principle. Vosskamp, like Lukács, emphasizes the absence of any sentimental attitude in the drama: the old world must be destroyed. But his conclusion is directly opposed to that of Lukács: *Faust* is not dialectical.

Vosskamp, however, adheres to a very simplistic conception of dialectics as some goal-directed panlogism, as a striving to crush the fragile individuality of the personality and the ecumenical spontaneity of the literary universe under the iron heel of the concept. This is, to say the least, a one-sided interpretation, even leaving aside the French neo-Hegelians who read the *Phenomenology* in a special way – precisely in the light of the fragile and concealed identity which Kierkegaard already found so lacking in Hegel and which Bloch defended (and, following him, Vosskamp too). Even without this, authentic Hegelian dialectics is full of dramatic content, and it is precisely in the *Phenomenology* that historical collisions acquire special tragic dimensions. There, dialectics is free of repressive political correctness and least of all corrupted with the totalitarian thinking of which it was suspected both by Popper (1945) and by the postmodernists (Derrida 1981).[42]

Indeed, Goethe did not subordinate the movement of *Faust* to laws of any kind; the events are to a considerable extent spontaneous and unpredictable and cannot be evaluated solely on the basis of some literary or other logic. Nor does Faust himself act in accordance with any plan given in advance. The living and deeply individual experience that Goethe propagates in *Faust* really is at times hard to reconcile with Hegelian constructions. 'The truly moving and radically substantive essence of the world is something intensive and not logical' (SO, p. 172).

But here, again, we shall have to make an exception for the *Phenomenology*, as the fate of the individual element is raised to the level of existential drama, while the dialectical dynamics are easily interpretable in the language of literature. From Bloch's argument it becomes clear that we have before us the movement of a constantly changing consciousness (or of its image, model, *Gestalt*). Just like heroes in Goethe, meanings (following Eckermann) are reflected in one another, and it is this play of reflections that constitutes the movement of tragedy – that is, the path of Faust's life. And the reflection of consciousness in itself or in another consciousness is the key theme of the *Phenomenology of Spirit* (Marx's famous statement that a human being becomes what it is only through recognizing the other as a human being is merely a later echo of Hegel's thought.) Bloch's own literary technique mimetically reproduces this kind of philosophy: as the interplay of reflections (Ueding 2009; Czajka 2006); but the objects of these reflections are now different; not forms of consciousness, but the histories and the meanings, the narratives and their 'moral'.

Here we can see further analogies. The Faustian principle is far from being as 'harmonious' as it might seem; rather, he moves along the laborious path of Hegelian consciousness. Faust intoxicates himself:

> Let us the sensual deeps explore,
> To quench the fervors of glowing passion!
> Let every marvel take form and fashion
> Through the impervious veil it wore!
> Plunge we in Time's tumultuous dance,
> In the rush and roll of Circumstance!
>
> (Faust I, 1750–5, trans. B. Taylor)

Recall Hegel:

> The life of spirit is not a life afraid of death and austerely saving itself from ruin; rather, it bears death calmly, and in death, it sustains itself. Spirit only wins its truth when it finds its feet within its absolute disruption. Spirit is . . . this power only when it looks the negative in the face and lingers with it. This lingering is the magical power that converts it into being. (32, cf. Encyclopedia, par. 382–3)

Another affinity of *Faust* and the *Phenomenology* is their mutual attack on the abstractions and rigid rationality of understanding. In particular, both the Preface to the *Phenomenology of Spirit* and the first part of *Faust* criticize a naive mathematicized rationalism. Goethe depicts the torments of Faust, who feels cramped within the confines of solidified dogmatic knowledge, and mocks these dogmas. This criticism is presented in the *Phenomenology* in an equally ironic form. Hegel does not merely present the realm of understanding lost in particulars and abstract schemas, but also proposes an alternative: the concepts of reason and then of spirit as knowledge 'of itself in its self-emptying', of an essence 'which is the movement of keeping parity with itself in its otherness' (759). Neither Hegel nor Goethe accept an interpretation of truth as an end result separated from its genesis; 'tabular' understanding, the idea that the true can be expressed in a single clear proposition (*Satz*), is alien to them both. The criticism of abstractions is one of the main features of that very experience of consciousness we were looking for, advocated both by Hegel and Goethe (Wieland 1992).

The fulfilled instant

This motif reappears in Bloch's interpretation of *Faust* over and over again. *Phenomenology* shares with *Faust* the movement 'of the restless consciousness through the spacious gallery of the world, the inadequate as Becoming the event' (PH, p. 1195; PHE, p. 1017),[43] and the basic *raison d'être* of this movement is the fulfilled instant that Bloch interprets in the spirit of his philosophy as close and intimate, as darkness and opacity. Of course this event of adequacy may be interpreted along various lines. It suffices to recall the religious philosophy of Kierkegaard or the secular aesthetics of Baudelaire (in his essay *The Painter of Modern Life*). Indeed, Hegel himself gave due recognition to the portrayal of instants in art that demonstrate eternal meaning, flickering through their evanescence. (See the characterization of Dutch painting in the *Lectures on Aesthetics*. (Hegel 1975, Vol. 1, pp. 597–600))

At the end of the second part, the blind Faust 'sees' the image of a free nation in a free land. Bloch interprets this unalienated existence as a brightening up of the darkness of the instant and in the spirit of a social utopia. Goethe's philosophy of nature is also of significance: the future realm is founded upon a harmony between man and nature.

Bloch also makes an important remark that literary depiction of the instant is fundamentally constrained – it is only a presentiment of the utopian but not its full content. Faust never experiences the decisive instant in reality, but merely imagines it, and the conditional mood in which he clothes his words is akin to myth or fiction (Jameson 1971). In this sense, the utopian impulse is organized as an allegory: it always refers to something else; it can never be found directly; it 'speaks' only through images and summons us to supplement, improve and interpret them. I shall return to this below, in the discussion of Benjamin and Adorno.

The goal of Faust's journey is an event that puts an end to alienation (PH, p. 1196), an event of liberation and redemption (Wieland 1992, p. 65).[44] The idea of the fulfilled instant is not abstract – it is an idea of such concreteness that there no longer remains any idea (PH, p. 1190f.), but only an experiment, the spiritual core of which, in Bloch, is the goal of bringing freedom for the whole of humankind.

At the beginning of the second part, Faust speaks to the Earth:

> And now beginnest, all thy gladness granting,
> A vigorous resolution to restore me,
> To seek that highest life (*zum höchsten Dasein*) for which I'm panting.
> (Faust II, 4683-5, trans. B. Taylor)

We have before us, on the one hand, an absolutely full being-present (*Dasein*), and, on the other hand, a special visionary, the messianic[45] 'here and now'. However, for Goethe this 'here and now' was a tragic irony: while Faust lapses into dreams of a future world, lemurs dig up his grave. In fact, Faust's grandiose 'revolutionary' design turns out to be an *abstract utopia*, remaining merely the vision of a ruler who did not hesitate to shed blood for the sake of realizing his idea. The conquest of the future, which the Marxist Bloch wants so much to justify, turns out to be ruinous, and the hope that Bloch wants to save, at least in a single instant, is debunked in the words of Mephistopheles, who calls this instant final, bad and empty.[46]

But is it debunked completely? 'The night seems deeper all around me,/Only within me is there gleaming light' (p. 420) – says the blind Faust, who has not ceased to hope and continues to envision with his inner eye a utopian dream that is unattainable from the point of view of current developments and inexplicable in terms of historical logic. He 'wants something impossible' (p. 282). The instant becomes the triumph of individuality as unique living concreteness (connected with the natural principle by the most intimate ties).

Renate Wieland rethinks this logic of individuality: the final instant is a moment of love and perfect openness to the other, a moment at which independent people turn to each other, and not the dissolution of objecthood as an absolute subject (Wieland 1992, p. 51).

> Eternal, fire of bliss,
> Glow of love's bond this is,
> Pain in the heart, seething,
> Rapture divine, foaming.
> Arrows, come, piercing me,
> Spears, compelling me,
> Clubs, you may shatter me,
> Lightning may flash through me!
> So passes the nullity
> Of all unreality,
> And from the lasting star
> Shines Love's eternal core (Faust II, 11854-65; trans. A. S. Kline).

Thus speaks the Father Ecstaticus at the end of the tragedy. The 'pain of love' (*Liebesqual*), the scenes from nature – mountain gorges, forests, cliffs and deserts animated by the love that created them and depicted by Goethe in dazzling, living images; the world's mystical bounty, unpredictability and at the same time – and paradoxically! – its mysterious proportionality, constant changeability and incompleteness, all this is not really consistent either with general conceptions of *Bildung* or with popular dialectical constructions (this concerns especially the schematism of Lukács). In addition, it is hardly worth comparing (as Wieland also often does) the ending of *Faust* with the finale of the *Phenomenology of Spirit*, if only because in the first case, however 'objective' the whole second part of the tragedy may be and however epic its scale, it takes us back to individuality, something quite uncharacteristic of Hegel, for whom at the higher levels of development consciousness is spirit: 'this absolute substance which constitutes the unity of its oppositions in their complete freedom and self-sufficiency, namely, in the oppositions of the various self-consciousnesses existing for themselves: The *I* that is *We* and the *We* that is *I*' (177).

Faust is not the sole figure whom Bloch proposes as an indicative image of 'venturing beyond the limits'. Another character who appears in his work is Don Juan, who surrenders himself to his altogether this-worldly passion and fights against outmoded, petrified vestiges of the past. The Promethean nature of Don Juan (first exposed by Bloch in a 1928 article on the staging of the Mozart opera)[47] is, among other things, the devotion to the immediate moment and a cult of momentary passion and masculinity. Curiously enough, in a letter to Kracauer, Bloch refers to his article, stating that although Don Juan is a revolutionary, this does not mean that *any* passionate enthusiasm is revolutionary, too. 'What is a matter of indifference from the point of view of the tragic drama is not a matter of indifference from the point of view of the revolution' (Br I, p. 287). Thus, Bloch repudiates the cult of blind and self-sufficient radicalism,[48] while showing that the tragic principle possesses the most diverse ethical and aesthetic potentialities.

Bloch considered the utopian coda of *Faust* to be more humanistic and less abstract than the absolute knowing portrayed at the end of the *Phenomenology* – that is, literature appears to be more 'lifelike' and animated than philosophy. Here one also could find the crux of the disagreement between Bloch and Hegel. Literature has room for the unexpected, for sensual experience, for the fragmented and the fortuitous, for astonishment, the mystical, the spontaneous and the figurative; it has room for nature, irreducible to the conceptual schemas of the subject. But such opposition between literature and philosophy is not altogether justified: either for Hegel who narrated his *Phenomenology* guided by a literary imagination towards absolute knowing, reaching the highest point of ambivalence, at which the ability of consciousness to appropriate its other attains its limit[49]; or for Goethe, who clearly saw the drama of ideas in *Faust* (especially in its second part). Both Goethe and Hegel fearlessly speak of the absolute and trace the development of spirit in language. After all, is not the aesthetic act itself a visible embodiment of the absolute idea?

The way in which Bloch correlates *Faust* with the *Phenomenology* seems to suggest a new approach to interpreting the grounds and premises of Hegelian dialectics. What we need to account for is the manifestation of the spirit itself, its life in finite and historically limited human beings. This appearance of spirit underlies the *entire* Hegelian project, inasmuch as without the *Phenomenology of Spirit* the entire construction of the *Logic* would be groundless.[50] The intricacies of the personal and social being of a modern individual, the tragic nature of existence, the religious experience and the social fabric of history – all this is addressed both by the *Phenomenology of Spirit* and by *Faust*. And it is upon this material that the majestic structure of Hegel's system, to which the *Phenomenology* serves as an introduction, is ultimately erected. To grasp the essence of dialectics one should pass through the storms of human life, experience and overcome doubts, despair, disruption, conflicts with the community and much else.

This literary background of Hegelian thinking is the most appropriate in our context, to take stock, posing problematic questions with equally doubtful possible answers: what could Bloch inherit from Lukács? I would propose to connect the dots calling by name some decisive points of the narrative attempted so far.

Bloch's interest in *The Metaphysics of Tragedy* clearly demonstrated that the realm of their communication with Lukács was defined by literary forms. However, beginning with *The Theory of the Novel*, another axis emerged, and this was defined by the philosophy of history. Lukács's messianic reading of Marx and a more orthodox view of Goethe and Hegel suggest that these constellations were not arbitrary. To associate the ideas of *Bildung* and negativity with the fate of individuality traced by Goethe in *Faust* and in *Meister* meant to discover the elementary structure of modern historicity. And this, again, was done with recourse to literary figures making use of various frameworks – ranging from aesthetic speculation and essayism to Blochian thought-images, sometimes intentionally simplified to make them reveal their poetic energy. To (re)think history as literary forms, to find the words or images commensurable with the paradoxes of the utopian, to be able to formulate them at all – these were the ultimate stakes of their common philosophical enterprise.

Bloch saw in Lukács something that was dangerous and hazardous to adopt: *the philosophical passion*. It only could allow Lukács to accept, as one accepts a monastic vow, a system of ideas and likewise – sweepingly, in a single moment – to deny it. For Bloch, Lukács was an example of a vivid, active, albeit not fully realized hope, an example of a man who took the idea of *praxis* seriously, who lived by mediations and who never distinguished, following Hegel, the theory of struggle and the struggle for theory – neither in politics, nor in art.

Notes

1   The article was supposed to be named *Metaphysik des Dramatisch-Tragischen*; the editors of the *Logos* journal, where the text was first published, insisted on the simpler formulation (Cf. the letter to Leo Popper in: Lukács 1982, p. 173).
2   Despite the disagreements, Benjamin has taken much from Nietzsche, who claimed that the only genuine dramatic form was the classical drama, the Dionysian-Apollonian tragedy destroyed by the Socratic spirit of reflection, and that the return was possible only by restoring the lost myth (see, for instance: Fehér 1985b).
3   Curiously, the problem of form in Lukács can be traced to the notions of 'drive toward abstraction' of the art critic Wilhelm Worringer (the author of *Abstraction and Empathy*). It also builds upon Simmel's (1918) views on the human alienation from the world (particularly, in the famous article *On the Concept and the Tragedy of Culture*). But where Simmel saw an irreparable, fatal discrepancy between life and form, between an individual and his creations and moreover, an incredible, inconceivable transition from life to form, Lukács saw a possibility of overcoming and radically transfiguring life. While Simmel merely ascertained the discrepancy between the soul and the frozen, reified forms, Lukács in those years looked for new forms that would be adequate for the new soul. A more detailed account can be found in Thaler (2003, pp. 30-1, 92).
4   Due to the publication (abridged) of *The Metaphysics of Tragedy* in the journal *Logos* (Lukács 1911), this text gained attention and there were more discussions around it in 1910-11 compared to other essays collected in *The Soul and Form*. Lukács sent his article and later the book to a number of prominent intellectuals of the time, among them Ziegler, Buber, Simmel and Ernst Robert Curtius.
5   Cf. Antigone's words: 'Thou livest; but my life hath long been given to death, that so I might serve the dead' (Sophocles, *Antigone*, 546-7, trans. R. Jebb).
6   For young Lukács, Hebbel's work formed the aesthetic canon and constituted the origin of the modern drama (Lukács 1981, p. 242).

7   The subject of tragedy is also discussed in Lukács's and Bloch's correspondence, but in only one letter, where Bloch talks too hastily and too generally (Br I, pp. 40–1).
8   In the first edition this text was a part of a large section under the general title *Comic Hero*, of which only the discussion of *The Metaphysics of Tragedy* remained in the second edition.
9   Lehmann (1985, p. 540f.) shows that form is powerless in Bloch, it does not create reality and cannot alter it by itself. Later Bloch avoids the notion of form altogether, and rather examines symbol and allegory.
10 The problem of historicity of form was also clearly perceived by Lukács (cf. his letter to Ernst: Lukács 1982, p. 282), who wrote *The History of the Development of Modern Drama* and later the *The Theory of the Novel*, which clearly deal with the philosophy of history. Lukács realized that in the theory of tragedy one has to convincingly show how the tragic is different from other artistic forms. However, in the *metaphysics* of tragedy he posed himself other, more abstract philosophical goals. Historical or sociological analysis of any kind is completely irrelevant here. Bloch continues this line of criticism also in *The Principle of Hope*, where he accuses Lukács, among other things, of not accepting the idea of sacrifice as fundamental for tragedy (Benjamin also considered the idea of sacrifice to be central), for disregarding not only the social and historical context in which the hero finds himself, but also traditional forms of fate and retribution (PH, p. 1375).
11 Bloch himself, according to his students' recollection, had the same attitude towards his own texts, constantly reformulating and rewriting them (Ueding 2009, p. 189).
12 Interestingly, Bloch might have had an impact on Lukács's further development and an interpretation of Ernst's *Ariadne on Naxos* along religious lines (Thaler 2003, p. 81). The longing for the new God is for a short time preferred to the irreligious and uncompromising ethics of the tragic hero.
13 In a letter to Frank Benseler, Lukács pointed out that he took it from someone's characterization of the French philosopher Alain (Benseler 2002).
14 However, one could understand 'the right' as an 'idealistic' projection of the future, a refusal to immerse into the thick materiality of the empirical world and an orientation towards the utopian horizons (Schmidt 1985, p. 36).
15 According to a different interpretation Bloch speaks here not of Lukács, but of Max Scheler (Pelletier 2008, p. 231).
16 Cf., for instance, a characteristic appearance of Alyosha Karamazov in the decisive episode of *The Star of Redemption* (Rosenzweig 1988, p. 317).
17 The words in parenthesis appeared in the first edition: GU1, p. 357. However, this whole section of the book could have been evoked not as much by the sophiological dreams of Soloviev, but rather by the acquaintance of and communication with the poet Margarete Susman (see: Czajka 2003).
18 Bloch later referred to Proust to rehabilitate 'bourgeois' literature and in dealing with Benjamin, whose name in Germany was often associated with Proust – both formally (he was one of the first translators) and substantially. Cf. a short characterization in *The Heritage of our Times*, where Proust's world is described as an attempt to bring back the time which, even as it had been originally experienced, was already gone, and the attempt to stand before the judge, who is no more (EZ, p. 242f.).
19 He even speaks of *epopee* as of an adventure, a soul's journey through the incomplete world, its path towards the unknown end (GU1, p. 255).
20 Though Lukács accuses Fichte and Hegel of idealism, he contends that in Fichte 'we see . . . the origin of the philosophical tendency to press forward to a conception

of the subject which can be thought of as the creator of the totality of content' (HCC, p. 122f.). Cf. Rockmore 1992.
21 Cf. also the letter to Lukács from 19 July 1911 (Br I, pp. 45–8). Schmidt traces the evolution of Bloch's views and notes that while in *The Spirit of Utopia* Bloch called for a building of oneself up into the blue, into the unknown, he ends the book on Thomas Müntzer in a completely different way — invoking the 'dark, heavy soil' (1985, p. 20). However, already in *The Spirit of Utopia* Bloch mentions the apocalyptic possibility of the end of nature, of the physical death of the Universe (Schmidt 1985, p. 118, cf.: GU1, p. 438), while having extensively edited the monograph on Müntzer for its publication in the collected works.
22 On Hegel in this context see: GU2, p. 235. For Weber's concept see, for instance: Weber (1958). I owe this reference to Greg Yudin.
23 Curiously, Lukács uses the notion of utopia only in the negative sense and precisely in this respect criticizes Bloch's book on Müntzer. The differentiation between 'the concrete' and 'the abstract' utopia in Bloch's subsequent works is apparently triggered precisely by Lukács' critique.
24 Scholars debate the exact moment when Bloch turned to Marxism – in 1923 under Lukács's influence or much later, after the Nazi rise to power. The former opinion is held among others by Peter Zudeick (1980) and Hans-Ernst Schiller (1982). Ujma (1995), drawing on Dietschy (1988) and Bloch's articles of that time, maintains that Bloch finally identified himself as a Marxist only in the beginning of the 1930s, reacting against the rightist menace. Bloch himself testifies to this, for instance in a letter to Thomas Mann (Br II, pp. 692–3).
25 See, for instance: EZ, pp. 379–81. See also: Ujma 1995, pp. 74–86. Ujma argues that Bloch could have adopted this notion from the second (1922) edition of Karl Barth's *The Epistle to the Romans*.
26 In another form this recollection is given in Bloch's essay *Niemandsland* (S, p. 190). There the context is linked to the perception of the enormous universe, in which the human soul becomes lost, which nevertheless (this is how Bloch conveys the words of his 'wise friend'), if it was asked, would reply nonsense, for 'it has read neither Plato, nor Kant'.
27 Curiously, Bloch's non-party status was already perceived as distinguishing him from Lukács in the 1960s (Bartsch 1969).
28 'Jubiläum der Renegaten' in PM, pp. 225–35. This article, first published in 1937 in the journal *Die neue Weltbühne*, could well be compared to Carl Schmitt's notorious text *The Führer Defends the Law* and Heidegger's speech *The Self-Assertion of the German University*. Cf. also a disgraceful text of 1937, *Kritik einer Prozeßkritik*, several repulsive formulations in *Bucharins Schlußwort* (both texts in: *Vom Hasard zur Katastrophe*) or a later passage from *The Principle of Hope*: 'Without factions in love, with an equally concrete pole of hatred, there is no genuine love; without *partiality* of the revolutionary class standpoint there only remains backward idealism instead of forward practice'. (PH, p. 319; PHE, p. 274).
29 In Goethe's eyes, Hegel's positive attitude towards Goethe's theory of colour more than compensated for and 'outweighed' his views regarding *Naturphilosophie*, which in other contexts Goethe found quite unacceptable.
30 G. W. F. Hegel, *Phenomenology of Spirit*, par. 360. Further quotations from this work are given in the new English translation of the work by Terry Pinkard forthcoming from Cambridge University Press and available at http://terrypinkard.weebly.com/phenomenology-of-spirit-page.html; paragraph numbers are shown in the text. The text is reproduced with the consent of the translator.

31 Here there is a play on words, based on the idiom 'sich das Leben nehmen' – literally, 'take to oneself life' or 'deprive oneself of life'.
32 Self-consciousness passes into a new stage – 'the Law of the Heart' – and here, as several commentators on the *Phenomenology* have observed, the focus shifts to other literary characters: the Savoy priest in Jean-Jacques Rousseau's *Émile*, Woldemar in F. H. Jacobi's novel of the same name, Schiller's *Don Carlos*, or the characters of F. Hölderlin. (Siep 2000, p. 152).
33 However, Hegel scholars have long doubted – and not without grounds – the authenticity of this part of the *Aesthetics*. (Gethmann-Siefert and Stemmrich-Köhler 1983).
34 Lukács refers to a letter that Goethe sent to Schiller at the time when he was working on Faust, in which he writes: 'nature is unfathomable for the very reason that no one man cannot comprehend it, although humanity, as a whole, might be able to comprehend it' (Schiller and Goethe 1890, p. 56). Compare also the characteristic (almost Hegelian) statement from *Poetry and Truth*: 'If, now, during our own lifetime, we see that performed by others, for which we ourselves felt an earlier call, but had been obliged to give it up, with much besides, then the beautiful feeling enters the mind that only mankind together is the true man, and that the individual can only be joyous and happy when he has the courage to feel himself in the whole.' (Goethe 1864, p. 332).
35 See the first publication of this text in *Neue Welt* (1949. 4.), pp. 71–86. Of course, Bloch was interested in *Faust* before, but in *The Spirit of Utopia* in the centre of his attention was not Faust, but Gretchen – the female element, embodying the essence of utopian mystery (GU2, p. 266).
36 Bloch, of course, also devotes much time to criticizing the Platonic anamnesis in the same spirit, being careful, however, to clarify that Plato himself was the creator of a utopia who strove to realize his ideas in Syracuse. (See, for instance: EM, p. 163; Habermas 1971, p. 148).
37 Cf. the political interpretation of the same idea: 'The factor of subjective contradiction, though only together with the contradiction that has arisen objectively within the history of the class struggle, supplements the material dialectic. This subjectively negative violence leads by a revolutionary path away from simple catastrophe, which would be an ordinary negation: as a strengthening of the productive, explosive character of objective contradictions' (SO, p. 150).
38 One should perhaps note that Goethe's philosophical views (like Schelling's) cannot, of course, be reduced to Spinozism or naturalistic pantheism. What Bloch describes is merely an important tendency.
39 Note, again, that classifying various versions of dialectics is only relevant as a conventional schema utilized by Bloch, but not necessarily of general validity.
40 Theodor Adorno, for example, refused to understand *Faust* in a neo-Kantian spirit; he considered, however, that the moving force in *Faust* is not the laws of dialectics but the power of oblivion, which enables the chief hero to live and act (Adorno 1991).
41 Oittinen (2001) shows, in particular, how the Hegelian concept of the 'cunning of reason' was misused to justify Stalinist and fascist terror and how inconsistent Lukács was in this case in refusing to apply Hegelian philosophy of history to the analysis of fascism.
42 Of course, Derrida's attitude towards Hegel is much more complex, but the drive of deconstructivist philosophy is still associated today with the rejection of dialectical teleology and the 'economy' of Hegelian sublation.

43 Cf. *Faust's* finale: Das Unzulängliche,/Hier wird's Ereignis (in Bloch: 'das Unzulängliche als Werden zum Ereignis').
44 On the whole, Wieland interprets the sphere of aesthetic appearance (*Schein*) in the spirit of Adorno as an irremovable residue resisting dialectical totalization.
45 Bloch's metaphysics of the moment can even be rendered closer to us through Paul's words: 'Listen, I will tell you a mystery: we will not sleep, but we will all be changed in a moment, in the twinkling of an eye, at the last trumpet. For the trumpet will sound, and the dead will be raised imperishable, and we will be changed' (1 Cor. 15:51–52).
46 Den letzten, schlechten, leeren Augenblick,/Der Arme wünscht ihn festzuhalten./ Der mir so kräftig widerstand/Die Zeit wird Herr, der Greis hier liegt im Sand./Die Uhr steht still – (Faust II, 11589–93).
47 Partly republished in PH, 1180–88. See Ujma 1995.
48 It was precisely for this that Bloch and his supporters were subsequently unjustly rebuked by Schelsky (1979). Schelsky asserts that intoxicated passion for revolution and millenarian anticipation of a new order disorient and undermine the ability to deal appropriately with illusions, irrespective of the nature of the latter – be they fascist illusions (to which Schelsky himself fell prey in his youth) or communist ones.
49 An important passage from *Phenomenology of Spirit* (754) enacts the revealed religion as the birthplace of the highest form of spirit, incorporating into itself all the torments and longings of the preceding stages – these latter being invoked once more and recollected.
50 'In the said treatise [*Phenomenology of Spirit* – I. B.], immediate consciousness is also that which in the science comes first and immediately and is therefore a presupposition; but in logic the presupposition is what has proved itself to be the result of that preceding consideration, namely the idea as pure knowledge' (Hegel 2010, p. 47).

3

Eschatology and Messianism: Bloch with Buber, Landauer and Rosenzweig

Before we move on to another important historical constellation (Bloch-Benjamin), it is necessary to show the place of the 'revolutionary gnosis' in Bloch's philosophy – a set of ideas he attempted to graft into Marxist theory, imparting socialist ideology of liberation with new historical overtones.

Norbert Bolz (1997) once commented that 'the Frankfurt philosophers so elegantly concealed under the titles of aesthetics and "social theory" . . . all-permeating theology' In this context Bloch's work 'had an advantage of clearness' (p. 40).

The religious origin of Bloch's ideas is beyond all doubt. But we could be even more sure that in the context of any traditional religion, his philosophy would necessarily be deemed heretical. Religious thinking had nevertheless influenced Bloch in various significant ways that I will attempt to locate and specify.

Early Bloch's world view was clearly defined by religious and mystical ideas of various kinds. Mysticism became part of the theory of immediate spiritual experience, beyond a mere concept. In a heartfelt letter to Lukács in 1911, having outlined his vision of the coming kingdom, he proclaims without a trace of joke: 'I am a paraclete, and the people I have been sent to, will experience and comprehend the coming of God' (Br I, p. 67). *The Spirit of Utopia* is a prophetic text, with an elevated style, long breathless sentences, indulging in its own suggestive imagery. A major role in this experience was played by Bloch's first wife Else von Stritzky, who became for Bloch a model of genuine holiness, innocence and crystal purity of religious sense.

In his dissertation on Rickert, Bloch complements the 'motor' intention of knowledge that guides itself outwards, imparting it with a mystical temporality, inwardly directed and immersing the subjectivity to the core, in the innermost mystery of each object. This is a kind of anti-intentionality or reversal movement that became Bloch's philosophical drive. The mystical function of knowledge consists in 'collecting' things and transfiguring them in accordance with the self. The mystical side of things is their hidden, not-yet-manifest absolute essence, complementing time, created by the motor intention, with the space of the new, emerging world (TL, pp. 112–14). From that point, the mystical transcends the limits of the usual givenness of the world and enters the conceptual arsenal of utopian philosophy. There is nothing surprising in this intellectual development. And it is not just about the obvious influence of German mystics and speculative thought on Bloch. Religious discourse gave utopian philosophy the necessary *universalist perspective,* allowing it to address absolute claims (Münz-Koenen 1997, p. 58).

Later, after attacking irrationalism (which was already present in *The Spirit of Utopia*) Bloch became more reserved in talking about mystical insights, replacing the call for a new church and prayer (GU2, p. 346) with the Marxist ideals of unalienated social being; and the search for God – with the dialectical interaction between human labour and becoming nature. But the denial of ordinary, one-dimensional scientific rationality was retained in the later works, for the very foundation of his utopian philosophical project opposes the tenets of understanding and common sense. Bloch's philosophy is above all subject to affective conviction, even faith, rather than rational reconstruction following strict epistemological standards.

The negative programme of *The Spirit of Utopia* and *Thomas Müntzer* is the critique of rational analytical thinking and of the inert conservative political mechanisms associated with it. This perspective also saliently manifests Bloch's readings of mystical literature. It is no accident that he called his doctrine *political mysticism* (GU1, p. 410), in contrast, for instance, to the conservatism of Carl Schmitt (1996), who also analysed the origins of early modern religious and political forms and sought to explain their stability.

Bloch's messianic orientation follows quite naturally from his general philosophical stance. The structure of his argument that singles out the 'Not-yet' as the Absolute to come can be read as the theological promise of messianic thinking. The anticipation of utopian totality is further formulated in a symbolic language that links various temporal orders and, in prefiguring the coming of the Messiah, binds them together in quite different domains of experience.[1]

In the first edition of *The Spirit of Utopia* Bloch attempted a re-examination of various esoteric ideas that were extremely popular at the time, such as theosophy (GU1, pp. 238–42). He mentions here the search for the new domains of philosophy as the case for the new style and 'even for a revived mysticism' (GU1, p. 73). However, it is hardly possible to subscribe Bloch to a single doctrine. The traces of various esoteric teachings remain in his early texts, exposing his attempt at integrating heterogeneous meanings.

Bloch evidently drew his inspiration both from primary sources and from various compilations that he came across. In particular, he owed his knowledge of Jewish mysticism, and especially of the book of *Zohar*, according to his own testimony, to the four-volume compilation *The Philosophy of History* (1824–53) by F. J. Molitor (1779–1860). Molitor was a friend and a student of Baader and an expert in the Jewish religion and esotericism.[2] Bloch also used other works, for example, the occult books of the nineteenth century theosophist Franz Hartmann (Landmann 1982, p. 167). This reading could partly explain the manifest eclecticism of Bloch's esoteric intuitions, his unwillingness to adhere to a single tradition and to strictly follow it, in the search for an all-encompassing synthesis.

Being gnostic: Bloch's shibboleth

It is common to acknowledge the gnostic influence on Bloch. But what is gnosticism, how should it be defined and why can Bloch be called a gnostic? It is impossible to give an unequivocal and completely satisfactory definition of gnosticism,[3] and I would use this term loosely to refer to a certain complex of ideas.

Gnosis is mainly understood as a hidden knowledge, only accessible to the consecrated, of both the origins of the universe and the future redemption (which is also possible only for the chosen). *Gnosticism* is usually referred to as a heterogeneous collection of religious doctrines, created in the second century. Importantly, it is the revealed *knowledge* of the architecture and the fate of the universe that becomes the key to opening all the doors for the gnostic. The soul is thrown into the world, created not by the genuine God (who is absolutely exorbitant and unknowable), but by an evil demiurge. The souls of the chosen preserve the God-given sparks, which give one hope of redemption – the return of all things to the true God, from whom they have fallen apart. The gnosis as a performative conjunction of the knower (gnostic) and the object of knowledge (the sparks within the depths of subjectivity) is the process of restoration of the lost unity. Redemption (*Erlösung*) for a gnostic happens *instantaneously* and is connected to the innermost part of his soul, which touches God.

More common gnostic motives include ontological and epistemological *dualism*, inevitable scepticism towards positive scientific knowledge and progress (see GU2, p. 241), the notion of the external world and bodily reality as a massive illusion[4] reposing on chaos, the hope of overcoming this illusion through immersion in oneself and the ecstatic experience. Gnosis is needed to transcend the profane, to show things their 'utopian fate' (GU1, p. 339), to grasp the universal struggle between the light and the darkness and to find one's place in this process.

Bloch's negative theology is permeated by gnostic concepts and images. In particular, he refers to Basilides (GU2, pp. 245–6; AC, p. 289) and Marcion (AC, pp. 237–43); gnosis is recurrently mentioned in *The Principle of Hope*. (See, for instance: PH, pp. 382, 841, 857). Bloch was largely inspired to read the gnostics in Heidelberg in 1911 by Lukács, whose fascination with gnostic thought grew at the moment of their closest association. Of course, Bloch was also influenced by Schelling (Pauen 1994, p. 214) and the general vogue for gnosticism in German culture of that time.

Gnostic imagery does not disappear from Bloch's later work either. Universal darkness and the new light that marks the hope brought by new art appear in the articles on Expressionism of the 1930s (Ujma 1995, p. 236f.). *The Principle of Hope* begins with a gnostic pasticcio: 'Who are we? Where do we come from? Where are we going? What are we waiting for? What awaits us?' (PH, p. 1; PHE, p. 3).[5] It is these questions that a gnostic must answer, and Bloch was obviously donning this role for himself. This passage, which Jacob Taubes (Taubes 1996, p. 177) takes as a kind of variation on Marcion interpreted through Adolf von Harnack (the question of whether Marcion, the heretical writer of the second century A. D., was in fact a gnostic, will not be examined in detail here), characterizes an important postulate of utopian philosophy: there becomes *through us* something altogether new in the world, which is the product of the darkest vagaries of our capabilities.

All of the world-renouncing pathos that was so characteristic of gnostics can be found in Bloch: '[T]his world is an error, and void; in the face of absolute truth it has only the right to be destroyed' (GU2, p. 287; SU, p. 229). Nature is a prison cell in which humanity languors (GU2, p. 336f.). The wretched and fallen material world guided by the power of darkness is opposed by the force of subjectivity. The final contours of the new world will only become discernible after the apocalyptic overthrow. The secret knowledge helps bring about this revolution. Bloch reiterates the keywords: the God-given spark and the hidden being of the divine in the depths of the human soul (GU2, pp. 48, 257); the dualism of God the creator and God the redeemer, God of love, who has not come yet (GU1, p. 441; GU2, p. 335). This is, in fact, a deeper meaning of Bloch's atheism: not just to get rid of the authority and hierarchy of the transcendent, but also to establish a gnostic theodicy – to redeem the future, coming God from the sinfulness of the worldly (Bolz 1997).

The 'wicked' God acts under different masks, but everywhere as an enemy, as a bloody tyrant, 'reputable Lord for reputable lords', for whom the only law is his own might, the sovereign of the world of injustice and oppression, of the inert and slowly decomposing pagan kingdom. Inert because it does not allow the powers of soul to illuminate the world; decomposing because without the mystical light, the world will not fulfil its destiny; it will not go beyond shallow and dismal self-reference, that is, beyond its own finitude.

Here is another gnostic argument in Bloch:

> The unknowing around us is the final ground for the manifestation of this world, and for precisely this reason does knowing, the lightning flash of a future knowledge striking unerringly into our darkness . . . constitute . . . the inevitably sufficient ground for the manifestation, for the arrival in the other world. (GU2, p. 227, SU, p. 229; cf.: GU1, p. 389)

The very notion that knowledge is an instrument of transforming the world and redeeming it, the claim that to be saved one has to acquire a knowledge of some sort, constitutes the link between gnosticism and Marxism. Not surprisingly, Bloch gave the concluding part of *The Spirit of Utopia* a title that would at first glance seem eccentric – 'Karl Marx, Death, and the Apocalypse'.[6] Marx insisted that it was *the knowledge* of the laws of capitalism that should explode the world. The major force of the revolution in Marxism is the understanding that the end of capitalism is inevitable and a clear vision of deep injustices in the institutions of capitalist exploitation. Gnostics, to be sure, meant a different knowledge, but Bloch was rather drawn by their revolutionary passion, and for that sake, he was able to overlook the confused nature of some gnostic mythologemes.

Early Bloch's eschatology is undoubtedly influenced by Marcion. The affinity went so far that later Bloch found himself as an *alter ego* of this writer: within the circle of the initiated in the GDR he was called Marcion (Pauen 1992a, p. 40). Following this subversive philosophy Bloch proclaims the radical destruction of the old world and its equally radical renewal. It happens in the depths of the soul, but 'the things are awakening together with us', they 'are looking for their poet' (GU1, pp. 335, 387) and the whole world experiences a utopian rebirth.

Along with *The Spirit of Utopia* another book was being written, Adolf von Harnack's *Marcion: The Gospel of the Alien God*, published in 1921, where the doctrine of Marcion was declared the key for understanding the emergence of Christianity as a separate religion. The rejection of Judaism, the Old Testament and the connection between God the Father and Christ, together with the institution of an entirely new religion, were the defining features of Marcionism that contributed, according to Harnack, to the autonomization of Christianity.

It has to be mentioned that Harnack's ideas appeared in the centre of a heated political debate in the Germany of the 1920s. The critique of Judaic religion, Marcion's peculiar 'anti-Semitism'[7] and Harnack's proposal to remove the Old Testament from the Christian canon (Harnack 1921, p. 214) did not promote a peaceful dialogue between Christians and Jews. It is hard to say whether these ideas were a factor in or a consequence of the growing general anti-Semitism, but one thing is clear: at the time they were interpreted in a rather unambiguous way (Cf. Buber 1963, p. 151ff.)

In this context Bloch's syncretism, dealing with Marcion as the exponent of radical messianism and therefore – of the deepest truth of Jewish spirituality – is manifest. One could say, of course, that by Jewish spirituality Bloch meant a special messianic movement in Jewish mysticism (Scholem 1986 [1963]); however he does not make any similar differentiations. Marcion's 'metaphysical anti-Semitism' is valued much higher than the 'holy *economy*' of the Old testament, in which the messianic heavens for 'propaedeutic reasons' descend to earth (GU1, p. 330). Marcion proclaims *the radical other*, together with Paul, whom he considers an ally, opposing Jewish law to the Gospels. At the same time Marcion's asceticism does not exclude humanism in Bloch's eyes: the rebellion against religious dogma and authority implies among other things a turn to the human (AC, pp. 238–40).

Of course, not all of the gnostic ideas were integrated into Bloch's thinking. For instance, even though he uses the gnostic concept of *pleroma* (divine fullness), he says almost nothing of the transcendental genesis, avoiding the entirety of complex and entangled mythological speculations in gnosticism (Christen 1979, p. 60), which, moreover, existed in different, at times hardly reconcilable, versions. Rather, he is interested in the radical dualism of these teachings and the notion of the hidden life of the human soul – as the key to the redemption of the world (Pauen 1994, p. 250; GU2, p. 346).

Interestingly, the idea of an active and becoming God, redeeming the world, human kind and also himself, occurs in Rosenzweig's *The Star of Redemption*. Discussing the eternity of God, he writes that for Him redemption, creation and revelation coincide, for He stands beyond time – it is human kind and the profane world that requires time in order to be saved. The finite and time-related distinctions between the Saviour and the saved are invalid for the eternal God (Rosenzweig 1988, p. 303). 'It is only in Redemption that God becomes that which the human spirit, in its temerity, constantly sought everywhere and affirmed everywhere, yet without ever having found it, for this was not yet: the One and the All' (Rosenzweig 1988, p. 266; Rosenzweig 2005, p. 256).

The dependence of God's fate on the fate of the world is an important idea for Martin Buber, discussed in his early lectures on Jewish religiosity. Bloch's eschatology is organized in a similar way: the final Judgement awaits both God and man (GU1, p. 439). The same idea would appear a little later in Scheler: 'The becoming of God and human being are from the beginning mutually correlated' (Scheler 1991, p. 92).

Of course, it is difficult to imagine the divine life without any recourse to anthropomorphism, hence the complex cosmic metaphoric in Rosenzweig and the ambiguous, mysterious passages in Bloch, referring to an unusual experience. Hence, the final formula: 'The world is untrue, but it wants to return home through man and through truth' (GU2, p. 347; SU, p. 279).

Later Bloch would combine the pathos of total rejection of the world with the notion of clarifying *the mystery of humanity*. Rejecting the contemporary world, the human being does not lose anything, on the contrary – she finds her own self (AC, p. 240). However, in Bloch's earlier gnosticism this human being is consumed by the Nietzschean fire, for the radicalism of gnostic ideas, just as any other absolute negation of the world, always burns, and the history of Harnack's reception bears witness to this.

Adopting the gnostic style of thinking, Bloch does not subscribe to the gnostic mythology. The estrangement of the individual from the reality surrounding her, the lapsed world of the profane, cannot be abolished by describing experiences in abstract allegories or traditional symbols. The gnostic myth, pompous and burdened by details, is insufficient for Bloch; he seeks, armed with dualistic metaphysics, to import into his text the moment of personal immediacy and in doing so to make a transition from myth to history.

Eschatology and apocalyptics

Bloch's interest in apocalyptics and messianism was in tune with his times, 'imbued with the anxious sense of an impetuous, unstoppable, even involuntary movement forward, with the vague sensation of historical outgrowth' and for which the apocalyptics of the past 'becomes . . . the historical mirror . . ., a means of spiritual orientation' (Bulgakov 1993, p. 377f.). It is no accident that Osip Mandelstam at approximately the same time 'heard with the sharpness of ears caught by the sound of a distant threshing machine in the field the burgeoning and increase, not of the barley in its ear, not of the northern apple, but of the world, the capitalist world, that was ripening in order to fall!' (1965, p. 111).

The initial situation of Bloch's apocalyptic philosophy is the experience of fractured and meaningless existence, the feeling of total degradation, which was so common to the intellectuals of his time. World War I embodied for him the collapse of European culture and the total victory of rational machinery. The disintegration of reality and total ethical uncertainty in the *fin de siècle* were, however, not equivalent to immorality. Intellectuals were *searching* for new values, registering the despair and the loss of former identity. Apocalyptics and messianism, especially among the young and educated Europeans, were the reaction to secularization and an attempt to build a new culture and a new metaphysics.

It is difficult to separate the gnostic and the apocalyptic tendencies in Bloch (Christen 1979, p. 55). In fact, the chiliastic attitudes, that is, the prophecies of the Thousand Year Reign of Christ, originated from gnostic ideas; moreover, the Gnosis itself was often construed as a philosophy of history, recounting the Fall. Of course, the evaluation of this history is negative: like gnostics, Bloch does not believe in the progress of reason. However, contempt for rational scientific knowledge is combined in him with a positive evaluation of the broadening of the capabilities of science: like theosophists, Bloch is not against its 'sublation' to synthesis with occult knowledge (GU1, p. 240).

The deliverance from the world infected by instrumental rationality occurs within the depths of the soul. The initial situation and diagnosis of modernity, which served as the point of departure for both Bloch and Lukács, is well formulated in Weber:

> Since asceticism undertook to remodel the world and to work out its ideals in the world, material goods have gained an increasing and finally an inexorable power over the lives of men as at no previous period in history. To-day the spirit of religious asceticism – whether finally, who knows? – has escaped from the cage. But victorious capitalism, since it rests on mechanical foundations, needs its support no longer. (Weber 2005, p. 124)

The apocalyptic mood was exacerbated by the World War.

> Who was defended?
> – asks Bloch in *The Spirit of Utopia*. –
>
> Foul, wretched profiteers. What was young had to fall, was forced to die for ends so alien and inimical to the spirit, but the despicable ones were saved, and now they sit there in their comfortable drawing rooms. The artists defended the middlemen ... a triumph of stupidity, guarded by the gendarme, acclaimed by the intellectuals. (GU1, p. 9; SU, p. 1)

The feeling that the world has been disenchanted and broken down can be found not only in Bloch's texts but also in the Expressionists of his generation, to whom he owes so much (GU2, p. 212).

The immediate form of grasping the mysteries of the new world is through art. In *The Spirit of Utopia* the mystical attitude is naturally juxtaposed onto and inspired by *expressionist painting*. In the discussion of Van Gogh and Cezanne (GU2, pp. 45–8) Bloch relates his thinking to expressionist aesthetics and finds in contemporary art an 'integral ecstatic contemplation' of subjectivity (GU1, p. 47). Owing to the supernatural power of art, things cease to be a lifeless entourage, an eternal tautology, and when we encounter ourselves in them, we see, at last, the human face. This animated mystical universe responds to us as the panhuman ('*makantropos*'); as the tautology dissolves, and a new world is born. The heritage of Expressionism (and Jewish mysticism in Buber's version, see Pauen 1992a, p. 27) is also manifest in the attention to the simple, often imperceptible things inhabiting the everyday – recall the description of a pitcher in the beginning of *The Spirit of Utopia*. Aesthetics becomes the basis for the philosophy of history, and the mystical experience of art easily transforms into eschatology. The new eschatological clarity grants us the truth, 'that takes no more, but gives, comprehends no more, but nominates with works and prayers' (GU1, p. 388f.).

The art of the 1910–20s, that was for many the sermon of rot and decay, attracted Bloch as he saw it as an axis of his epoch. Not only music, but also language (a more transparent medium) became for him the elements of messianic comprehension; reading of allegories turned into a gesture pointing at the unknown. The Messiah had to come off the page, had to be experienced as part of the Now; he represents new time for Bloch – the ability to make the words sound new. But one can only grasp the call of the Messiah by a hermeneutic effort, trying to decipher the future. This amounted to living with history and in history, not being satisfied by repetition, opening in oneself the ability to see the excess and the folds of historical time.

The eschatological mood was widespread in expressionist literature. It emerged as an awareness of a rupture between the world of the artist's mystical contemplation and the real world. The instant in which the ideal and the reality coincide is postponed here until the end of history; the mystical experience is complemented by the eschatological event of the apocalypse. This historical dimension is not always present in ecstatic religiosity, whereas in Bloch's texts it is felt from the very beginning (GU1, p. 383).

Eschatology and messianism in *The Spirit of Utopia* is the rejection of any half-heartedness, of any reservations and spiritual compromises. One of Bloch's Russian contemporaries put it quite clearly:

> Not a gradual evolution and progress, at the end of which, after all the ordeals of history, everything would be ended . . . as in the teachings of modern socialism, but a world and historical catastrophe separates the present *aion* from the future one. (Bulgakov 1993, p. 400)

In his radical and heretical revolutionary pathos Bloch is merciless towards traditional religious values. For him Lucifer was the first revolutionary (GU1, p. 441f.), he awaits the new God together with Marcion (Ibid., p. 330f., 381). Bloch's eschatologism is a political programme, to which the book on Müntzer bears testimony. Falsely ascribing complex cosmological speculations to Müntzer, Bloch nevertheless successfully uses his image to show that the consciousness of the coming Judgement becomes not only a part of inner life, but also an element of political struggle, which abolishes all previous history. The goal of messianism in this context is to hasten the end of this world.

> [T]he goal of this battle is . . . that the removal of the physical world will be met with purified souls, with the souls' finally discovered *Absolute [Überhaupt]*, with the unriven Paracletan guardian spirit of what is inmost, of the Servants, with the word from the essence, with the keyword of that Holy Spirit who for his part could let nature, this rubbish heap of error, disappear so completely that for the evil ones, as for Satan, one would not even need a gravestone, let alone a hell. (GU2, p. 342; SU, p. 275)

Eschatologism is also a special style, manifest in Bloch's early texts – the style of an intense anticipation of a catastrophe, where there is room for elevated, at times even high soaring proclamations, for hysterical cries, as well as for accurately grasped figures of time. By the way, it is straightforward to see here the parallels with Russian theurgical aesthetics, originating with Vladimir Solovyov and developed by Vyacheslav Ivanov and Andrei Bely. Many basic sources of Bely's essays (Nietzsche, Ibsen, Steiner) were also paradigmatic for the young Bloch, but apart from this common background, the affinity of aspirations is also evident:

> Only one way is left for us: the way of rebirth; the creativity of life, just as life itself, depends on our transfiguration . . . to blow up history itself for the sake of absolute values, *not yet discovered by consciousness* [italics mine – I. B.], such is the sinister conclusion to be drawn from Nietzsche's lyric and Ibsen's drama.

To explode with one's century in the striving for genuine reality is the only means not to perish. (Bely 1994, p. 217)

It is a foundational feature of the apocalyptic consciousness that the world is judged from the perspective of its complete disappearance. Bloch does not wish to postpone the realization of utopia into the indefinite future, he is unwilling to accept Kant's argument of infinite progress towards perfection, hence his attention to the everyday and the metaphysics of the moment. But the immersion into oneself is not an enclosure within oneself, a rebellion against the defective world is necessary.

Bloch thus oscillates between the mystical presentism of the instant and the eschatological overtones of the revealed religions. It is not entirely clear how to reconcile the complete and unconditional destruction of the old world with the urge to uncover the mysteries within our soul and to give meaning to the world of everyday life. But while concentrating on one's own inwardness distorts the historical optic, the apocalyptic prevents one from seeing the genuine present (Christen 1979, p. 73), it drags the instant into the whirlpool of historical movement, which imposes on our actual being its concerns and perspectives. All the paradoxicality of a utopian project, to which we shall return later, is already manifest here.

Messianism is opposed to traditional religiosity, disregarding it as a dismal dogma. However, the destruction of the sanctuaries can be explained as a restoration of the genuine order and the return to the Golden Age. In fact, the tension between restorationist and utopian tendencies defines the entire history of Jewish messianism. For Bloch such a return is not the result of historically immanent evolutionary forces, causally determined by some preceding development; instead he speaks of an intrusion from without, abrupt and unpredictable (relating him to both Rosenzweig and Benjamin) (Scholem 1986; Rabinbach 1997). The God-given spark can flare at any moment, in any matter, even the most mediocre and ridiculous, and here gnosticism and (superconfessionary) messianism coincide.

Bloch's eschatology draws both on Christian and Judaic religious traditions. In *The Spirit of Utopia*, images of the apocalypse are continually borrowed from *The Revelation* (the black, 'grim' sun, the bloody moon, white clothes etc.).[8] But more important for Bloch are the revolutionary heresies, and above all the figure of Joachim of Fiore, a famous prophet of the Third Kingdom. Joachim talks not of the other world, but prophesies the institution of the new world on this earth, the brotherly community of free people (EZ, pp. 132–8). The obvious anarchism of Christian heretics, who expected the world beyond material production to come, fit well into Bloch's utopian project. But Bloch was neither a Christian writer nor a full-fledged Christian heretic. He was, rather, under the immediate impact of Judaic tradition.

Judaic filiations

In 1919 in Interlaken, Switzerland, young Gershom Scholem accompanied by Benjamin entered Bloch's room and was astounded to find on his desk a book by the German anti-Semitic scholar Johann Andreas Eisenmenger entitled *Judaism Unmasked (Entdecktes Judenthum*, 1700). Scholem looked at Bloch in astonishment, but Bloch explained that he had a great time reading the book, for the author, a parody of a scientist, did not realize that by exposing the blasphemies and extensively quoting Jewish authors, he was in fact opening up the treasury of the Jewish thought. Scholem, according to his own testimony, had a chance to see for himself that Bloch turned out to be right (Scholem 1975b, p. 102f.; 1975a, p. 110).[9]

Though Bloch was born to a Jewish family, his parents were quite far from the religious rites, and he himself never observed any of them. Talking to the Israeli ambassador in the 1960s Bloch said that he was not an assimilated Jew, on the contrary, he had assimilated himself into Judaism (Landmann 1982, p. 161). However, the Jewish intellectual tradition did have an impact on Bloch. Thus, in 1918 he characterizes himself as a man who is associated with Jewish culture (Br I, p. 232f.).

There were many points of contact with Judaism. For instance, Bloch's love for music as a special, non-figurative art could be interpreted in the context of his early philosophical aesthetics opposed to any complete forms, like Jews, who reject any images of God (Lellouche 2008, p. 120). Scholem in his notes on the 'Jewish question' emphasized the particular meaning given to the practice of questioning and answering in Jewish thought (see Dubbels 2011, p. 139). Any new answer produces new questions, and this glimmering of challenges and replies that came in Bloch under the title of the 'inconstruable question' comes very close to the ever-changing and never-perfect utopian image. The secret history of the world, the anticipation of the Messiah, the hope for redemption – all of these affects and images, which long since had been inherent in Jewish culture, maintained by the people deprived of homeland, became central both for Bloch and for several generations of other prominent German-Jewish thinkers.

These people lived in the conditions of a catastrophe that unfolded many times on different levels. The first and the biggest crisis of the turn of the century was the secularization, the sudden emptiness of a religious idea, the reduction of Jewish religion to an abstract ritual. Another one was the loss of identity due to assimilation. An excellent illustration of these conflicts is provided by Franz Kafka's *Letter* to his father. Finally, when the pan-European catastrophe – the World War – began, Jewish writers in Germany felt if not the coming of the apocalypse, then at least the beginning of a new, important era, that had to be understood, in which one had to find one's way.

Bloch's existential philosophy was deeply influenced by Martin Buber (1878–1965) although later Bloch was careful to renounce any such associations (Krochmalnik 1993). They knew each other, both attended (although in different periods) Simmel's seminar in Berlin. Buber's texts have for some time become both the intellectual/stylistic paradigmatic model, and a field of demarcation and critique – not only for Bloch, but also for many other German-Jewish intellectuals, among them Lukács, Benjamin, Scholem and Rosenzweig. Buber was a prolific author of philosophical prose, his expressive manner of writing gave new meanings to the Jewish idea, provided it with a new spiritual and political content, having shown that the heritage of Jewish mysticism is not just a romantic veil, but that it can be made a part of the everyday innermost life of each person. Therefore if Jewish mysticism began to interest Bloch, it was to a large extent due to Buber.

In *The Heritage of Our Times* of 1935, Bloch the Marxist already compares Buber to Hermann Keyserling (a philosopher who clearly did not fit into the Marxist canon) and labels mysticism as 'irresponsible windbaggery' (EZ, p. 149; HT, p. 135). But in *The Spirit of Utopia* he was evidently influenced by Buber's early work.[10] They have in common the idea of discovering and awakening one's inner I, the hidden self irreducible to the superficial narcissistic subjectivity obsessed with itself. The domain both Buber and Bloch sought to explore in order to link the sacred and the profane history was in everyday experience: its sacred dimensions were put in a simple, often prosaic context.

Buber's mysticism, and not the rationalistic progressism of Hermann Cohen,[11] defined the style which Bloch adopted in relation to Jewish wisdom. One should not forget, however, the emphasis on the separation of myth (in which uncertain and mysterious future is hardly possible) from religion in the *Ethics of Pure Will*, the emphasis that made prophetic messianism the central moment of shaping and comprehending history (Hamacher 2006, p. 177).

Jews in early Buber (1916) and in Bloch are a people prone not to contemplation, but to action, to the active creation of themselves in history. Early Bloch's metaphysics of subjectivity was surprisingly congenial to other Jewish principles. For instance, in his correspondence with Eugen Rosenstock-Huessy, Rosenzweig characterizes Judaism as a religion, which, unlike Christianity that strives to involve the whole world in its orbit, constantly problematizes itself, practices a retreat into itself, strives to find within itself the entire world (Mosès 2006, p. 65). Jewish prophets portrayed so eloquently by Buber are also heroes of utopian philosophy, guided by an internal imperative, the will to theocracy and hatred of any forms of this-worldly oppression and religious hierarchy.

Apparently, Bloch owed to Buber's books his interest in Hasidism, and first of all the legends and anecdotes of Jewish life collected by Buber. Bloch liked the stories of Baal Shem, especially the one that tells of a drunkard not observing the Sabbath and in whose house Baal Shem spent the night and before whom he fell to his knees, having recognized in him God's chosen, walking on the water. This incognito that lives within things and events, a mystery that is meant to be uncovered one day (Landmann 1982, p. 166), was reinterpreted as utopian.

However, it is worth noting several reservations. The fundamental characteristics of Jewish religion attempted by Cohen (monotheism as striving for the One and ideology of humanism as a messianic vision of future humanity) are in fact very close to Bloch's discussion of Jewishness in *The Spirit of Utopia*. Cohen's providential interpretation of history and his ethical socialism, as well as the idea of a postulate, ethical dimension that is elevated above the givenness of human life, are quite commensurable with Bloch's utopian messianism. In particular, Cohen refers to the end of days:

> Let it be the Sometimes to which any politics must aspire; and any reality orient itself . . . only the future should be the guiding star of politics and hence religion. The reality brought by the "messianic days" should be not the end of the world and humanity, but rather the beginning of the new times, new world . . . and the new humanity on Earth. (Cited in: Hamacher 2006, p. 177)

Bloch was also tending towards the universal dimension of the messianic idea. However, Cohen had the notion of the infinite, asymptotic approximation of the ideal goal. For Bloch the apocalypticist, this kind of utopia, as we shall see, was unacceptable.

Curiously, Cohen's 'logic of the origin' that proposed to commence the epistemic experience with the infinitely small differential found a clear correspondence in Blochian logic of the dark and imperceptible instant (Pelletier 2008). This shows that Bloch was deeply involved in the philosophical discussion around Cohen, without, however, explicitly dealing with either his theory of knowledge, or philosophy of history.

Generally, Bloch did not share Buber's Zionist views that made him popular among the Jewish youth. For justice's sake we have to mention that the early Buber considered not the exodus of Jews but the overcoming of internal boundaries, the internal spiritual liberation and transformation, to be of real significance. In his polemics with Cohen he makes a double move by establishing the development of the national self-consciousness as a necessary way to achieve a universal goal envisaged by Cohen (Dubbels 2011, p. 236). To fulfill its historical mission beyond any national boundaries, the Jewish people, Buber claimed, should create a centripetal movement to find itself, and this self-encounter as an attainment of an absolute identity is the only real way to transcend and to actualize it, again, to fulfil and to abolish oneself by this fulfilment.

In any case Zionism as an ideology of the nation-state ran counter to the cosmopolitanism and socialist world-view of Bloch the Marcionite, just as it ran counter to the mystical anarchism of another Jewish radical – Gustav Landauer (1870–1919), the author of *Scepticism and Mysticism* (1903) and *The Revolution* (1907), a friend to Buber, Kropotkin and Margarete Susman, who was also a close friend of Bloch. Bloch considered the Zionist ideals to be a profanation of Jewish mysticism, as a banal outcome of the movement for global liberation. Bloch and Landauer's attention in 1917 was fixed on Russia, not on Israel (Löwy 1992).[12] Neither Bloch nor Benjamin and Landauer approved of Buber's militaristic pathos during World War I.

Landauer's radical socialism was surely germane to that of Bloch, to the point that plagiarism became, though untenably so, a suspicion (Pelletier 2008). Along with their general political stance they shared an interest in mystical and heretical traditions (Landauer translated and published the Meister Eckhart anthology – the edition Bloch surely knew) and the idea of reconfiguring the mythical energies coming from conservative nationalist ideas and of directing them to the left. Bloch in many respects inherits Landauer's discontented attitude towards traditional or 'cold' Marxism that they both considered not radical enough and too neutral in its attempts to become scientific.

Landauer attacked the contemporary state, lamented when diagnosing a corrupt modernity and urged to return to the medieval commune, to universal brotherhood, which, rather in line with Jewish eschatology and German Romanticism, was conceived of as the restoration of the Golden Age and as a complete demise of existing institutions. He was a prolific writer who believed in the transformative power of his discursive gestures and identified an ecstatic vision of a poet with the evocation of a future community, and an appeal for socialism. This general attitude also manifests an important affinity to Bloch.

Rebelling against stagnant ideology and otherworldly religiosity, Landauer believed in the possibility of instantly changing the world into a global socialist community, and tied this transformation (under Buber's influence) to the universal historical mission of the Jewish people, who know no borders and no nation-states, led by no one but prophets – Moses, Christ and Spinoza. Bloch, undoubtedly, felt Landauer's influence to a certain degree, which is evident in *The Spirit of Utopia*, where anarchism is combined with spiritual aristocratism and where utopia is understood in a revolutionary, activist sense. The same can be said of *Thomas Müntzer*, in the way it glorifies a socialistic religion and suggests working with a not-yet-accomplished past. Landauer also invoked the concept of utopia in his *Revolution*, but only to attack the deterministic philosophy of history interpreting the historical process as the sequence of 'topias' and 'utopias' (Pelletier 2008). At times Bloch was even more radical than Landauer who distanced himself from the possible apocalyptic consequences of his views (Dubbels 2011).

Another author important in this context is Rosenzweig, 'the Jewish Bloch' (Kaufmann 1997, p. 48), who constructed a philosophy of history out of the intensive experience of the instant. (Both Bloch and Benjamin were acquainted with Rosenzweig and visited him regularly in the 1920s (Ujma 1995, p. 102.)) This was the experience of symbolic unity in the religious community paired with a persistent and tense anticipation of redemption animating the time of history and giving it meaning. Rosenzweig's anticipation implies that the community must live in a situation where the Kingdom is just about to come, and redemption is just about to happen. This extreme intensity of experience of time bares an already familiar paradox: we balance on the brink between the cult of the instant, the condensation of history in one moment and a constant postponing of history's finale into the future, the awaiting of the Messiah. Rosenzweig's concept of an origin, as well as Bloch's homeland, is restated as an end: in its experience of eternity the Jewish community inverts the traditional temporal order.

In the first edition of *The Spirit of Utopia* there is a chapter called 'Symbol: Jews' (GU1, pp. 319–31), written already in 1912. Bloch reconstructs the attitudes of contemporaneous Jewish intellectuals and forces them into his historical context. Jewish world-view is seen as a refusal to accept the world,[13] an urge to transform life on the basis of justice and spirituality, and messianism as an obsession with a super-worldly goal for all humanity, not just the Jewish people (GU1, p. 321f.). Indeed, this understanding of the Jewish element is directly translated into Blochian language: the new Jewry is inherently utopian.

Such reappropriation of messianism is probably inspired by Cohen and Landauer, but could be found in the Jewish sources as well. Towards the end of *The Spirit of Utopia* Bloch provides an extensive quote, emphasizing the embeddedness of his philosophy in the Judaic tradition:

> "Know this," says an old manuscript of the Zohar[14] . . ., "know that there is a twofold view of any world. One shows its external aspect, namely the general laws of this world in its external form. The other shows the inner essence of this world, namely the quintessence of the souls of men. Accordingly there are also two degrees of action, namely works and ascetic disciplines; works are for perfecting worlds with respect to their externality, but prayers are for causing one world to be contained in the other, and raising it up." Within such a functional correlation of disburdening and spirit, Marxism and religion, united in the will to the Kingdom,

flows the ultimate master system of all the tributaries: the Soul, the Messiah, and the Apocalypse, which represents the act of awakening in totality, provide the final impulses to do and to know, form the a priori of all politics and culture. (GU2, p. 345f.; SU, p. 278)

The world of Jewish life envisaged by Rosenzweig is in a similar condition: any particular thing in this world has, apart from its usual existence and purpose, a kind of a 'second bottom', a different dimension, through which the coming world shines (Rosenzweig 1988, pp. 341f.). This duality is wholly overcome and the blessing is granted to all the nations, not a single thing will remain forsaken, not a single righteous man will be left behind the door to the temple of eternal life.

Bloch's utopian gesture implies that someone who managed to grasp oneself with one's inner eye and dissolve the darkness and the opaque veil of one's own consciousness is capable of completely transforming the world. This idea builds upon the Nietzschean conception of the *Übermensch* (with its dynamic search and the joyful affirmation of life), but also the Judaic notions of the divine consummation, of *Shekhinah* (divine presence), which has fallen away into the finite world and is capable of returning to God only through human action.[15] Buber and Bloch agree that redemption is in the hands of the human being, who must, in the familiar figure of self-comprehension, experience one's soul in its authenticity, in its bareness, to feel the integrity of one's own self and its unity with the world; that original oneness, that lies at the root of any duality.

There is another important dimension of the Jewish tradition: the notion of the Messiah, fulfilling his historical mission only when humanity has matured and is ready to meet him. Bloch finds this messianism in the sacred Jewish texts: he refers to the *Gemara* claiming that the last is far more important than the first, that at the root of the origin ('alpha') lies the event of the consummation ('omega'), that which has not yet occurred, but glimmers through the present. Adam Kadmon, the proto-human, is defined by the panhuman (*makantropos*), awaited by the coming times. Bloch grounds his doctrine of utopian anticipation in a Kabbalistic reunification of the scattered spiritual forces, or sparks.

He also relies on Sabbateanism and the religion of joy, following Baal Shem's dictum that 'joy is higher than law' (GU1, p. 330; Lellouche 2008, p. 61f.). Commentators find the echoes of Lurianic Kabbalah (Jacobson 2003, p. 252) in Bloch's descriptions of the coming tragic times, when the world will become completely godless, and in his invoking 'the sparks of the end', which we carry on our journey – even though he could have taken these metaphors from gnostics as well. In fact, as Pauen (1992a) shows, this imagery could be traced back to the Stoics and even to Heraclitus.

Scholem recognized the embodiment of the utopian tradition of messianism in Bloch's oeuvre. Scholem contends that Bloch owes his insights to 'the energy and depth of mystical inspiration', and not 'to the jungle of his Marxist rhapsodies' (Scholem 1986, p. 13). But why does Scholem emphasize Bloch's contribution? Probably because he saw the affinity between Bloch's secularized mysticism and his own attempts to free the Jewish religion from stagnancy, to shake its dogmas by indicating the unstable and pluralistic field of interpretations inherent in it (Dubbels 2011, p. 142). He saw in *The Spirit of Utopia* if not the letter, then the spirit of Jewish eschatology, and in its mysterious formulas – the allegories pronounced by prophets predicting the end of the world after all of history was revealed to them, disillusioned with the profane history and obsessed with the anticipation of the end. Bloch inherits their energy and inspiration.

The notion that the glimmers of the future can be found in the present are ubiquitous in Jewish mysticism (Landmann 1982, p. 167f.). Self-encounter – the aim and the meaning of human transformation in *The Spirit of Utopia* – is described also in the mystical techniques of prophetic Kabbalah, in the school of Abraham Abulafia (Scholem 1955, p. 141ff.). At a certain moment of Kabbalist's meditation 'that which is within will manifest itself without, and through the power of sheer imagination will take on the form of the polished mirror . . . Whereupon one sees that his inmost being is something outside of himself' (Scholem 1955, p. 155). One cannot help recalling the main slogan of *The Spirit of Utopia* – the search for ways in which the inward can become outward, and the outward turn inward.

The figure of Jesus Christ and the problem of the Jewish attitude towards Christianity in *The Spirit of Utopia* deserve a separate mention. Bloch observes the complete denouncement on the part of the older generations and a surprisingly positive attitude to Christ of the younger Jews. Commenting on *The Epistle to the Romans*, he argues that the Jewish people always played an important role for Paul (see Rom. 10–11) and that Christ always lived in its heart as a messianic spirit.

The aggadic literature always knew *the suffering Messiah*. Bloch quotes Isaiah (53) talking about the suffering God, and mentions the Jewish theologians who compared this theological figure with Christ, meaning the Messiah from the house of Joseph, that is the Messiah of the end of times, who does not bring the new world, but dies for the old (in contrast to the Messiah from the house of David – who restores to the rightful place the former dynasty, which existed prior to the political schism among the Jews). This reference also perfectly corresponds to Buber's vision of Judaism (see Dubbels 2011, p. 246f.)

However, the Jews never accepted Christ, the Jewish spirit 'stuck in the empty formalistic traditionalism and a completely sober, abstract deism' (GU1, p. 330), the Jews lost the former zeal of their faith. But 'in our deepest, and nameless yet, innermost secrecy the last, unknown Christ is sleeping, the conqueror of coldness, emptiness, world and God, Dionysos, theurg of enormous powers, foremost felt by Moses, and dressed, but not embodied by soft-hearted Jesus' (GU1, p. 332). Saying 'Christ', Bloch means the new Messiah, the anointed one, and not Jesus. The central role of Jesus, Scholem claimed, was the result of Buber's influence. One way or another, one cannot call Bloch a Christian, not least in this respect: he was awaiting the 'new' Christ. The key element here is precisely the attitude of the new Jewish generation that can overcome both the statics of its own tradition and the tautology of the Second Coming monopolized by the alienated institutions of the authoritarian church.

Was the Jewish element decisive for Bloch or did he simply subordinate it to the aims of his philosophy, striking the sparks of utopian ideas from Jewish wisdom? Maybe Habermas is right in saying that Bloch was a follower of Schelling and the Romanticists who actively appropriated Kabbalistic ideas, and that his Jewish training is, quite naturally, a part of a purely German spirit, eagerly learning from the Jews (Habermas cited in Ujma 1995, p. 12). His effort to integrate various traditions leads us to Bloch's Christian origins.

Christian heretics

> ... but ourselves also, who have the first fruits of the Spirit, even we ourselves groan within ourselves, waiting for adoption, the redemption of our body. For we were saved in hope, but hope that is seen is not hope. For who hopes for that which he sees? But if we hope for that which we don't see, we wait for it with patience. In the same way, the Spirit also helps our weaknesses, for we don't know how to pray as we ought. But the Spirit himself makes intercession for us with groanings which can't be uttered.
>
> (Rom. 8: 23–26)

Bloch's philosophy was profoundly influenced by Christianity in general and various forms of Christian mysticism in particular. Any ideas, including the ones borrowed from Jewish or gnostic tradition, were being reinterpreted in view of the Christian perspective on humanity and history. One year before his death, in conversation with J. M. Palmier, Bloch stressed that he is not a believing Jew and that the roots of his thinking are Christian (Tagträume, p. 109). Indeed, Bloch interprets the Talmudic formula 'Kiddush HaShem' ('sanctification of the name', an important practice in Judaism) as the Christian *Lord's Prayer*. Repudiating the classical ontology of recollection, Bloch discovered in Christianity a religion of revolutionary anticipation of a future world. And in early works he even awaited 'a radical renewal of Catholicism from the spirit of the Franciscan life and Eckhartian, Dominican mystics' (TM, p. 103).[16]

However, in Christianity Bloch also searched for the elements that were closer to his revolutionary dissent. In the later work *Atheism in Christianity* he interprets the Old Testament Serpent almost in a Promethean fashion, as liberating humans, making them equal to God, revealing the world that lies beyond the one given by *Yahweh* the Demiurge. For instance, in *The Principle of Hope* he discusses the Ophites who worship the serpent[17] – the ambivalent image of absolute evil (also of the Original Sin) and of absolute wisdom (PH, p. 1495ff.). The construction of the *Tower of Babel* is reformulated as an audacious revolutionary defiance against the divine power's authority and the hierarchic structures associated with it (AC, p. 119). It is precisely the God of Exodus, God of Moses, and not the traditional religious God, who for Bloch is the true utopian Absolute. Another subversive Bible figure appearing in the later work is Job (AC, p. 155ff.). Here the gnostic dualism reappears, for Bloch's Job awaits the new God.

Christ is distinguished by Bloch precisely because he was neither a dreamer nor a warrior fighting like Bar Kokhba for the existing order of things. His ideals led him away from the authoritarianism of the Jewish religion towards the new kingdom of the end-times, and in this sense the Blochian Christ becomes one of the highest examples of *Jewish* apocalyptics (AC, p. 182f.). All these considerations are further developed into the idea of atheism underlying Bloch's later understanding of the messianic idea (PH, p. 1413; cf. the idea of 'heroic-mystical atheism' in GU1, p. 230).

Bloch did not accept the mysticism of blood and was not satisfied with Paul's rendering of Jesus's atoning sacrifice. Jesus becomes the Messiah *despite* His death, and not *due to it*. Bloch's Jesus realizes himself not merely as a Son of God, but as a human being: the one who passes the torch of the messianic idea to the Holy Spirit, the spirit of consolation (PH, p. 1489ff.), and ultimately to the entire liberated humanity. We do not stop, we go even further than Christ, and here lies a clear boundary between Bloch and the most 'liberal' versions of Christianity, for which there is nothing new after Christ, and His coming is that very absolute event, which contains both our past and our future (Denecke 1993, pp. 72–5).

Christian mysticism also plays an important role for Bloch, for in the experience of the instant and in anticipating the consummation of the world one can discern that illumination of the soul, which the Christian mystics interpreted as the experience of the singular individual. The most salient figure of mystical thought relevant here is the birth of God in the innermost depths of the human soul, of which Eckhart speaks in his sermon *On Eternal Birth*. This experience cannot be expressed in either image or word or anything external at all, it appears only when all the outer is forgotten, including the self, when God speaks the sacred Word. However, Bloch makes some reservations quoting this passage:

> in Eckhart, as forcefully as he immediately asks, "Where is he that was born King of the Jews?,"[18] the light-substance is still very high, very remote in space, shifted away from the subject and the We to the supradivine God, into the highest depths, into vertiginous depths of angelic light, which truly can least of all contain, resolve, the only secret, the secret of our nearness. Rather it must be the moment just lived; it alone, its darkness, is the only darkness, its light is the only light, its word is the primordial concept that resolves everything. Nothing sublime lives whose sublimity is not such that it conveys a presentiment of our future freedom, an initial interference by the "Kingdom"; indeed Messiah himself (in Collossians 3:4),[19] the bringer of absolute adequation, is nothing but the finally uncovered face of our unceasingly nearest depth. (GU2, p. 246f.; SU, p. 195f.)

Eckhart exempts the birth of God from any temporal order, and this eternal moment merging together various times stays in a problematic relationship with the utopian perspective that is intimately connected to the uncertainty and fragility inherent in the experience of temporality. Eckhartian mysticism lacked a historical dimension, and this was something Bloch wanted to impart into it.

Finally, the inspired visions of Jakob Böhme combined with alchemical experimentation had a remarkable impact on Bloch and his later speculative philosophy of nature. Böhme was another Christian mystic (and a heretic!), who instituted a new heterodoxy. Böhme was an emblematic figure during Bloch's formative years (particularly, Böhme's teachings interested Buber to a very large extent; Russian religious philosophers were also fascinated by the Böhmean speculation). The volitive impulse Böhme places at the origin of the world corresponds to the utopian energy of human and natural being in Bloch's work. Böhme's metaphors (such as the metaphor of the inner mirror referring to the incomprehensible Absolute), his plastic language producing physically tangible concepts of light and dark, of illumination, of torments, trembling, and fermenting of material being, his dualistic natural philosophy – all of this easily penetrated Bloch's utopian philosophy from the very beginning.

However, early Bloch's gnostic rebelliousness explicitly contradicted the doctrines of Christian mystics. Gnostic radicalism, the ideology of 'the great refusal', cannot be easily reconciled with Neoplatonism and continualist metaphysics, and the hatred towards nature – with the natural philosophy of, say, Böhme. Despite Bloch's later proximity to the tradition of Böhme, Baader and Schelling with their ideas of the becoming nature that realize messianic possibilities, some of his early ideological dispositions are still quite alien to this intellectual tradition.

Did Bloch seek to synthesize Christianity and Judaism? The writer Anna Lesznai in her 1912 diary notes that Bloch's proximity to Talmud borders on Catholicism (quoted in Gluck 1985, p. 160) and Paul Honigsheim, the member of the Weber circle, calls him a 'catholisizing Jewish apocalypticist' (quoted in Zudeick 1987, p. 46). In the early, never completed 'System of theoretical messianism', Bloch clearly sought a synthesis in which Jesus would have been a preliminary, latent Jewish Messiah (GU1, p. 328). Most probably, he was guided by the example of Molitor attempting to see the single root of Christianity and Judaism in mystical experience and their confluence in the eschatological perspective.

Hesitant conclusions: Tensions within messianic thought

Bloch's philosophy is messianic in many respects. This judgement is based not only on stylistic features of his early work or evocations of Messiah in the *Spirit of Utopia*. In describing the messianic time Scholem stressed the logic of the inversion inherent in it (see the analysis in Dubbels 2011, p. 133ff.) The seeming completeness and closure of the past as well as the alleged openness of the future are questioned as soon as the messianic time arrives. The time itself becomes reversible. It is telling that Bloch's theory of non-contemporaneity and his earlier attempts to work with the past and to evoke the seemingly foregone figures and meanings were precisely a messianic project.

The contradictions inherent in Bloch's eschatology and pertaining to messianic thinking in general are notorious; however, it is worth articulating them once again.

Radicalism and peremptoriness cannot easily be reconciled with the idea of uncertainty and instability of the utopian. The young Bloch regarded his prophecy as a result of a certain spiritual, artistic revelation, uncompromising in its self-assertion. But where is the room for humanism and the radical *incompleteness* and understatements of human beings in the world? Later Bloch would try to come to grips with these features of the utopian vision, whereas the prophetic tone by and large moves to the background.

The utopian aspiration of the new world is a creation that brings with itself a total destruction. Our own political and ethical action in history seems meaningless and powerless compared to the transcendent intervention of the utopian.[20] This problem is present both in the Christian and in the Judaic apocalyptics. In *The Spirit of Utopia* and especially in *Thomas Müntzer*, Bloch clearly gravitates towards the activist solution, subsequently ascribing the active participation in the bringing of a better future not only to the leaders of heretical sects, but also to the Old Testament prophets (AC, p. 133). In *Thomas Müntzer* he also places this issue in the context of an inner-Christian polemic and defends the Eckhartian idea of the divine spark against Luther's emphasis on the full impuissance of the human (TM, p. 140).

The problem of messianic action and its integration into history is a very old one. The young Hegel, for instance, in a 1795 letter to Schelling reproduced their mutual shibboleth: 'May the Kingdom of God come, and our hands not be idle!' (1984, p. 32). Buber also wrote about the active contribution of an individual to redemption in *The Three Speeches on Judaism*, which had an impact on the young Bloch.

However, the link between human action and messianic redemption remains vague and so do the moral guidelines. Small wonder that the anarchist tendencies of Judaic messianism confront the world of Halakha, the legally organized structures of Jewish life. Hasidism offered a different model: *individual* atonement resting solely in individual action was separated from messianic redemption, which pertained to the *community as a whole* and rested solely with God (Scholem 1955). The Christian world-view is also close to such an understanding. The Kingdom of God is within us. But when we glimpse eternity and the absolute nature of God through prayer, this does not mean that such communication can have a historical impact: history moves in its own way and at some point it will end.

This tension between the individual and the collective had another form that played a significant role in the writings of German-Jewish intellectuals of that time and shaped their philosophy of history (I mean here the contradictions of Zionism, that demonstrate a paradoxical coexistence of its universal aspiration and national particularism.)[21] The messianic idea seems to belong to the Jewish people, that – by elevating the whole world – loses its identity of the chosen nation.

Bloch is unwilling to describe redemption as a result of the predetermined, but secret divine plan; nor is he tending to completely entrust responsibility for redemption onto the human being (Rabinbach 1997). On the one hand he discards the idea of progressive and deterministic historical process with an outcome that is known in advance; and, on the other, he places at the centre of this process the final event of redemption, thus subordinating history to the expected instant of the messianic coming.

It could be claimed, for example, that in Jewish apocalyptics chiliasm (the anticipation of a thousand-year kingdom *in history*) and eschatology (as transcending history, located beyond human actions, aspirations, beyond historical time) are combined, whereas in Christianity they are clearly separated (Bulgakov 1993). But is this distinction satisfactory? Bloch also finds himself in an ambivalent situation, praising Jesus, but running into a paradox: that is, for a Christian, the events of real history are simply incommensurable with the secret history of redemption, for they sit outside human history, have to be moved beyond its limits – both in the causal sense and in the temporal perspective. As Schweppenhäuser succinctly noted, 'without history the spirit cannot be realized, but within history it cannot remain any more' (1985, p. 169).

Hence the tensions between mysticism and eschatology: for Bloch, especially in the later period, mysticism in its common form is untenable, he is sceptical towards reviving the old forms of mystical life (PH, p. 1540). A mystic places the experience of wholeness, of unity, *into the present*, achieves the extreme intensity and ultimately the abolition of time; whereas the utopian philosopher, the prophet of the 'Not-Yet-Being', promises the messianic kingdom and the end of times only in the future (TE, p. 185). This tension translates into a conflict between contemplative attitude and activism. But maybe Bloch's most important philosophical effort was directed at reconciling (perhaps clashing together) the being-out-of-present with the being-out-of-tomorrow, to turn the absolute presence into the absolute promise, to show that they can be joined together.

How can we find the mediating links between the internal transformation of life, between the rejuvenation of the soul and the reorganization of the world? How to avoid both extreme subjectivism (unacceptable to Bloch even in *The Spirit of Utopia*) and sectarianism?[22] Rosenzweig found a solution that reveals his Hegelian inspiration. He dismissed both the conception of the messianic intervention into history independent of individuals, and the model of the steady progressive historical movement. A person cannot bring redemption closer, but a *people* can – as a church, a collective body, members of which meticulously observe their religious rites, honour their law and live according to their meta-historical symbolic time (Mosès 2006, p. 93). And the tread of history is visible in this ritual act. We saw that Lukács (at the time of his interest in Hegel) came to a similar solution, having identified the Messiah with the collective unity, though bound by different ties, but also solely capable of truly winning the future.

If we follow Scholem, then the primary difference between the Judaic and the Christian messianism is that the very situation of deliverance, of redemption for Jews cannot be hidden, the apocalypse is an event that unfolds in the space of social history, in the community; whereas Christian thinkers have always spoken of redemption in the depths of the soul, of the inner purity of the spirit amidst the sinful and God-forsaken world. German-Jewish authors of the early twentieth century, Bloch among them, deemed such a position weak and quietist. However, without Christianity, Jewish messianism could not have won the intensity of historical occurrence.

All these tensions stem not only from the logical inconsistencies of any affective gesture (which is, assuredly, constitutive of Bloch's philosophy), but also from the multitude of historical layers, the crossovers between different traditions. They are, at times, reflected in the unbearable eclecticism of revolutionary gnosis, which seamlessly combines Marxism and mysticism, religious hopes with the rebellion against ecclesiastical authority, and the urge of the solitary – that naked soul that finds its genuine face – with the vision of the utopian community. The mixture of styles and meanings in Bloch can be also correlated to the stylistic revolution that Erich Auerbach linked in *Mimesis* to the transition from the Antique to the Judaeo-Christian culture (Faber 2006).

Balancing incessantly among these – hardly rationally resolvable – paradoxes, Bloch and his readers recognize that in spite of them, utopian philosophy is still possible – as an artistic and political project, as a practical way of life inspired by heretical religiosity.

One of the most substantial and most popular characteristics of the philosophical habitus in Bloch and at the same time almost a precise formulation of his mysticism – is *transcending without the transcendent*. Despite all the dissimilarity, one cannot resist the temptation to compare it to another formula that emerged in entirely different circumstances – the slogan of Jacques Derrida (1999), which he put forward in response to the criticism of his book *Spectres of Marx*: 'messianic without messianism' or 'anticipation without anticipation'. It is the anticipation of something that a fortiori exceeds any possible expectations. Derrida sees in this complex structure of 'without' an undeconstructible basis of an event, of a revolution, of justice, which always precedes deconstruction of messianic meanings itself – deconstruction that comprises the very essence of utopia, for Bloch's intentions lie beyond any presently imaginable forms.

The problem of messianism, once laid out in religious terms and subsequently combined with Marxism, was recurrently discussed in various works of Walter Benjamin. His texts provide answers and perspectives to many of the problems I dealt with in this chapter. Benjamin's vision helped to reframe these issues in ways that were unexpected and momentous for twentieth-century philosophy. Benjamin's relation to Bloch's messianism can hardly be overlooked. Various and not always clear-cut situations of their mutual influence and polemic, of their attraction and repulsion should not just illustrate their intellectual biographies, but rather guide us in the search for new strategies and forms of doing and interpreting *messianic philosophy*.

Notes

1 See Dubbels (2011), who makes the case for a symbolic interpretation of Bloch's early messianism.
2 Characteristically, it was precisely the reading of Molitor that inspired Gershom Scholem to study Jewish mysticism (See Mosès 2006, p. 268).
3 A preliminary conclusion was drawn at a conference in Messina 1966 r. See Bianchi 1970. See also: Jonas 1975; Bolz 1984; Pauen 1992; Hanegraaf 2006, p. 403ff.).
4 Cf. in Bloch on the contempt for the body: GU1, p. 417.
5 Cf.: *Excerpta ex Theodoto* by Clement of Alexandria: 'The knowledge of who we were, and what we have become, where we were or where we were placed, whither we hasten, from what we are redeemed, what birth is and what rebirth' (78, 2). Similar passages can be found, of course, in *The Spirit of Utopia* (GU2, pp. 285, 343).
6 Incidentally, the initial title of the whole book was *Music and the Apocalypse*.
7 Of course, it is inadequate to call historical Marcion an anti-Semite – we only imply an interpretation of his ideas.
8 Revelation. 3: 5, 6: 12–14, cf. GU2, pp. 344, 338f.
9 In this article Scholem claims that Bloch's entire philosophy is a desperate attempt to link the incompatible – Marxism and mysticism – and that he cannot consider Bloch as atheist.
10 In general Buber's influence is well shown in Christen (1979) and mentioned by Scholem (1999, pp. 172f.). See also Wołkowicz 1988; Mendes-Flohr 1991, pp. 102–5.
11 In Bloch's youth German academic philosophy was under an enormous influence of neo-Kantianism. In 1909, Bloch sent his dissertation to Cohen (Mendes-Flohr 1983).
12 Of course, Bloch at the time was interested not as much by the 'real', but by an 'ideal', mythic Russia – the land populated by Dostoyevsky's heroes and, in Rilke's words, bordering on God.

13 Scholem in his book on Jewish mysticism provides a midrash perfectly illustrating this characteristic. God creates a human, who remembers (in the Platonic sense) all the archetypes, all the pure essences, that lay in the basis of the world. But immediately after birth the child *forgets* all about it, for if he were to remember the eternal ideas and at the same time observe the chaos of the real world, he would go insane (Scholem 1955, p. 92).

14 In the letter to M. Landman dated 30 January 1978, Scholem rather contemptuously indicates that what is implied is not the book of Zohar, but a well-known Lurianic manuscript cited in Molitor (Scholem 1999, p. 173).

15 Bloch talks of *Shekhinah*, for instance, in GU1, p. 385. See also the passage on the coming kingdom of Sabbath (GU2, p. 339).

16 This renovation of the idea (but not the reality!) of Catholicism is linked to the notion of the church as a locus of the total utopian renewal (see Bolz 1987, p. 307). It would be interesting to compare this messianic conception with the hopes attached to the Catholic idea by Max Scheler and Carl Schmitt.

17 See John 3:14, where Jesus is compared to the serpent, whom God ordered Moses to make (Numbers 21: 9), so that those bitten by the snake would survive. Bloch thinks that these are the traces of an original Biblical conception, removed by the later editing (AC, p. 102).

18 In the beginning of the sermon 'On Ignorance' Eckhart cites Matthew (2, 2).

19 'When Christ, who is our life, shall appear, then shall ye also appear with him in glory' (KJV).

20 Kracauer in his review of *Thomas Müntzer* discusses, among other things, the problem of *theurgy* (Kracauer 1990, pp. 196–204). Later, Bloch could not accept that only the human could bring about the highest good. But the objective element, insofar as it is active, has to possess the creative power. It is here that the basis for the notion of subject-nature is laid.

21 A good source, especially with regard to the early writings of Buber, is Dubbels (2011), who shows how Buber subsequently tried to overcome these difficulties in his ethics of dialogue.

22 In the history of Jewish mysticism one could draw a similar distinction between the universalism of the Sabbathean movement and early Hasidism.

4

The Form of the Messianic: Bloch and Benjamin

In Charles Baudelaire's critical essay *Exposition Universelle de 1855* there is a passage so significant for our subject that it makes sense to quote it at length:

> There is yet another, and very fashionable, error which I am anxious to avoid like the very devil. I refer to the idea of "progress". This gloomy beacon, invention of present-day philosophizing, licensed without guarantee of Nature or of God – this modem lantern throws a stream of darkness upon all the objects of knowledge; liberty melts away, discipline vanishes. Anyone who wants to see his way clear through history must first and foremost extinguish this treacherous beacon. This grotesque idea . . . has discharged each man from his duty, has delivered each soul from its responsibility and has released the will from all the bonds imposed upon it by the love of the Beautiful. And if this disastrous folly lasts for long, the dwindling races of the earth will fall into the drivelling slumber of decrepitude upon the pillow of their destiny . . .
>
> But where, I ask you, is the guarantee that this progress will continue overnight? For that is how the disciples of the philosophers of steam and sulphur matches understand it; progress only appears to them in the form of an unending series. . . . It does not exist, I tell you, except in your credulity and your fatuity.
>
> I leave on one side the question of deciding whether . . . proceeding as it does by a stubborn negation of itself, it would not turn out to be a perpetually renewed form of suicide, and whether, shut up in the fiery circle of divine logic, it would not be like the scorpion which stings itself with its own terrible tail – progress, that eternal desideratum which is its own eternal despair!
>
> Transported into the sphere of the imagination . . . the idea of progress takes the stage with a gigantic absurdity, a grotesqueness which reaches nightmarish heights. The theory can no longer be upheld. The facts are too palpable, too well known. They mock at sophistry and confront it without flinching. In the poetic and artistic order, the true prophets are seldom preceded by forerunners. Every efflorescence is spontaneous, individual. Was Signorelli really the begetter of Michelangelo? Did Perugino contain Raphael? The artist stems only from himself. His own works are the only promises that he makes to the coming centuries. . . . He dies childless. He has been his own *king*, his own *priest*, his own *God*. (1955, pp. 198–200; Mosès 2006, pp. 173–4)

Walter Benjamin, who, in the last 20 or so years, has come to be considered one of the most significant German philosophers of the previous century, to a large extent relied on Baudelaire's critical position in *The Arcades Project* – his last and unfinished *magnum opus*. The way of thinking exemplified by Baudelaire was revived by Benjamin with respect to the ethical (the idea of progress deprives us of the ability to act freely, renders *the action* impossible), the aesthetic (irrelevance of a linear, progressive theory of art – each masterpiece creates history anew) and the political (simple causal relations between different moments of history deprive us of the ability to find our own way in it).

The differences of Bloch's and Lukács's aesthetic programmes were organized around similar lines: Bloch was exceptionally attentive to the discontinuities of the homogenous space of art, to its unique, idiosyncratic and 'non-simultaneous' aspects. Hence, within the domain of Marxist aesthetics, Bloch can be regarded as Benjamin's ally. However, this characteristic requires further qualifications, and a closer look complicates this comparative story further.

In Benjamin's work, the aesthetics of the avant-garde go hand in hand with his interest in theology. A miraculous combination of absolute despair and a longing for a new world – the substantial element of the expressionist era – gives birth to a tragic image of history, populated by the fragile shadows of finite human existence, an image altogether alien to the traditional Marxist philosophy. Benjamin experienced, recognized and brilliantly described this state of melancholy as the demise of bourgeois modernist culture, which was construed by Bloch and Lukács as 'an era of absolute sinfulness.' Social critique, variations on Marxist themes and analysis of popular culture could be associated with both Bloch and Benjamin. It was these theoretical credentials that made Benjamin a prophet of the contemporary world, a world lost among endless popular images supplied by the media.

Bloch once recounted the traits that appealed to him in Benjamin. He mentioned the deciphering of the inconspicuous in the manner of a detective story (both of them admired this genre, see LA, pp. 242–63; GS IV, pp. 381–3. See also: Brecht 1992), the technique of montage (which disjoins the proximate, while bringing together what is usually distant), the attention to strange, apparently meaningless things and events. They also shared particular subjects as a texture of philosophy, such as images of childhood. Bloch was always amazed at just how vivid and how expressive was Benjamin's perception, how he thought of the world as of an encrypted text (even though he never mentioned Benjamin's interest in graphology, which his friend certainly had, as well as a passion for alchemy and old books).

Collective emotions was another subject that they both espoused. Benjamin in his later works tried to explain collective emotions relying on Marxist instruments (*The Arcades Project*, as Irving Wohlfahrt (2006, p. 263) notes, could be called *History and the Collective Unconsciousness*), while Bloch integrated them into his theory of 'daydreaming', where not only individuals but social groups themselves dream of a better world. Benjamin describes the drowsy nineteenth century as surrounded by things, which, like dreams, reflect the living conditions of social classes. They need to *wake up,* and they will be awakened by an historian, inspired by the messianic. The image of an era that sleeps, dreams, awaits or becomes disappointed is a favourite figure of thought both in Bloch and Benjamin.

Engaging in a sort of implicit competition with Benjamin, Bloch produces several texts; one of them – *Silence and Mirrors* – even begins with a reflection about a friend (in fact, Benjamin), who 'sees everyone very clearly, himself somewhat less so'. As if reporting their conversation, Bloch invites his friend to characterize the inhabitant of his own room following Sherlock Holmes's method and relying on just a few of his possessions. In response, the trembling lips of his converser remind the author of a story from Herodotus.[1] He tells of a pharaoh Psammetic, who, having been taken prisoner, meets along his way first his daughter, now a slave, and remains silent; and when he meets his son, being taken to the execution, the pharaoh remains unmoved. Finally, when the pharaoh saw a porter from his army with his hands in fetters he cried out and lamented his fate with great force. Why did the king cry out only when he saw his servant? – Bloch asks. Maybe it was the last drop that brought the sorrow of this steadfast man to overflowing? (this is, by the way, Montaigne's interpretation). But this answer is too obvious to be plausible, the story is about a great pharaoh, not an ordinary citizen. What if the pharaoh was too proud to cry, what if his pride deprived him of spontaneity, preventing him from expressing his feelings immediately, being able to mourn his children's fate only with a delay? This explanation is also imperfect because it is built upon a historically bound emotion and renders the appearance of the servant too accidental. Bloch suggests that we should interpret this scene as a way to see the darkness of the Here and Now, and to encounter oneself. The most distant, mundane, unobtrusive, pushed away into the outskirts of our world, something barely lingering on the horizon, suddenly becomes a mirror in which we can see the merciless truth about ourselves, that makes the darkness dissipate and brings ultimate clarity (S, p. 108ff.).[2] This unpretentious story related by Bloch and Benjamin can reveal a lot, especially in their historical situation, which is arguably much closer to us than to the times of Herodotus or Montaigne.

Traces of biographies

Scholem reports that Bloch first met Benjamin in the spring of 1919[3] in Bern, Switzerland. Benjamin came there to complete his education and to write his first dissertation. They were introduced to each other by Hugo Ball, at that time a famous anti-war publicist, poet and one of the founders of Dadaism. Bloch lived close to Ball in Interlaken (Ball met him as soon as he came to Bern in 1917), they worked together in *Die Freie Zeitung*. Its authors held anti-Prussian and anti-militarist views. The atmosphere was highly politicized, and even though at that time Benjamin avoided politics, his new friends prompted him to read Georges Sorel (and that led Benjamin to write *The Critique of Violence*). Ball then published his book *Critique of the German Intelligentsia*, in which, as well as in his articles, he advocated a religious anarchism in the spirit of Thomas Müntzer and called for a renewal of culture and spirit, declaring this intelligentsia as its prophet (without, however, having anything to do with Marx who criticized French utopian socialism and Russian anarchism. For a more detailed account, see: Kambas 1996).

In the middle of September 1919, Benjamin writes a letter to Scholem informing his friend that he is currently reading *The Spirit of Utopia* and that he will relate to his new acquaintance everything he finds praiseworthy in the book. 'Unfortunately, not everything in it is deserving of approval. Indeed, sometimes it leaves me overcome with impatience. The author has certainly already transcended the book' (CWB, p. 147). Several days later, in a letter to Ernst Schoen, Benjamin characterizes Bloch as the only outstanding person that he has met in Switzerland. He then notes about *The Spirit of Utopia:*

> It exhibits enormous deficiencies. Nonetheless, I am indebted to the book for much that is substantive, and the author is ten times better than his book. . . . [This] is nevertheless the only book on which, as a truly contemporaneous and contemporary utterance, I can take my own measure. *Because*: the author stands alone and philosophically stands up for his cause, while almost everything we read today of a philosophical nature written by our contemporaries is derivative and adulterated'. (CWB, p. 148)

In November Benjamin reports to Scholem that he has already added glosses to the book in order to review the book. He was still writing in January 1920 (it took him three months to finish, which, he confessed, was incredibly long), and in a letter to Scholem he says that the review would be 'highly detailed, highly academic, highly and decidedly laudatory, highly and esoterically critical' (CWB, p. 158). Because Benjamin was also trying to set his score with Expressionism he read Kandinsky's *Concerning the Spiritual in Art* on this occasion. Speaking of *The Spirit of Utopia* in the February letter to Schoen, Benjamin remarked that he agreed to write the review because he felt sympathy towards Bloch. He noted that several points central to *The Spirit of Utopia* coincided with his own position; however, in general their understanding of philosophy is diametrically opposed. The book is imbued with a will to expression, and the decisive question was, according to Benjamin, whether Bloch would be able to express the new in him, which had outgrown his own work (CWB, p. 158).

In February Scholem writes to Benjamin a letter criticizing *The Spirit of Utopia*. He concentrates on the notion of *Kiddush Hashem* (sanctification of the Name, an important precept of Judaism), about which Bloch writes:

> The Father and the Son, or the Logos and the Holy Spirit are just the sign and the direction, in which this great and principal word is moving, the word that reveals the origin, Kiddush Hashem, the sanctification of the divine Name, the innermost verbum mirificum of the absolute knowledge. (GU1, p. 381)

At the very end of the book Bloch mentions the righteous men, through whom God dwells in the world, who hold the sanctification of the name in their hands, thus appointing (*Ernennung*), performing the divine (GU1, p. 445).

Without more precise qualifications Scholem criticized Bloch's Christology (the issue at stake was most probably that Christ was always potentially present in the life and history of the Jewish people and that Jews sooner or later would turn to Christianity as an embodiment of the messianic spirit), his loose treatment of the sources, and a persistent ambiguity in identifying himself as a Jew or as a non-Jew (this, by the way, can be seen in the notes that Scholem made in his several copies of the early editions of *The Spirit of Utopia*).[4] But Scholem (and Benjamin who followed his friend and sometimes relied on his opinion) was most annoyed with Bloch's *dependence on Buber*.[5]

The relations between Scholem and Buber were complicated, and such a harsh reaction was quite understandable. The sanctification of the Name, the mutual penetration of the human and the divine in a kind of historical dynamic happening, the dependence of the fate of God and of the world on human action – all of these themes in early Buber's work certainly attracted Bloch. Scholem blamed Bloch for historical inconsistency, inherited from Buber and manifesting in Buber's 'stigmata' that mark the whole text.[6] Scholem cannot accept the idea that the body of Christ is the substance of history.[7] He is concerned that Bloch's 'perversions' in the philosophy of history are imbued with 'an awful mechanical law conformity' (something which Benjamin would later attack in the *Theses on the Philosophy of History*). 'Bloch's world', Scholem continues, 'is, of course, not topsy-turvy, but there are signs indicating that it is illusory, and this illusion is the one that is of a differential distance from reality' (1975a, p. 114f.).

Benjamin replied to Scholem saying that there is nothing he could add – he agreed completely. Besides Bloch's Christology being absolutely 'unworthy of discussion', the book lacks an acceptable theory of knowledge. Benjamin did not report his lines pertaining to this topic because he sent Scholem the whole thing. However, having repudiated the epistemological foundation of the book, Benjamin 'refutes it *en bloc*'. Once again he stresses that the review contains a complimentary account of Bloch's better points, which is itself grounded in the objective merits of the book; but he reiterates that Bloch's book has nothing in common with his own philosophical thinking. Still, owing to their friendship at Interlaken, Benjamin sacrifices his review of Bloch's precocious and premature book – sacrifices it to his belief in its author.

What does Benjamin mean when talks about theory of knowledge? What did he himself have to offer at that time? Today we know that already in the early 1920s Benjamin's theory of knowledge was, in fact, his metaphysics developed in *On the Program of the Coming Philosophy, On Language as Such and on the Language of Man* and later in the *Epistemo-Critical Prologue* to the book on the tragic drama. The former two had been already written in 1916 and it is clear that Bloch was unfamiliar with Benjamin's ideas, for the questions Benjamin posed had no clear answers in *The Spirit of Utopia*. Benjamin's lost review could thus become one of the most fascinating documents in the philosophical history of the 1920s. Nowadays, apart from engaging in philosophical speculation, we can only analyse and compare the conclusions derived from different metaphysical foundations.

In December 1920 in a letter to Scholem Benjamin mentions among his prosaic sketches a *Fantasy on a Passage from the Spirit of Utopia* (CWB, p. 170),[8] yet after this Bloch's name is invoked rarely and on private occasions. They meet on Capri, where life was cheaper and more peaceful. At times, they tried light drugs (Benjamin produced a protocol of these experiments),[9] and they talked a lot in Paris in 1926 (*Über Walter Benjamin*, p. 16). In *Traces* there is a sketch in the genre of a 'cityscape', recounting how a revolutionary consciousness invaded the streets of Paris, and that not only people, but also things, and the whole atmosphere of the big city testified to it (S, pp. 22–6). This sketch dates from their time in Paris together, and is largely written as a development of Benjamin's surrealist technique (Czajka 2006, pp. 87, 98).

In the late 1920s Bloch clearly comes under the influence of Benjamin: his *Hieroglyphs of the Nineteenth Century* and *Rescuing Wagner through Surrealistic Colportage* are undoubtedly a product of his contact with Benjamin, who at that time was opening the avant-garde to philosophy. Bloch's attitude towards surrealism (recognition of its revolutionary potential), together with his peculiar vision of the past century – through the details of interior, stylistic subtleties, enabling him to grasp the whole essence of social life and the true potential of social protest – are clearly inspired by his communication with Benjamin himself and his texts. It is exactly after this that Bloch started to thematize the collective unconscious of the bourgeoisie – that is, taking into account the relevant critique of Jung, who for him was too right-wing.

Their relationship deteriorated when Benjamin started to suspect plagiarism on Bloch's part,[10] to which I will return in a discussion around *One-way Street*. The first version of a review written by Bloch is rather critical, but later having talked to Benjamin (Ujma 1995, p. 256f.) he significantly softened his position. While initially he compared Benjamin's urban images to the *Neue Sachlichkeit* (New Objectivity) movement that he dismissed, claiming that it turns the stillness into an apology for the *status quo*, later, having included his review in *The Heritage of Our Times* he completely shifted his emphases – of which he carefully notified Benjamin in a letter (Br II, p. 658).[11]

Despite the quarrels, inevitable between such sensitive characters, Benjamin and Bloch, judging by their exchanges in the 1930s,[12] never stopped communicating and taking interest in each other's lives until the very end.

> I was often asked what were the topics of our conversations. . . . Since we had a common inclination towards the insignificant things, details, often unnoticed . . . due to this common interest in the twists and turns, from which decisive conclusions could be drawn, we were talking, to put it in the style of the 18th century, *de omnibus rebus et de quibusdam aliis*. (Über Walter Benjamin, p. 17)

One of these talks is described in Benjamin's *The Arcades Project*, where he recalls how he told Bloch about his work, saying that it is analogous to the splitting of the atom, freeing the unprecedented forces of history, exploding history from within, while Bloch replied: 'History displays its Scotland Yard badge'. Apparently, he meant Benjamin's 'detective' technique (GS V, 1, p. 578; AP, p. 463, see also Ujma 1995, p. 127f.).

Bloch, who inherited a great deal from Simmel (whom he called a surrealist, the title later reserved for Benjamin in Bloch's parlance), praises Benjamin's tendency to read carefully, his propensity towards a 'micro-philological' analysis, enabling and encouraging a metaphysical interpretation of the insignificant, so that it could invade the context without being inscribed into it or subsumed by its magic.

Messianic subtexts of history

> *In the nights of annihilation of the last war the frame of mankind was shaken by a feeling that resembled the bliss of the epileptic. And the revolts that followed it were the first attempt of mankind to bring the new body under its control. The power of*

the proletariat is the measure of its convalescence. If it is not gripped to the very marrow by the discipline of this power, no pacifist polemics will save it. Living substance conquers the frenzy of destruction only in the ecstasy of procreation.
(GS IV. S. 148; OWS, p. 104)

The problem of messianism is probably the most interesting philosophical point where Bloch and Benjamin confront each other. The key dilemma of messianism was already mentioned above: to what extent does a human being really participate in the messianic redemption, can people really act as makers of their history – not just the immanent, but also the radically other; can they act towards the abolition of history as such and what would it mean? Or will the Messiah himself, regardless of our actions, save this world, complete it and establish a new kingdom beyond time? Can we already become witnesses of the messianic kingdom, live side by side with the Messiah (Sholem reports that this was exactly what Benjamin's attitude looked like, see Jacobson 2003, p. 25), or should we just wait, without trying to prepare his coming?

Benjamin was definitely concerned with these issues. A short text written in 1921 and known as the *Theological-political Fragment* addresses this:

Only the Messiah himself consummates all history, in the sense that he alone redeems, creates its relation to the Messianic. For this reason nothing historical can relate itself on its own account to anything Messianic. Therefore the Kingdom of God is not the telos of the historical dynamic[13]; it cannot be set as a goal. From the standpoint of history it is not the goal, but the end.[14] Therefore the order of the profane cannot be built up on the idea of the Divine Kingdom, and therefore theocracy has no political, but only a religious meaning. To have repudiated with utmost vehemence the political significance of theocracy is the cardinal merit of Bloch's *Spirit of Utopia*.

The profane should be erected on the idea of happiness. The relation of this order to the messianic is one of the essential teachings of the philosophy of history. It is the precondition of a mystical conception of history, containing a problem that can be represented figuratively. If one arrow points to the goal towards which the profane dynamic moves, and another marks the direction of the Messianic intensity, then certainly the quest of free humanity for happiness runs counter to the Messianic direction; but just as a force can, through acting, increase another that is acting in the opposite direction, so the order of the profane assists, through profanity, in the coming of the Messianic Kingdom.[15] The profane, therefore, although not itself a category of this Kingdom, is a decisive category of its quietest approach. For in happiness, all that is earthly seeks its downfall, and only in good fortune is its downfall destined to find it. Whereas, admittedly, the immediate Messianic intensity of the heart, of the inner man in isolation, passes through misfortune, as suffering. To the spiritual *restitutio in integrum*, which introduces immortality, corresponds to a worldly restitution that leads to an eternity of downfall, and the rhythm of an eternally transient worldly existence, transient in its totality and its spatiality but also in its temporality. The rhythm of Messianic nature is happiness. For nature is Messianic by reason of its eternal and total passing away.

To strive after such passing, even for those stages of man that are nature, is the task of world politics, whose method must be called nihilism. (GS II. S. 203f.; OWS, p. 155f.)

Benjamin's central thesis is that only the messianic idea makes history meaningful, without it one cannot grasp either historical eventness or historical accomplishment. But this very accomplishment ends with the coming of the Messiah, together with the end of all other profane, worldly oppositions. Without the intrusion of thought, like without the Augustinian grace (however strange this theological parallel may seem), any political activity is useless. The Messiah puts an end to the world that lives in anticipation.

Benjamin proclaims the absolute separation of the profane and the messianic order, which is located beyond history and accomplishes it at the same time. In this he follows a traditional religious logic: the event of the apocalypse happens beyond time (Rev. 10, 6), and to say that it happens *before* or *after* is, strictly speaking, incorrect. We can conceive of the apocalyptic event only *figuratively*, *symbolically*. There is not and there cannot be a conceptual definition of a messianic event. By reducing the coming of the Messiah to the immanent logic of historical development, we turn it into simply another act of this history, which contradicts the essential meaning of such emergence. The abolition of temporal power becomes temporal itself, and instead of a spiritual revolution we end up with another zilch, a political coup. The divine violence in this world can only be manifest as annihilation, and only in the world-to-come can it act differently (GS VI, p. 99). In the *Theses* Benjamin would construe the coming of the Messiah not just as an abolition of time, but as its utmost saturation. The redemption was envisaged as a fullness of time.

The primary antipode of Benjamin's messianic philosophy is the deterministic picture of historical progress – he demands revolutionary intervention in history. While for Marx revolutions were the locomotives of world history, Benjamin's mankind that is inside this locomotive desperately reaches for the emergency brake (GS I, 3, p. 1232): a revolution is an attempt, sometimes successful, but often not, to hold up the wheel of history, to slow down its movement.

The messianic kingdom is not the aim of history, but its end. Like Bloch, Benjamin does not accept the linear or teleological view of history and cannot agree that history 'automatically' engenders redemption within itself; on the contrary, it always misses the mark. This radical break with the idea of progress, as well as with religious thinking, which puts the messianic kingdom at the end of history, prompts some to talk of the 'atheological' nature of Benjamin's *Fragment*, as far as religion presupposes messianic teleology (Hamacher 2006, p. 178f.). But Gérard Raulet (1997, p. 188, 191) sees in Benjamin's rationalization of theology and critique of theocracy a tradition initiated by Spinoza's *Tractatus Theologico-Politicus*.

It is clear that terms used by Benjamin, such as an important concept of 'remembrance' (*Eingedenken*) applied to a historian's work, had for him an indubitable theological meaning (GS V, 1, p. 588f.), which was not without Bloch's influence. (Cf.: GU2, pp. 215f., 260, 339. Benjamin himself acknowledges this: GS V, 2, p. 1006).

Benjamin reiterates his critique of the linear and causal view of the historical process in the *Theses* on the philosophy of history, where he urges to break the monotonous chain of events, to grasp their specific constellation, a particular intensity of historical time emerging when mankind – both in the past and in the future – faces a threat.[16]

The reference to *The Spirit of Utopia* in the *Fragment* was puzzling for many. Some thought that this was a disguised critique of Zionism framed with Bloch's assistance (Wohlfahrt 1986, p. 118; Jacobson 2003, p. 241).[17] Zionism, an idea of a theocratic Jewish state, around which the philosophy of history was supposed to have been built, was addressed in *The Spirit of Utopia*, as we have seen above. This is why Jacob Taubes (2006) labelled both Bloch and Benjamin Marcionists, and not adherents of Jewish messianism, and claimed that the real message of the *Fragment* was actually a critique of Jewish political theology, along the lines of Marcion's radical vision of history (And Paul's as a 'teacher' of Marcion. Giorgio Agamben also draws Paul and Marcion together. See also Arndt 2012 for Bloch's reception of Paul). Jewish messianism, as it was demonstrated by Scholem, is 'public', it happens in the space of collective identity, and therefore is political in significance; while Benjamin in the *Fragment* maintained that true messianism is devoid of theocratic meaning. At the same time Taubes (2006, p. 56f.) criticizes Scholem's dichotomy, pointing out that the function of the community or of some public action in Christianity is no less significant than in Judaism – giving pietism as an example. Taubes thus reduces the problem of messianism not to the tension between Judaism and Christianity (where the former appears as a 'political' and the latter – as a 'spiritual' form of religion) but rather to the internal conflict among the Jews, playing out between traditionalism and zealotism – a revolutionary movement within Judaism. He calls Paul and Marcion zealots as well. Taubes's argument coincides with Bloch's interpretation of Marcion's theology as one advanced by a rebellion against tradition, discarding any historical mediation between the old and the new kingdom (AC, p. 241f.).

Of course, the straightforward and schematic opposition of Judaism and Christianity made by Scholem cannot be considered fully satisfactory. It is one of those conjectural schemes that are easy to criticize. However, one could question Taubes's idea that Benjamin was *not* a Jewish thinker.

For instance, as Astrid Deuber-Mankowsky (2002) maintains, Taubes did not fully understand Scholem's distinction. The dichotomy proposed by Scholem is more complex – the 'external', the public redemption or salvation has a special significance in the context of the extra-historical, or transcendent; while 'the internal', purely individual element is tied to worldly history and thus has a dubious legitimacy. Private eschatological considerations may turn out to be arbitrary, and a person who considers himself a Messiah could very well be mistaken just because he has excessive confidence in himself. Benjamin, on this view, remains a purely Jewish thinker, retaining from Cohen a prohibition on idolatry – a mental discipline prohibiting the celebration of the human striving to become god and the confusion of knowledge and faith.

This is how Deuber-Mankowsky interprets a passage from Benjamin's letter to Scholem, where he summarizes his unpublished review of *The Spirit of Utopia* mentioning his epistemological criticism of the book. It is noteworthy that Cohen connects this uncritical (I would say – dialectical) merging of human and God within Christianity, insisting that Judaism alone has retained a pure and radical distinction between them. Bloch's theory of knowledge is unsatisfactory in Benjamin's view, because it overinflates the role of knowledge[18] – the role that exclusively pertains to the Messiah, the final and the absolute instance of truth (Wunder 1997, p. 101). Interpreted in this fashion, Benjamin appears to be not only a critic of Bloch's (and, allegedly, Buber's) Christology, but also an opponent of gnosticism, of the notion of redemption through knowledge. Challenging the political significance of theocracy would then amount to criticism of mediation in an attempt to strictly separate the two spheres – the divine and the human, religion and reason (or politics), logic and ethics – to prevent the secularization of religious notions and the emanation of the messianic from historical subjectivity (Cf. also a similar position: Wißkirchen 1987, p. 64).

Richard Wolin (1982, p. 25f.) interprets the difference between Bloch's and Benjamin's aesthetics in a similar way. Both Bloch and Benjamin, he supposes, ascribe to the work of art a special power to transcend a particular historical narrowness and to grant one a place within a utopian, redeemed being. However, Benjamin does not go so far as to postulate an immediate ontological *bond* between art and the utopian end of time.

Nevertheless, an analysis of this sort runs into several obvious limitations. On the one hand, the possibilities of secularization were always immanent in Christianity, and were often actualized. Historically Bloch could, indeed, easily be perceived by Scholem and Benjamin as refusing to strictly distinguish Christianity and Judaism. But secular versions of Christian ideas are one thing, while the Christianity of the Gospels, clearly stating: 'My kingdom is not of this world' (John 18: 36), is entirely different. Benjamin's theocratic anarchism does not in any way contradict *such* Christianity.[19] It is also not entirely clear *what* Judaism we are referring to, since 'Jewish' philosophy can among other things be 'Kantian' (Cohen), or 'Hegelian' (as, for example, in Lurianic Kabbalah).

Deuber-Mankowsky's Bloch is an apologist of progressism and teleological philosophy of history, which suppresses the bygone, 'the unsuccessful' generations; and the favourable mention of *The Spirit of Utopia* in the *Fragment* would be a mere expression of hope, which Benjamin, judging from their correspondence, associated with Bloch himself and his ideas, but not with this book.

However, one probably should not rhyme the dialectical mediation between the world and the human being with the inexorable determinism of historical process; these notions do not necessarily presuppose one another. Bloch did not accept either the absolute and implacable regularity in history, or the total scepticism concerning the possibility of discovering such laws.[20] In fact, Bloch's messianism is to a large extent due to the fact that in *The Spirit of Utopia* the motives of an unmediatable, unrationalizable historical dynamic are evident – something the *Fragment* would link to the coming of the Messiah. It is not accidental that for the younger Bloch both the Good (as the highest value in the ethical hierarchy), the musical (as the principal art, the apogee of the revolutionary aesthetic), and the metaphysical bear witness to a utopia that cannot be realized in the earthly realm (GU2, p. 201). And that is why, when later Bloch attacks, say, the theology of Rudolf Otto or Karl Barth for their radical separation of man from God, Bloch at the same time unconsciously criticizes his own earlier radicalism and the gnostic contempt for the mundane world (AC, pp. 72–80).

Moreover, there persists an ambiguity in any Kantianism, which at the time was associated with a tragic break, as a loss of a synthetic element. History became a scaffold for the ominous 'Hume's guillotine': the separation between the 'is' and the 'ought' turned into the execution of meaning. This sort of critique can be found in the 'archaeologic' passages of *History and Class Consciousness* with its deconstruction of bourgeois science, as shown above. It is also ascribed to Bloch by Adorno (1991, p. 206), who interestingly does so, saying that this view (that the Kantian separation of consciousness from the thing-in-itself is peculiar to the world of capitalist materialism) is common to both Bloch and Benjamin!

Finally, there is another important point. The radical distinction between the religious (theological, messianic) element and the political in Benjamin is not so remote from their absolute identification: they are the two sides of the very same process. How else could we understand the mystical link between the profane and the messianic, which leads the political actuality of this world towards the Kingdom? Thus, a possible critique of Bloch's political apocalyptics might be suddenly turned into a favourable stance towards this messianic figure.

Bloch's *teleology* should not be viewed as a teleology 'from above', subordinated to some *a priori*, higher, presumably true element; rather, it is a teleology 'from below', which does not follow pre-existing laws; on the contrary, it creates them from itself (Schmidt 1985, pp. 37–8, 67, 119–20). And if one thinks of it on the model of a living organism, then it is inhabited by creatures whose genetic programme is not given once and for all, who live in accordance with permanently changing laws. And we can at most become imbued with the rhythm of this movement, enter into it.

Bloch's philosophy *is not teleological in a sense of a given goal*. It is, rather, a philosophy of action organized around Marxist *praxis* and a philosophy of an unaccomplished universe. However, what was especially appealing for Benjamin was that in the early work Bloch advanced *an apocalyptic philosophy*.

> The quintessence of the highest, evident objects also does not obey any of the world-spirit's pyramids of ideas, but is purely part of the inventory of the exodus-spirit, and only from such explosively understood, anti-mundane knowledge, directed toward the outcome and not the origin of the world, will the *verbum mirificum* sound, will the features of the identical substance of every moral-mystical symbol-intention take shape. (GU2, p. 259; SU, p. 206)

Indeed, one should not bow down before the state here and now, and the theocratic principle cannot serve as a basis of politics. But human activity in history, which in Benjamin's *Fragment* remains a revolutionary melancholy and nihilism, and in the theses *On the Concept of History* is aimed at redeeming the past, in Bloch is augmented by *action*, which cannot be mediated, in which different elements of history combine for the sake of the future and where *we* are to struggle for our own liberation. The interruption of time and the break of the historical continuum are necessary, but not sufficient for such an activist view of history (Schiller 1991), inexorably gravitating towards Marxism in the spirit of *History and Class Consciousness*. It is not accidental, as already mentioned, that Bloch in his review of this book stresses the moment of *decision,* so immensely significant for that epoch, when, for example, the concept of 'the state of exception' was being developed in political philosophy (by Carl Schmitt, but also taken up by Benjamin). This active element was placed at the very root of the utopian dialectic, which overcomes both the eternal amorphous mutability in the spirit of Bergson (GU2, p. 258f.), and formal Platonic pre-determinateness (Schmidt 1985, p. 120). Otherwise Bloch could not state the 'inconstruable question' – something that eventually eludes any possible mediations, without, however, letting us give up the whole business of asking it. The final aim does not freeze the utopian event and does not make it conform to its logic. Bloch takes pains to separate uncertainty and quietism.

In the context of the political ideas of *The Spirit of Utopia* one could interpret Benjamin's reference as a development of several Blochian ideas. Numerous invectives against the governmental apparatus in *The Spirit of Utopia* manifest a search for the new social organization, in which there will be no place for the state. *The Spirit of Utopia* is pervaded by anarchist visions. Even in 1929 in a letter to Kracauer, characterizing the discussions that he held with Lukács in Vienna, Bloch characterizes Lukács's position as a communist one, while ascribing to himself anarchic views (Br I, p. 322). Bloch, like Buber, does not see theocracy as a new authoritarian instance, but a rejection of traditional political forms and power relations in the epoch when 'whoever among us does not worship his belly worships the state; everything else has sunk to the level of a joke, of entertainment' (GU1, 9; SU, p. 2). Elsewhere he says:

> It is because the state became independent and its independence became an end in itself, and because it makes positive claims, in the most peremptory way suppressing the power of the nation, – that the – once liberal – idea of the citizenship was transformed into the most awful servitude bowed under the abstract power of state autonomy. (GU1, p. 401, see also p. 410)

Instead of the government an invisible church should come – the spiritual brotherhood of the elected few, which will become the new utopian kingdom, that very 'third kingdom', which humanity, wallowing in political conflict and tired of tyranny, long awaits.

Norbert Bolz considers Bloch's standpoint in the second edition of *The Spirit of Utopia* much closer to Benjamin's than the one in the first edition, where he says that 'in the mystery of the kingdom the worldly organization takes possession of its immediately operative, immediately deducting metaphysics' (GU1, p. 411; See: Bolz 1987, pp. 306–7. Cf. also: GU2, 307, but also 346, where Bloch speaks of a 'functional relation' between Marxism and religion). But Bloch is not very concerned with the earthly organization – primarily because before the coming of the new age, politics is intertwined with the arrangement of material life, with the satisfaction of the most basic needs, whereas in the messianic kingdom it would be detached from this task (that very 'worldly organization') and thus elevated.

All that is most 'interesting' in political life will become the basis of the new kingdom. It is thus not really important anymore how the profane would be linked to the messianic: perhaps they would move in opposite directions so that the profane would unwittingly help bring about the Messiah, or perhaps material production would serve as a building block of the new.

A digression: Bloch and Kant

The Kantian doctrine, one way or another, is always present in Bloch's discourse, and philosophy of history is no exception.

The Spirit of Utopia and later *The Principle of Hope* correlate the Kantian thing-in-itself with the Not-Yet-Being; abandoning, along neo-Kantian lines, the idea of a rigid boundary between the phenomenal and the noumenal. In his search for the basis of the perceptive act, Bloch stays unwilling to put this basis into either the subject or the thing-in-itself alone. 'A question of being is not resolved, both for us and for its own self' (EM, p. 74; see Schiller 1991, p. 61ff.). Knowledge, he argues, is founded not by the transcendental subject with its a priori forms of sensibility and categories of understanding, but by certain intensities, the will, tension, *Gestalt* that can be located both in the object and in the subject. This is also related to the 'symbolic intention' of consciousness, which is realized in the works and the experience of art (Czajka 2006, p. 25f.)[21] – the directedness of consciousness towards something whole and at the same time towards the very aim itself, shining through the artistic forms.

It is, however, not the theory of knowledge, but Kant's *ethics* that was truly significant for utopian philosophy. Bloch was fascinated by the regulative ideas of reason, 'those basic limit concepts that can only be willed or thought, but not recognized' (GU2, p. 222; SU, p. 176). The *a priori* significance of moral postulates, separating the empirical world of theoretical regularities from the world of ethics, helps us to pick things out from the darkness, to clarify, to intuit. Even if it is only for one moment, our own 'intelligible character' and together with it the utopia of the 'highest good', is glimpsed. This makes the world shine with hope, and the action becomes free, directed to the 'kingdom of God, governed by the ethical laws' (SO, p. 497). Bloch's Kant seems to point at a completely different, 'second', or messianic world, refusing, unlike Bloch's Hegel, to reconcile the subject with this world. An ethical action cannot be grounded scientifically (early Bloch generally does not accept Hegelian rational mediations) but one can impart unto it an *a priori* unconditional significance. Postulates are not given, they are being defined, and this endless defining leads the subject of practical action to the Kantian ideal world – the kingdom of 'higher and . . . more productive intelligences' (GU2, p. 223, SU, p. 176). Over and above the ordinary causal connections of the phenomenal world we are affected by the 'idea of the unconditional', a source of 'moral-mystical'[22] inwardness.

This intention is fundamental for the metaphysics of subjectivity in *The Spirit of Utopia*. And in *Traces*, Bloch refers to Kant's lectures on psychology, in which Kant compares the moral sense with the organs of an unborn child. The child will need them in another world, just as we shall need our not-yet-developed abilities (S, p. 133). The world of morality affects the subject, and from this affective bond, a moral action is born. In fact, Bloch returns to the emotional, qualitative definitions, thus downplaying the formal basis of morality while explicitly or implicitly ascribing to the postulate both regulative and constitutive functions and also criticizing Cohen (Pelletier 2008, p. 269). He shows that in the world of moral categories our actions are wonderfully productive: thinking about them brings them into existence (GU1, p. 259).

The apparency of moral laws is the source of Bloch's 'militant optimism': it is the optimism not of rational certainty, but rather of the moral-mystical manifestation of utopia, making one act, *as if* it could be turned into reality. Moral 'as if' becomes in Bloch the theological 'Not-yet' (GU2, p. 224), and his protagonist becomes like Simmel's 'adventurer' who risks all 'on the hovering chance, on fate, on the more-or-less', burning his bridges and stepping into the mist, as if the road would lead him on, no matter what. 'The obscurities of fate are certainly no more transparent to him than to others; but he proceeds *as if they were*.' (Simmel 1997, p. 226, italics mine. – I. B.)

Bloch was also clearly influenced by the Kantian utopia of universal citizenship. In his *Idea for a Universal History*, Kant mentions chiliasm and the possibility of it being brought about. However, he does not have a definite position on the question of whether this aim is realistic and could be actually achieved, pointing instead at the inadequacy of our knowledge, for we are only in the beginning of the journey – both to eternal peace and to the state of world citizenship. What then is left to Bloch? The only thing that is left is the very pathos of the inner necessity to move towards this chiliasm, towards the *unconditionality of moral obligation*; but Bloch rejects the idea of a primordial natural plan to which the unfolding of history is subordinate. The subject for him is at the same time within history and outside of it, and so is the collective, which 'eccentrically to time as the inventory of Oughts' (GU2, p. 296; SU, p. 237), transcends the boundaries of its social and historical being. Kantian ideas of affective community, inter-subjective judgements of taste, the unity of ethics and aesthetics as a means of future emancipation, have also influenced Bloch (Münz-Koenen 1997, p. 43). In the end, his profane pathos and insistence on the *utopian will* acting from here, from within this world, are inspired not only by Nietzsche (who was for the young Bloch someone who attacked 'cold' intellectualism and rationalism), but also by Kantianism.

But Bloch is sceptical of the idea of infinite approximation, which is central to Kant and Cohen. Infinite progress does not allow the actualization of the new, the preconditions of which are laid, among other things, by the human acting in history. Here Bloch largely follows the critique of Kantian ethics in *The Phenomenology of Spirit*:

> the *culmination* of . . . progress has to be *put off to infinity*, since if that culmination were actually to arrive on the scene, moral consciousness would be sublated. This is so because *morality* is merely moral *consciousness* as the negative essence for which sensibility is merely of negative significance, that is, is merely *not in conformity with* pure duty. But in that harmony, *morality* as *consciousness* vanishes, that is, its *actuality* vanishes in the way that in moral *consciousness*, that is, actuality, its *harmony* vanishes. For that reason, the culmination is not actually to be reached. Instead, it is to be thought of merely as an *absolute task*, which is to say, a task which remains purely and simply a task. Nonetheless, at the same time its content is to be thought in terms of what purely and simply must *be*, and it must not remain a task whether or not consciousness is to be represented as sublated in this goal. In the dark remoteness of the infinity to which the attainment of the end consequently has to be postponed, there is no clear distinction to be made as to

which of these views is to be held. Strictly speaking, the determinate representation of this progress should be of no interest and ought not to be sought because it leads to contradictions – contradictions lying in a task which is both to remain a task and which is yet to be fulfilled, and in a morality which is not any more supposed to be consciousness and not any more supposed to be actual (603).

Hegel criticized Kant's notion of hope saying that it was too detached from the actual human sensuous or practical action, eventually resulting in the failure to act. In *The Phenomenology of Spirit* Hegel tried to develop his own ethics by looking at the relation of *hope* to the higher good from the point of view of the critical and dialectical notion of praxis (Simons 1981). Hegel discards the transcendental nature of Kantian postulates and opposes the view that they are grounded only in the rational ethical belief in the realization of a necessary and a universal goal.

Interestingly, Hegel relates hope to language. Through the mediation of this 'practical' logic of hope a clear image, an idea (*Vergegenwärtigung*) of the higher good, a new understanding of the unity of nature and freedom, of history and God are achieved. Simons believed that Bloch had taken up and developed this argument (see also SO, p. 491). For Bloch the ecstatic experience of 'insight', of partaking in the higher good is the mediator of the gospel, or the prophecy of hope. Bloch thus transforms Hegel's dynamic and practical understanding of hope into an expressive prophecy, an enlightened knowledge; the world itself is thought of as a game, begotten by language[23] and action. It is precisely through this creative linguistic action that the world can be transformed. This expressive utopian knowledge is formed through the overcoming of present circumstances, through the attempt to 'let Kant burn through Hegel' (GU2, p. 236; SU, p. 187), without binding the I into the objective system, and without turning the ethical-mystical insight into the solitary Don Quixotism of wishful thinking, without giving up too early, without turning away from history.

For Bloch the 'fulfilled moment' of the experience of hope turns out to be both internal, intimate and at the same time historically coloured. It is communicative-sensual, linked to expression, prophecy and a generation of the new; a painful and at the same time blissful language game, in which the historical game of world events is reflected.[24]

Bloch's dynamic metaphysics has the action of the *autonomous subject* at its core. It is not accidental that both Kant and Marx appear in the first edition of *The Spirit of Utopia*: the former as the author of postulates that 'open up' the rigid world of natural necessity, connecting the 'ought' to the 'is'; and the latter as a prophet preaching intolerance of social injustice and urging political action. At the same time the role of action is such that a postulate does not remain a purely psychological phenomenon, it is not merely a result of the lonely introspection or a form expressing an unconditional moral ideal. Rather, we ourselves actively promote its implementation. The anticipation of a future kingdom in Bloch, contrary to a simple dream, is linked to an understanding of the attainability of utopia, with consciousness of the aim and of the distance that separates us from it (PH, p. 215f.; SO, p. 501). But even though Hegel gets rid of the infinite approximation, he leaves no space for autonomous human action. It is dissolved in the necessary unfolding of the world spirit (PH, p. 198), and here is where Kant comes into play.

Later Bloch would provide a standard critique of Kant's alleged ethical formalism and abstraction from social context, the influence of which is, however, inevitable and remains unrecognized. He views the abstraction of Kantian ethics in quite a Marxist fashion – as a reflection of bourgeois individualism with its abstractions. The unhistorical character of Kantian moral requirements exacerbates alienation and exploitation, and prevents the forces of social solidarity from serving the future. Instead of Kantian subjectivism, Bloch attempts to propose a real foundation for hope, and other forward-looking affects. One cannot separate the higher good from the immanence of being (PH, p. 1566, Schiller 1991, p. 75) through postulating that happiness and morality can coincide only in the world of the transcendent, the intelligible, which has nothing to do with the world that we inhabit. The possibility of transcending must be inherent in nature; Bloch achieves this possibility by ontologizing the content of Kantian postulates (Schiller 1991, pp. 80, 85). He insists that because being itself contains the 'oughts', as incompleteness and projectivity, utopian demands should also be *realizable*.

However, such criticism is levelled from the standpoint of the utopian *system*, and within it, the early 'moral-mystical' trembling of the normative is replaced by mere instrumentalization. Aims are normally conceived as known, as if we had already ended the discussion of the content of this very utopian 'Not-yet'. This question will be discussed in detail later with reference to Adorno's criticism of Bloch, so at this point I shall only remark that Kantian philosophy had a decisive significance for the very structure of the utopian in Bloch's work. It is under the banner of the categorical imperative – even with a 'revolver' in hand (GU2, p. 302) – that the utopian intention is constructed; and the absolute boundary that for Kant separates the natural world from the kingdom of freedom is problematized, among other things, as the essence of *messianism*.

But let us return to Benjamin's *Fragment*. Werner Hamacher, comparing Bloch and Benjamin, uses a quote from Jacob Böhme, which Bloch cites in the first edition of *The Spirit of Utopia*:

> But wilt thou know where God dwells, take away Nature and Creature, and then God is *All*. But thou wilt say, I cannot take away Nature and Creature from me; for if that were done, I should be nothing, therefore I must thus represent the Deity by an Image or *Resemblance*. But hearken my Brother, God says in *Moses [Exod., 20]*, *Thou shalt make thee an Image of my God*. And this is the right and nearest Way to God; for the *Image of God* to sink down in itself from all imprinted Images, and forsake all Images, Disputation, and Contention in itself and depart from Self Will, Desire and *Opinion*, and immerse itself merely and solely into the Eternal One. (GU1, p. 368f.)[25]

By quoting Böhme, Bloch wants to show the futility of the conceptual theoretical fixation of internal experience, the necessity of practical action that is aimed inwards, into the darkness and the flux of the soul. Such reasoning, Hamacher argues, is paradoxical: it is as if we remove the ground from beneath our feet, renouncing any possible imagery. And while Bloch the gnostic assumes a halfway position, separating the God of creation from the God of redemption, Benjamin's anarchic nihilism appears to be more consistent. Following Böhme, Benjamin rejects *any* possibility of mundane knowledge being related to the divine. Insisting on the absolute immanence of the mundane, 'purging' messianism and theology correspondingly, he deprives the profane of any ground outside itself. In *this*-world, the human must rely on itself in all its mortal and existential fragility. Inadvertently repeating the formula of Kant, who limited, bounded, suspended knowledge to make room for faith, Benjamin suspends the mundane to make room for the messianic. The mundane by this Kantian gesture abolishes itself (as does language in questioning itself, pointing to its own boundaries).[26] It turns out that the total immanentization of the world (Benjamin says 'of nature') and of the human being in the world, the extreme profanization of history, potentiation of the profane becomes – by way of a radical inversion – a source of genuine messianism, liberating us from the tautology of eternal recurrence (Raulet 1997, p. 193f.). The coming of the messianic kingdom is prepared not by the *Übermensches*, these blond beasts, but by the weak, the mortal losers, the defeated (if we recall the *Theses* on the philosophy of history), who nevertheless find the strength to be happy, understanding all their limitation and finitude.

One of the images of such messianism was for Benjamin a tragic hero going to one's doom and dying under the oppression of fate (Jacobson 2003, pp. 38–45; 2009, p. 218). In this theology of despair he is juxtaposed against the brave footstep of progress, against the mass optimism of those marching in line. And in him one could see not only the hero of Lukács's *Metaphysics of Tragedy*, but also the prophets of The Old Testament, who, in Buber's presentation, oppose political power and the charisma of political sovereignty in the name of genuine theocracy, thereby dooming themselves to a catastrophe (Bolz 1987, p. 296).

It is the presence of the weak and the oppressed, striving towards happiness, those hopeless for whose sake all hope is given to us (GS I, 1. p. 201), that defines the connection of Benjamin's philosophy of history both with Marxism and theology. Benjamin suggests that we look for the messianic in the intensity of this finitude, in the limit, at which language ceases, in the muteness that opens up to language and generally to the finite human knowledge. But let us ponder for a moment: was it not in the immanence, in the closest proximity of the dark moment that Bloch urged to look for the utopian truth? Was it not him who rebelled against the otherworldly authority, in almost Nietzschean terms urging to return to the profane?

The *Fragment* mentions people seeking happiness. This notion, grounding Western ethical reflection, can be thought of as a part of the internal polemics with the Kantian ethics of duty which attempts to separate the urge towards happiness from the higher good in the form of a moral absolute and, at the same time, to ground the notion of the immortality of the soul by the necessity of infinite approximation to this higher good. In Bloch's metaphysics of the instant, as we saw in Chapter 1, moments of *happiness*, of a perfect and universal insight into being, become the signs of the utopian (S, p. 217). The moments of happiness are an innuendo, a promise of the future unity of the self and the world; while the utopian search, the pursuit of happiness, and the urge for the new form this shimmering point, from which the transformation of society and nature can begin.

Benjamin, on the contrary, conceives this happiness pessimistically, since it is available only to finite beings, and therefore is the lot of the mortal: a sign that anticipates the fall and the decay awaiting all of us. Happiness is finite, but also infinite in its constant elusiveness, transience. It is the happiness of the angels who had the chance, according to the Kabbalistic tradition, to sing just one single time before the face of God, prior to their dissolution into nothingness. *Angelus Novus*, of which Benjamin talks in his 1933 essay, also strives for happiness, in which the revel of the unexpectedly new coincides with the bliss of repeating and recollecting something that has already happened. Here the discovery of the long forgotten and the outburst of the entirely new are paradoxically united. We shall return to this paradox in due course.

Benjamin links happiness not to the future, but to the past.

> [O]ur image of happiness is thoroughly coloured by the time to which the course of our own existence has assigned us. The kind of happiness that could arouse envy in us exists only in the air we have breathed. . . . In other words, our image of happiness is indissolubly bound up with the image of redemption. (IER, p. 253f.)

In these deeply meaningful words, among other things, one could find the essence of Benjamin's attitude towards both history and messianism. They could be interpreted as an attempt to find the way into history, and not 'jump out' of it (Deuber-Mankowsky 2002, p. 16).

Hamacher believes that the eschatological mood of *The Spirit of Utopia* is closer to Benjamin's position when Bloch speaks of *restitutio in integrum* (GU1, 42, p. 442),[27] which, however, leads us out of the 'labyrinth of the world', restores the genuine unity of the universe, unmercifully destroying the 'iron cage' built by the demiurge[28]; while in Benjamin it is the world itself, the internal rhythm of the world, the rhythm of fading and falling, the concentration of the immanent, in which messianic time is altogether different, which we can only bring closer by drawing it further away. Later, in *The Epistemo-Critical Prologue* Benjamin speaks of the salvation of the phenomena through ideas as the constellations and forms of synthesis, interpreting the phenomena anew.[29] This position can hardly be reconciled with Bloch's early radicalism, with his resolute intention to fully destroy the phenomenal world (Deuber-Mankowsky 2002, p. 10), even though the structure of the argument as well as its radicality remains the same.

Another important nuance relates to Bloch's distinctly pronounced emphasis on the individual, the personal event of the apocalypse – the dimension not discussed in detail by Benjamin's *Fragment*.[30] And here again we are faced with a notion, towards which all of messianism's antinomies gravitate – the notion of redemption (*Erlösung*).

Excursus: Redemption

The main term around which not only the Jewish messianism of Bloch and Benjamin is centred, but also messianic and eschatological ideas in general – is redemption, or deliverance (*Erlösung*).[31] The redeemer is the one who 'pays', 'buys humanity out' from the slavery of sin, thus saving it. In Christianity the fee comes in the form of the death on a cross, the blood of an innocent, spilled for the sake of humanity.

The main peculiarity of the Christian world-view is that redemption *has already taken place* and has brought into the world something which cannot be renounced any more, something that changed the course of history wholly and forever. For unorthodox German-Jewish philosophers this was not essential. Bloch is more Jewish than Christian here: it is not the Messiah who is important, but the idea embodied in him (Denecke 1993, p. 65).[32] *The Spirit of Utopia* reinterprets Christianity in this fashion.

The central text of the new vision is Rosenzweig's *The Star of Redemption*. Despite all the existential pathos, Rosenzweig makes the grammatical model of redemption the first-person *plural*, in a future tense. Redemption is the collective event, happening in the mode of *anticipation* (Mosès 2006, p. 108f.) – the anticipation of the final conclusion of all things, their end, 'the end before which all that has begun turns back to be engulfed in its beginning' (Rosenzweig 1988, p. 269; 2005, p. 259). Rosenzweig introduced the notion of redemption as unifying and completing the creation (accomplished in space) and revelation (which unfolds in time), implying a special status of God who redeems not only the world and the human, but also Himself. Redemption enters the world through the love of neighbour and religious ritual.

As already mentioned, the problem of redemption as a process is not only the problem of its subjective or objective nature, but also the problem of causality. An interesting solution is given in the system of Isaac Luria, praised by Bloch as one of the great Kabbalistic thinkers (PH, p. 1459). In fact, the Lurianic Kabbalah comprises much of the tensions encountered by a messianic philosophy of history. Deliverance, the restoration of things in their initial wholeness, is interpreted by Luria as a process of birth of the divine personality (*tikkun*), and this becomes, in part, the responsibility of humanity (Scholem 1955, pp. 273–80). Humanity must return all things into their original place, to reunite them with God.

> [E]very soul contains potentialities of this spiritual appearance, outraged and degraded by the fall of Adam, whose soul contained all souls. From this soul of all souls sparks have scattered in all directions and become diffused into matter. The problem is to reassemble them, to lift them to their proper place and to restore the spiritual nature of man in its original splendour as God conceived it. (Scholem 1955, p. 278)

Together with external history (which can be discontinuous, in which there is room for failures, backtracking or dead ends) there is also a secret history in which everyone contributes to collecting the pieces of the scattered truth and thus to the liberation of *Shekhinah* (divine presence) and its reunification with God, and *this* secret history *is uninterrupted.*

The notion that the external pattern might not match the internal history, but nevertheless be connected to it, is present throughout *The Spirit of Utopia* and undoubtedly creates the rhythm of Bloch's early philosophy. This invisible, tacit progress – invoked by Luria – delivers salvation right on time. But from the viewpoint of an external, profane history it occurs unexpectedly. At the same time the Messiah's role becomes unimportant; he merely completes history symbolically, like the big boss who cuts the ceremonial ribbon at the opening of a new building, without participating in its construction.

If we go back to Scholem's distinction between the Christian and the Jewish notion of redemption, then we are once again faced with the questions that always arise when one overly systematizes and simplifies religious philosophy of history (saying that it is often difficult to formulate problems without it). Can redemption in Christianity be considered 'subjective', tied to the life and the spiritual making of the soul? Or should it be as in Judaism, 'objective' (or perhaps 'inter-subjective'), public, inherently linked to the religious community and dependent on individual participation in the life of the religious body? Such opposition is invalidated as soon as one admits that, as already indicated above, individual redemption is not a particular feature of the Christian religion, and, what is more, the community, the church, plays an enormous role in Christianity. Conversely, in the Lurianic Kabbalah every individual becomes an integral part of the secret – and *universal* – history of redemption.

The debates around the role of the individual in redemption are not a mere reminiscence of medieval theological disputes on predestination and grace. The problem of religious community can be always posed in terms of individual alienation, of rigidity and inertia in religious institutions. The 'collective' is often regarded in exactly this way – as an external, ritualized, 'positive' (as early Hegel would have put it).[33] This tension is also quite strong in Rosenzweig who begins *The Star of Redemption* with the experience of a radical and irreducible individuality that resists any totalization, but then suppresses it in the image of inter-subjective religious collectivity (see Dubbels 2011). But, importantly, despite the primacy of the ecclesiastical, the collective element (in the Orthodox tradition – *sobornost*), the *personalist* element was also very strong in Christianity, because the church was always sanctified and bound together by the absolute person of Christ. This very aspect did not allow one to speak of the exclusively communitarian, supra-individual character of Christian religiosity. Bloch invoked this dynamic to protect the genuine church from ossification, he called it a 'revolutionary magic of the subject' – the theurgical power of philosophy, the mystical naming of God, that grants liberation (TM, p. 61, 203; GU1, p. 318).

Interestingly, Buber solves this very problem in the manner of Bloch's philosophy, or, more precisely, in the manner that they both inherited from Cohen. Fighting against the fetishization of the Jewish community as a chosen people, he shows that the attitude of the Jews towards their own chosenness is something critical and postulative, that their mission has *not yet been fulfilled*, that it is a problem, not completely solved, and thus there can be no points of rest, no false ritualization – and, hence, no rigidity – within the Jewish community (Buber 1966, p. 125; Bolz 1987, p. 295). Its life is the exemplary existence in the mode of the Not-Yet-Being.

Can we ascribe to Bloch a specific concept of redemption? Probably not. But *The Spirit of Utopia* undoubtedly manifests an urge to rephrase particular religious and philosophical traditions. Bloch deals with the Church *and* subjectivity, he calls for God and appeals to the righteous, through whom and in whom God dwells (GU1, p. 445; GU2, p. 346). A very important aspect of his early conception is the apocalyptic, catastrophic nature of redemption, which can be seen also in Benjamin's

Fragment. The only certain, indubitable connection of the messianic order to the profane is the abrupt and irreversible end. In saying this, both Benjamin and Bloch seem to settle the score with the rational 'sober' conception of the mundane world. Bloch frames this position within gnostic dualism and Benjamin's vision involves corporeal connotations ('transience') and melancholy. But both of them went further, to understand the significance of the indirect ('all the decisive blows are struck left-handed', Benjamin wrote in *One-Way Street*). These were the perceptions of historical time. Benjamin and Bloch saw the need to find some mode of existence amidst history, unfolding, it seemed, without their participation.

Temporalities

What matters for the dialectician is to have the wind of history in one's sails.
Thinking is for him: setting the sails. What is important is how they are set.
Words are his sails. The way they are set makes them into concepts.
(GS V, 1. p. 591; AP, p. 473)

Historicity in Bloch's philosophy is related not only to his Hegelian roots, his philosophy of history is permeated by utopian speculation. As we have seen earlier, the utopian is not formless, the inconstruable question has its own shape, or *Gestalt*, that must be unfolded, formulated, clarified (GU1, p. 365f.), and in this light history emerges, as a phenomenon and as a problem that fascinated Bloch.

Both Bloch and Benjamin tried to show how the past can help better discern the present and the future. Benjamin rethinks history as suddenly intervening into the present: The need to 'make the continuum of history explode' and to fan 'the spark of hope in the past' (*Illuminations*, pp. 255, 261). This requires the overcoming of the illusion of progress, of an uninterrupted and consecutive motion which leaves behind not only past victories, but also casualties which denounce the past to the victorious. The 'dialectical image' of the phenomena of the past, the 'involuntary recollection of redeemed mankind' (GS I, 3. p. 1233) is a monad, into which shuddering and shaken thought has turned. That is why Benjamin says that in *The Arcades Project* the fundamental concept for him is not that of progress, but rather *actualization*. This monad is closed, but still comprises within itself the totality of history (Schiller 1991, p. 26f.) for only then are we able to retain the past in its peculiarity, to read, at last, the whole text of history at the end of times (GS V, 1. p. 574ff.).[34] 'In Hegel . . . history itself judges people; whereas in Benjamin . . . people judge history' (Mosès 2006, p. 216).

Benjamin's historian is like the hero of García Márquez's *One Hundred Years of Solitude*, who eventually finds the genuine meaning in the chain of historical events amidst the collapsing world:

> Macondo was already a fearful whirlwind of dust and rubble being spun about by the wrath of the biblical hurricane when Aureliano . . . began to decipher the instant that he was living, deciphering it as he lived it . . . as if he were looking into a speaking mirror. . . . Before reaching the final line, however, he had already

understood that he would never leave that room, for it was foreseen that the city of mirrors (or mirages) would be wiped out by the wind and exiled from the memory of men at the precise moment when Aureliano Babilonia would finish deciphering the parchments. (The *One Hundred Years of Solitude*, trans. G. Rabassa 1970, p. 398f.)[35]

Drawing fragments from the past, compiling and citing them, a historian 'grasps the constellation which his own era has formed with a definite earlier one' (IER, p. 263).[36] One can understand and actualize a particular moment of the past only by forgetting what happened between this moment and the present, by denouncing continuity (GS V, 1., p. 587). In the actual present, in 'the Now', the unredeemed past, its recollection, or remembrance (*Eingedenken*) meets the unrealized future. At this point, actualization meets anticipation (Holz 1968; Raulet 2008).

History becomes plastic and stops following the logic of the winners, who have usurped the right to summarize and to qualify, like a genuine text that does not give itself up to the commentator's mercy. The relations between 'the Now' and the past are symbolic, and not temporal; metaphoric and not causal; in this the dialectical image, 'the dialectic at standstill', differs from the relation of the past to the present (GS V, 1., p. 576ff.), from the model of consecutive and deterministic development in linear historical time, where the past is completely lucid and accomplished, and the future derived from the present, hence, discerned and predetermined beforehand. It is as though a historian sewed together different layers of culture, and this mosaic is not only theoretically, but also politically interpretable, for it can face the urgent challenges of emancipation.

Bloch shares this vision and its messianic flavour: 'We've had enough of world history' (TM, p. 229), it is time to look for something else. Hans-Ernst Schiller shows that in *Thomas Müntzer*, Bloch, too, does not conceive of history as something completed and determined. A book dealing with the leader of peasant uprisings had to emerge in Germany of the time, so that the two epochs could meet, and the dead would return from the shadow of the dark moment to the living, so that the revolutionary proletariat would recognize itself in the rebellion of the medieval heretic (see also Letschka 1999). In this book history is presented as a series of ruptures, as a faltering search for an identity presented as a new form of *legend*, the 'self-encounter of history' (Bolz 1997, p. 48). Notably, like Benjamin in the *Theses*, Bloch emphasizes the moment of danger (Münz-Koenen 1997, p. 32; GU1, p. 332) that inflames revolutionary passion and inhabits the place where, in Hölderlin's words, that which saves grows.

Benjamin tries to register the past, torn out from the flow of time, to gather and concentrate it in one spot, while Bloch attacks the scientific conception of time as a transformed space (GU2, p. 252).[37] He believes that temporal relations should be grasped in a more flexible and pragmatically relevant way. We should be guided by the promise that what has not happened in the past, the unfinished is not gone forever, that we are left with a utopian bequest (Berghahn 1985, p. 12), that it takes only a breath, and the coals will fire up. Bloch later said that there is no recollection that related itself to the object in a completely detached fashion, one that was devoid of anticipation, of the desire to complete that which has not been accomplished (TE, p. 289f.). The theory of non-contemporaneity from *The Heritage of Our Times* is another way of dealing with this fascinating power of the past, with this inescapable craving for the subjunctive mood, with these echoes of freedom, the music of which, it seems, is gone forever, yet is one day capable of transforming our today to become a hymn of the new times.

The historical hermeneutics advanced by Bloch and Benjamin is based on the paradoxical combination of the unique, the unrepeatable constellation of circumstances and the recognition of the fundamental structures in them, as the fulfilment of utopian prophecies. History itself is discerned as such only in these constellations, dialectical images retained in consciousness (and through *Thomas Müntzer* in legends and the revolutionary hero), beyond which historicity itself loses any meaning.[38]

Bloch's construct – a palimpsest, on which the contours of the future world are inscribed – may be neatly supplemented by Benjamin's dialectical thesis: in the culture of every epoch one can discern something actual, imbued with the future that is 'alive'; and facing backwards, the spoiled, the obsolete resides. The latter sharpens the meaning of the former, making 'the progressive' even more progressive.

Benjamin proposes, as though hinting at Aristotle's logic of 'the third man', to divide this 'spoiled' and find in it yet more positive traits. This division can be continued *ad infinitum*, and ultimately 'the historical apocastasis' would allow one to appropriate the future in its entirety, to save it for the present (GS V, 1.; p. 571ff., see Letschka 1999, p. 50). Benjamin does not accept mechanical actualization, the immediate link between the present and the past. History does not have 'gears' that rotate with ever-increasing speed. Bloch, in rejecting the complete, fixed principles of historical development, actually professes the same notions.[39]

The proximity of Benjamin's *Jetztzeit* (Now-time)[40] and *Jetzt*, of which Bloch often writes, is not accidental. He comments: '*Jetztzeit* is the present time in which something forgotten long ago suddenly turns into the actual Now. But not as a romantic reprise: thus, the polis in the time of the French revolution was an actual Now' (Über Walter Benjamin, p. 20).[41]

Bloch associates this intervention with the critique of homogeneity and of something Benjamin called 'empty' time. The time filled with history is unrepeatable, as a dish of a good chef or a bouquet of a good gardener. And in this pluralistic universe, a star of the future rises, which, as Bloch emphasizes, trying to approach Benjamin's thinking, presupposes a dark, unclarified element, '*profound delight of early nightfall*' (GU2, p. 185; SU, p. 144).

Benjamin and Bloch employ – each in their own context – the new notion of contemporaneity as an instantaneous while incessant tension, resisting a nomological description, enabling to continuously settle the score with the past anew, to open new possibilities and to reject the mechanical reproduction of the past in the images of the future. While Benjamin saw this rupture as a sort of stasis, the impossibility of moving forward, a breaking, Bloch, rather, saw it as an actualization of possibilities, as a sharp, abrupt awakening of the utopian meanings. For Bloch the present is empty of historical pulsation, if it is devoid of utopia.

Such philosophy of history was linked to the overcoming of vulgar historical materialism. Bloch, Lukács and Benjamin – each in their own language – opposed the Marxism of the Second International, suggesting a new vision of history and socialism.

And in this they were clearly ahead of their time, distrusting idle talk about the 'laws of historical development'. Their instruments were social criticism and the utopian energy of messianism, capable of elevating a single individual and whole classes to the heights of the present moment, to feel, following Baudelaire, genuine contemporaneity and to wake up from the mythical hangover of the eternal recurrence, which promised only dark monotony and the horror of enslavement.

This inconvenient philosophy was not accepted right away. Only later, after World War II and concentration camps, would similar schemes take root in the humanities (in the form of, for example, Kuhn's thesis of incommensurability or the epistemological break in Althusser and Foucault), but their fate and their real contexts would be entirely different.

Inconspicuous blemishes of metaphysics

In philosophy Walter Benjamin and Ernst Bloch were those who moved thought closer to the objects by giving it a new, material and sensuous form of expression
(Holz 1968, p. 71f.)

In his attack on the ideology of progress and the traditional understanding of history, Benjamin did not renounce the notions of progress and development altogether; in fact he could not really jettison them. But he sees genuine progress in the invisible and the imperceptible, in the small things, through which rays of new life and gleams of new meanings emerge. Rephrasing Goethe's statement on Lichtenberg, Bloch recollects that wherever Benjamin touched on the details and the small things he managed to penetrate deep into the nature of a problem, to cast away the cliché and the commonplace stereotypes that interfere with perception (*Uber Walter Benjamin*, p. 21).

During the first encounter with Karola (then Bloch's fiancée, and later his wife) Benjamin, wandering pensively around Kurfürstendamm, replied to her question on what he was thinking about: 'My gracious lady, haven't you ever paid attention to the morbidity of these marzipan figures?' (Ibid., p. 18).

Bloch's words can be illustrated by passages from Benjamin's book *One-Way Street* (1928), which he reviewed and which captivated him to a great extent – a book that disguises itself as a collection of sketches on city life, but, in fact, combines urgent political journalism with the finest metaphysics. One of the sketches (*To the Public: Please Protect and Preserve These New Plantings*) goes like this:

> Do not all the questions of our lives, as we live, remain behind us like foliage obstructing our view?... We stride on, leave it behind, and from a distance it is indeed open to view, but indistinct, shadowy, and all the more enigmatically entangled...
>
> He who loves is attached not only to the "faults" of the beloved, not only to the whims and weaknesses of a woman. Wrinkles in the face, moles, shabby clothes and a lopsided walk bind him more lastingly and relentlessly than any beauty.... And why? If the theory is correct that feeling is not located in the head, that we sentiently experience a window, a cloud, a tree not in our brains, but, rather, in the place where we see it, then we are, in looking at our beloved, too, outside ourselves. But in a torment of tension and ravishness. Our feeling, dazzled, flutters like a flock

of birds in the woman's radiance. And as birds seek refuge in the leafy recesses of a tree, feelings escape into the shaded wrinkles, the awkward movements and inconspicuous blemishes of the body we love, where they can lie low in safety. And no passer-by would guess, that it is just here, in what is defective and censurable, that the fleeting darts of adoration nestle. (GS IV. S. 92; OWS, p. 51f.)

This text demonstrates many of Benjamin's favourite topics: the non-dispersed darkness of the past, eroticism, a sketch of the theory of knowledge which is centred on affect. 'Inconspicuous blemishes' of the beloved body, in which feeling seeks refuge, refer to those imperceptible details that Bloch talks about, but also to the phenomena that require salvation. This is not the place to talk about all the details of Benjamin's metaphysics, but we should demonstrate, at least, what Bloch refers to and why he was so attracted by *One-Way Street*.

In the review, written in 1928 (EZ, pp. 368–71), Bloch says that Benjamin's text is an example of surrealistic thinking.[42] It is like a city street, where no two houses look the same, where each shop offers a taste of the new and never-experienced ideas. Bloch, in a Bakhtinian gesture, juxtaposes the extinct and impotent 'higher' culture against the new, mass, 'market' phenomena that do not pretend to be aristocratic. Benjaminian 'revue form'[43] in philosophy genuinely penetrates modernity, 'as an imprint of that hollow space in which nothing can be closed any longer without lies, in which only parts now meet and mix' (EZ, p. 369; HT, p. 334f.). Thus the new philosophical form is a blow from the left, an improvisation, an unexpected combination, 'a falling away of the broken coherence . . . dreams, aphorisms, and passwords' (EZ, p. 369; HT, p. 335) – a photomontage composed of the signs of the epoch, a joining of the mythological and the everyday originating in Max Ernst and Jean Cocteau and evoking a recurring fascination with surrealistic paintings, films and texts. Montage is present also in Bloch's aesthetic theory, in his poetics, where he tried to shake the self-confident stability of the social mechanism by challenging stereotypical cultural forms[44] in the very canvas of the text. But to really achieve this one needs primarily,

> not ear or eye, not warmth, kindness, astonishment, but climatopathic sense of touch and taste. If a category of Bachofen's can be applied here, then a chtonic spirit has found its casing in this street-thinking, or more precisely, arcade-thinking. Just as sailing ships are stuck in a bottle, just as blossoming trees, and snow-covered towers seem enclosed and kept safe in those toy glass spheres that can be turned over, so philosophical assertions of the world are stuck beneath the glass of the shop windows (EZ, p. 370; HT, p. 336).

However, Bloch reminds Benjamin of *the danger of fetishization* of such small things.[45]

> Whereas precisely genuine images . . . of this literature . . . do not dwell in snail-shells or caves of Mithras, with a pane of glass in front, but in public process, as dialectical experiment-figures. . . . Surrealistic philosophizing is exemplary as polish and montage of fragments, which however very pluralistically and unrelatedly remain such. It is constitutive as montage which jointly builds real series of streets, such that not the intention but the fragment dies from the truth and is utilized for reality; even one-way streets have a goal. (EZ, p. 371; HT, p. 337)[46]

The last passage plays on Benjamin's words:

> Truth does not enter into relationships, particularly intentional ones. The object of knowledge, determined as it is by the intention inherent in the concept, is not the truth. Truth is an intentionless state of being, made up of ideas. The proper approach to it is not therefore one of intention and knowledge, but rather a total immersion and absorption in it. Truth is the death of intention. (OD, p. 35f.)[47]

Bloch could not agree with this 'platonic' doctrine of truth and later reacted to Benjamin's theory in the Hegelian style. Thus, on certain occasions Bloch retained an ambivalent attitude towards the notion of progress.[48] In the 1949 lecture *Marxist Propaedeutics and Once Again on Learning* Bloch cites Benjamin's *Epistemo-Critical Prologue* in the context of the *Bildung* problem (PA, pp. 256–9). He stresses the importance of thinking through the most minute details, the particulars, of showing the student – in the laboratory, in the seminar – how new knowledge is born along the lines of Benjamin's philosophical method: 'Tirelessly the process of thinking makes new beginnings, returning in a roundabout way to its original object. This continual pausing for breath is the mode most proper to the process of contemplation' (OD, p. 28).[49]

The intermittent, gushing, neurotic rhythm of the philosophical movement, which returns to its subject with a manic, almost Proustian persistence, clinging to the fragments of the mosaic, is the principal condition for grasping the whole. For Benjamin this attention to the separate parts of the 'material content' (*Sachgehalt*) arises because the value of an individual fragment (as the quality of glass in mosaic) is inversely proportional to its connection with the whole 'truth content' (*Wahrheitsgehalt*). A montage technique is opposed in its right to the continuous narrative, to the system in which every element is in its place. Such internal connection appears illusive to Benjamin – his world has already become different. And Bloch, who praised contemporaneous art for its use of montage and saw in it the philosophical achievement of Benjamin's *One-Way Street*, shares with Benjamin his 'productive scepticism', comparable 'to a pause of breath, after which thought can be totally and unhurriedly concentrated even on the very minutest object without the slightest inhibition' (OD, pp. 44–5).

Benjamin's philosophy, Bloch argues in his review, turns into a stroll along the city, a philosopher becomes a detective. Such a method teaches us modesty and self-restraint and warns us against constructing castles in the sky, against grandiose, pompous generalizations. (As an example of a theoretician of an opposite type Bloch mentions Friedrich Gundolf, a student of George, whom Benjamin argued against in his work on Goethe's *Elective Affinities*.) A detective cannot afford to miss an element in the deductive process, his attentive eye resists the false and insolent polyhistors, who always abound in the humanities – be it in the times of Bloch and Benjamin or today.

But Bloch contested the fetishization of the 'micrological technique', otherwise the examples in the boundless and disorderly multitude, unfolded in every direction, would lose their references. A salient example is the difference in the childhood images they invoked: frozen, mute, melancholic figures of recollection, like snapshots – in

Benjamin; and intense, imbued with enthusiasm of youth and premonitions – in Bloch. Bloch's recollections return to what has not yet ended, or what is located outside time altogether, and always correlated with an active search for oneself here and now (Czajka 2006, p. 156ff.).

Bloch did not see any utopian positivity in Benjamin's montage as it lacked an indication of a historical subject. He attached a crucial significance to such a concentration of force, combining the subjective and the utopian intention in the particular historical moment. Incidentally, as an example of scientific precision coupled with broadness of perspective, Bloch, in 1949, points at Hegel's *Phenomenology of Spirit*.

In 1934, in a long and bitter letter to Adorno, responding to his criticism, Bloch attacks the Benjaminian (and Adornian) form of philosophy (Br II, p. 429f.). The essential, the important, when stripped of its temporal context in the hands of such a 'philology', becomes dead; its life is driven out of it. Bloch doubts that reification can be overcome by carrying it to the extreme point; he quotes *The Spirit of Utopia* and notes that there he 'already deals with praxis and with the genuine, namely the red (that is, communist. — IB) mystery and, in decisive cases, never else with the ornamental seals and astral myths[50] . . . or, alternatively, with those ornamental seals only, which are invaded by a self-actualizing philosophy' (Br II, p. 430). His own texts, Bloch claims, should not be regarded as a poor version of those of Benjamin's – they have their own meaning. Benjamin's melancholy for them is the most inappropriate affect.

This perceived difference is taken up by Ernst Osterkamp (1978) who emphasizes Benjamin's relative neglect towards the dimension of the future and his appreciation of 'unmediated', or 'abstract' utopias fully detached from history. For Benjamin, utopia remained a negative concept: 'not the final fulfilment of the historically possible, but rather the destruction of historical possibilities' (p. 118).

Richard Wolin (1982, p. 26) finds a general explanation of this confrontation: Bloch, Wolin argues, puts more emphasis on philosophy and subordinates his aesthetics to the utopian truth; while Benjamin was first and foremost a literary critic, unwilling to subdue works of art to abstract ontological or epistemological principles. Probably, this is not totally true. After all, Bloch and Benjamin were both engaged in philosophy as well as literary criticism.

It is not accidental that Bloch mentions 'praxis' in the letter to Adorno. Benjamin remained for him an aesthete, an ideologue, even if very important and significant. He saw his own texts in a much more revolutionary and activist light. This is also the reason for Bloch's optimism, the belief that the utopian impulse is sufficient *by itself* to change the world in the direction of a better future; and that this performative utopian restlessness is a source of incessant transformation. In Bloch's perspective the pieces of the former epic wholeness of the world are not just a token of melancholic oppression of life, but a fragment of the future, a part of 'the multiverse', in which one could conjure its utopian fate. At the same time he identifies Benjamin – despite a deep respect for his ideas – with surrealists, implying that his Parisian friend has gotten too carried away by dreams, aimlessly flâneuring along a one-way street. This is also the root of their aesthetic disagreements or alternate readings; for instance, in the interpretation of a principle central for both of them, of montage – the device that became central to the *The Arcades Project*. But for Benjamin montage remained an interruption, a destruction, turned into dismantling demontage and ultimately frozen over in a sinister still life.

Benjamin himself saw it differently. The method of estrangement remained for him an element of political practice, and the dashed vision of history was always linked to the moment of decision, and not just a fragment of internal life or an aesthetic experience, to be simply registered or infinitely prolonged (Mosès 2006, pp. 203–4, 208).[51] Benjamin, who, as time went by, gravitated more and more towards critical theory and his own version of historical materialism, apparently saw his own work as an element of emancipation and collective awakening. Therefore it is hard to completely agree with Heinz Eidam who drew the difference between Bloch and Benjamin on the grounds that according to the *Epistemo-Critical Prologue* there is no question that could be posed to truth as a whole, while in Bloch the answer to the 'inconstruable question' is formed by the very intention to pose it. (Eidam 1992, p. 64). Both Benjamin and Bloch deemed their philosophy performative, through truth manifesting and actualizing itself (TE, p. 170). Linked to it is the enigma of questioning, the impossibility of catching and registering the instant, its darkness – the experience governing *The Spirit of Utopia* and *Traces*. Benjamin's optics is different: he displays things in a showcase, under the glass only to make them more eloquent, so that their very silence, this unbearable stasis would bear witness to history and to our part in it.

Even the early metaphysical notion of the idea – as of an objective interpretation that shows itself and cannot be questioned (Hörisch 1982) by truth – can be construed in a utopian fashion.

> The idea is a monad – the pre-stabilized representation of phenomena resides within it, as in their objective interpretation. . . . And so the real world could well constitute a *task*, in the sense that it would be a question of penetrating so deeply into everything real as to reveal thereby an objective interpretation of the world. (OD, p. 47f., emphasis added)

Such interpretation is just one step away from a real transformation of the world (Holz 1968, p. 98f.). History itself sets such a restless, disharmonic attitude, the feeling of permanent alertness, extreme intensity, which can be felt in the *Theses*, drawing the past into the vortex of the *Jetztzeit* and defending such a vision of the future, in which 'every second of time' would be 'the strait gate through which the Messiah might enter' (IER, p. 264).[52] Without this active element a critique of the nomological perspective on historical progress would just become another form of discourse, reminiscent of the German Historical school, with its idea of the uniqueness of each epoch and the inadequacy of universalism in the humanities. Benjamin did oppose mediations of historicism as technologies of deception, but not mediations as such. His ambivalence towards Hegelian schemes finds a perfect correspondence in Bloch's relation to Hegel, opposing dialectics in favour of mystical utopian immediacy, but then embracing it in the form of Marxist praxis.

Moreover, one should not forget the most common affinity of Bloch's and Benjamin's positions in terms of politics. And it is not just about Marxism and Antifascism.

Bloch's political mission was more than compatible with the one proclaimed by Benjamin:

> [T]o cultivate fields where, until now, only madness has reigned. Forge ahead with the whetted axe of reason, looking neither right nor left so as not to succumb to the horror that beckons from deep in the primeval forest. Every ground must at some point have been made arable by reason, must have been cleared of the undergrowth of delusion and myth. (GS V, 1. p. 570f., AP, p. 456f.)

Let us recall another image – a poem, *The Voyage*, which concludes Baudelaire's *Les Fleures du Mal*. Here are its two concluding stanzas:

> Ô Mort, vieux capitaine, il est temps! levons l'ancre!
> Ce pays nous ennuie, ô Mort! Appareillons!
> Si le ciel et la mer sont noirs comme de l'encre,
> Nos cœurs que tu connais sont remplis de rayons!
>
> Verse-nous ton poison pour qu'il nous réconforte!
> Nous voulons, tant ce feu nous brûle le cerveau,
> Plonger au fond du gouffre, Enfer ou Ciel, qu'importe?
> Au fond de l'Inconnu pour trouver *du nouveau*!

Baudelaire's hero could well have been a hero for both Bloch and Benjamin. Benjamin would emphasize that the hero sails into death, that it is his last voyage, and that it is death who is the captain, leading the ship away from this world, anywhere, just to escape the ennui. And Bloch, had he taken part in this imaginary dialogue, would have noted that despite all this the hero is not languished by the premonition of death, does not bow down before it, and is not afraid of the unknown that gapes before him, but rather incessantly seeks the new.

In the search for the truth of history, in trying to understand his own time, Benjamin saw its forms, like Goethe who saw the *Urphänomen*, he tried to show, to teach this vision (GS V, 1. pp. 573–4, 592; Mosès 2006, p. 180f.). The idea of *Urphänomen* was also significant to Bloch (Czajka, 2006, p. 276). But what Benjamin preferred to the 'pagan' language of Goethe, was the Jewish – *historical* – context, in which the *Urphänomen* is *the immediately visible*, that which Benjamin called the origin, the *Ursprung* of nineteenth-century culture. And in order to better understand what pictures appeared before Benjamin one has to transpose this visible origin from the eternal interconnections of natural philosophy to the philosophy of history. 'The death of intention', defining truth in the book on tragic drama, became in *The Arcades Project* the moment of truth, the second in which truth is saturated with time to the limit, explodes and together with it a truly historical time or a time of historical truth is born (GS V, 1. p. 577f.) Benjamin's own *now-time* disposed him to such a conception.

Allegories

In late 1934 Bloch sent a copy of *The Heritage of Our Times* to Benjamin with a comment that in his next book he would touch upon *Goethe's Elective Affinities* and

The Origin of German Tragic Drama in a more profound and earnest way (Br II, p. 659). The war prevented Bloch from publishing anything, but the manuscripts of that time (1934–38) became the basis for *The Problem of Materialism*, *The Tübingen Introduction in Philosophy* and *Experimentum Mundi* and indeed these books contain traces of work with Benjamin's texts.

In particular, Benjamin's book on tragic drama[53] influenced Bloch's understanding of allegory and symbol, and became the basic concepts of his aesthetics. Benjamin relies upon the ides of romantic philosopher Friedrich Creuzer who defined a symbol as a kind of instantaneous, holistic intuition of an unfamiliar connection that powerfully asserts itself and an allegory as a symbolic form that unfolds in time. Benjamin construes allegory as a type of montage technique that connects disjointed symbolic forms. 'With every idea[54] the moment of expression coincides with a veritable eruption of images, which gives rise to a chaotic mass of metaphors' (OD, p. 173).[55]

Bloch in his rendering of Benjamin's notion of allegory emphasizes the triumph of death and decay in the allegoric universe of tragic drama – a universe inhabited by the dead, for allegory is itself a decomposition of the holistic sense. And while the symbol for Benjamin is a visible connection of the finite and the infinite, in which the transcendent element manifests itself, allegory (particularly a baroque one) presents the world as incomplete, fractured and transient. As a result, the self-sufficient and enclosed symbolic universe disintegrates.

Benjamin's style makes death reappear in unexpected contexts: in the description of a bourgeois interior ('fittingly housing' a dead body) or of a hy-spy, with a child looking for Easter eggs hidden in the 'empty eye-sockets' of the room (OWS, pp. 49, 74). In *Traces* a similar style emerges, with a passenger's pride and happiness at the departure of a train or a ship suddenly reinterpreted as a welcoming of death, and the triumphant, joyful arrival associated with the forthcoming resurrection (S, p. 131).

Allegories as open structures of meaning play an important role in Bloch's utopian philosophy: one can interpret the elements of allegoric comparison in an infinite number of ways, it is as though allegory glimmers to reveal something new all the time, and in this 'wealth of vagueness' (PH, p. 200; PHE, p. 175) one cannot foresee them all. But it is not enough to simply fix one's eye upon this glimmering: Bloch urges to clarify the darkness and the mystery hidden behind the inflorescence of symbols and allegories and therefore act to play out today's and tomorrow's plays of the world. In his manuscript 'Simile, Allegory, Symbol' (1934) Bloch deals with literary imagery as a challenge to reality. At stake is the possibility of simile as a kind of contradiction within the world of objects, as an internal denial of their being-in-itself, to use Sartre's expression, of their prosaic givenness. Benjamin's 'dialectics of the image' is labelled 'very aesthete-like, very contemplative, but suitable' to complement the dialectic of nature (Logos der Materie, p. 375).

For Benjamin allegories are the central phenomena of baroque culture, he mentions their dependence on the subject, the allegorist, capable, with an alchemical gesture, of giving a different interpretation to the faded and petrified images.[56] Symbols, on the contrary, depend first and foremost on the actual content to which they refer and this content is, Benjamin argues, single and holistic. But in the case of an allegory this only means that the subject is also a part of the world and that his capacity to manipulate meanings is to a large extent dependent on the actual arrangement of historical reality. Benjamin's allegorist inhabits the melancholic universe of tragic play, he arranges new associations, searching in vain for a single, original meaning. He is expelled from the symbolic paradise and reminds of humanity awaiting the Messiah and striving for happiness. In this search, as we already know, the allegorist is aided by an historian, whose work dwells in between the world of despair and catastrophe and the world of redemption, between the baroque darkness and the light of messianic hope.

In his theory of allegory and symbol (TE, pp. 334–44, see also PH, p. 446) Bloch, first, explicitly acknowledges Benjamin's achievements in overcoming the inadequate classicist definition of allegory as of a frozen sensual embodiment of abstract concepts. Allegories are not background sceneries for abstractions (PH, p. 200f.), they refer to something through something different, but Bloch makes the meaning of an allegory dependent on archetypes, certain original figurative structures, subject to historical change and reflecting the hopes of humanity.

Secondly, Bloch relates allegoric structures to art (and to polytheistic religions), and associates symbolic forms with monotheistic religion. Allegoric movement is centrifugal and symbolic is centripetal with respect to the point of identity of the signified and the signifier. In the symbol as in a unity of that which is (i.e. the symbol itself) and that which is not (*yet*), we are shown a certain *unified* meaning-image pointing outside itself. In *The Principle of Hope* Bloch defines the difference between the symbol and the allegory with respect to the historical process: symbols point to a finite, single and total aim, while allegories are the signs of the utopian within the historical process (PH, p. 951; Paetzold 1974, p. 105). Allegories are related to the singular, the scattered, the transient and to otherness (*Alteritas*); symbols, on the contrary, reveal unity (*Unitas*) in the diverse. Such enfolding and unfolding, a pulsation of symbolic forms in search of the correspondence between the internal and the external constitutes not only the life of art, but also the life of the world which is composed according to Bloch, of 'real-ciphers' (PH, p. 203; PHE, p. 177), that hint at not-yet-revealed content. The images of dreams and desires are vivid, refer to one another, involved in the play of mutual reactions (PH, p. 199). Here Bloch's basic epistemological intuition, again, becomes visible: the point is not that by describing the world symbolically and discovering new meanings in it we simply find out something we did not know before – it is essential for any symbolization that the world itself is incomplete, only then does the symbol become productive. This is the reason why something standing behind the symbol does not give us final clarity. And this is exactly why Benjamin's interpretation of artworks as ruins and fragments, not as complete, self-contained forms, is so important for Bloch (M, p. 415; PH, p. 253; see also Kessler 2006, p. 113).

In this common search Bloch and Benjamin solved a problem that is hard to define precisely; one can only describe it from various angles in the hope of illuminating it. Bloch's 'revolutionary gnosis' and his wonderful style in *Traces* are echoed by Benjamin's metaphysical essays and in another point of their mutual engagement: *mysticism*.

Bloch and Benjamin as secular mystics

What is mysticism? There are two simple answers to this question. The first one would be historical. We could simply indicate the historical traditions that were once referred to as mysticism. Then people like Meister Eckhart and Mechthild of Magdeburg, Isaac Luria and Jakob Böhme would march before us. All sorts of spiritual communities were called (or called themselves) mystic – Orphics and Pythagoreans, Gnostics and Scholastics of the St Victor's school, Byzantine Hesychasts and Renaissance alchemists. One could call Loyola's spiritual practices and the materials of *Acéphale* society mystical, as well as *cognitio Dei experimentalis* in medieval theology or Joyce's epiphanies.

Yet, there is another way – to construct a phenomenology of the mystical, to single out what is common to all or almost all mystics and corresponds to the common intuition ascribed to them. Mystical is always something mysterious, enigmatic, unobjectifiable and unmediatable, hence unspeakable, inexpressible.

Historical context – relevant to Bloch – was reconstructed above. His early philosophy, one way or another was apparently influenced by mystical traditions. In Benjamin's case it is also obvious that his inspiration came not only from Jewish mysticism (his interest was, of course, due to his friend Scholem), but also from within the German tradition, especially romanticism, – primarily in the philosophy of language (Menninghaus 1980).

But what to do with the appearances of the mystical; how do mystical ideas 'function' in Benjamin's and Bloch's texts, and, generally, to what extent can they be called mystics?

The most significant characteristic of mystical texts is the reference to a certain specific personal and religious *experience* – the experience of immediate communication and/or attainment of identity with the divine. Bloch and Benjamin, strictly speaking, do not conceptualize this experience as such, as though it were absent. In fact, however, it is mediated by the (quasi)theological and philosophical speculation embedded in the literary form. A mystic's concentration becomes the impetus for a literary expression.

Stories and sketches from *Traces* provide a good reference point here. Anna Czajka demonstrates the peculiarities of Bloch's literary style referring to Erich Auerbach's distinction between epic and biblical styles (Czajka 2006, p. 216). Auerbach distinguished the Bible from the Homerian *epos*, arguing that the biblical text replaces the absolute immanentism of the narrative with a new otherworldly dimension, pointing to something completely different that does not coincide with the text; it is visible only through and by its narrative. Similarly, Bloch often does not provide a complete, exhaustive description, he just outlines with a few hasty strokes the contours of the situation that allow several shapes to appear briefly; but for all the schematism he succeeds in hinting at the deeper meaning behind them, he makes the text mysterious and laconic, prompting the reader's attention.

In *Traces* there is a story about a Viennese actor, who was coming home one evening going through a tenderloin district and saw a girl sticking out of the window and inviting him to come because she would do it in a 'Mexican' style. Promising to come another time, he walked by, but after several quarters got curious about the meaning of her words. When he came back, intending to find an explanation, he could find neither the house nor the girl touting him, and only later it became clear that once in a hundred years an angel descends to earth in the shape of a Viennese prostitute. The angel cannot stand the morals of the earthly life and is ready to reveal a great mystery that can change the human world completely. But until that moment nobody was able to understand this strange message, and the angel always returned to the heavens. Perhaps now he will never come again (S, p. 79f.).

This story, apart from the already familiar feeling of mysteriousness that is hidden within the everyday life, in fact contains the typical internal conflict of the mystical standpoint: the unspeakable, impenetrable nature of the mystical truth (for it is conferred immediately). Perhaps, we could never completely understand or at least clarify this vague basis of the world, but it does not mean that we should lose hope, on the contrary, one should master the secret language of things and the clandestine text of history. This leads to another mystical theme – the illumination of the dark moment by deciphering the mysteries of inwardness and by cultivating sensitivity to the inner light. It is naturally congruent to the gnostic metaphorics of light, darkness and the human souls as scattered sparks – something we already encountered in the texts of Bloch and Lukács.

The mystical poetics of Bloch and Benjamin becomes apparent in that both the texts and the reader seem to be suspended; what is revealed is not just the urgent necessity but the difficulty, perhaps even the impossibility, of illumination. Bloch recognizes that in the uneasy exploration of the mystical universe a contact with illusions, spectres, mirages is inescapable. They do not simply add mysteriousness to the world, or merely obstruct the path towards the aim – they are, rather, a part of this world, and in the dynamic universe it is not always possible to know for sure whether something was a mirage/myth/tale or a reality. We do not (yet) have the highest instance, to which we can appeal, which would deliver the final judgement. Moreover, the very essence of human life, its existential meaning as an incessant search for oneself, cannot be separated from mysteries and spectres. Life would not be fully lived, the path would not be walked to the end, if there were no illusions to overcome (however not in the manner of Odysseus, who ties himself to the mast, but like Orpheus, who enters in a dialogue with the sirens (S, p. 187f.)), if there are no riddles and no blind alleys, which we follow in this search. According to Adorno (1991, p. 209), Bloch would rather label all philosophy a mere illusion, semblance, than lose heart and embrace the positive, solid foundations of existence.

Mysticism is generally hostile to scientific knowledge. With such an inclination to figurativeness, dealing with life that is always tested by literature, Bloch could not grasp the not-yet-actualized being from a detached empirical position. However, an epistemological interpretation of his philosophy (there is simply something that we do not yet know, and this is the only reason for the incompleteness of the world) may also seem legitimate. Benjamin emphasized this negative moment as well: 'Someone who wants to know how the "redeemed mankind" will be organized, what are the necessary conditions of achieving this organization and when could we expect this achievement to come – puts the questions that have no answer' (GS I, 3. p. 1232).

However, such a reading would be misplaced with regard to the spirit of the time and, in general, the style of Bloch's early texts, aspiring to become prophetic and thus inseparable from an obsessive aspiration towards the basic elements through concentration and maximal 'compression' of the utopian material (S, p. 90). This 'spirit of the time' lived also in the essays of early Lukács and in the first texts of Benjamin. Bloch's figures – be it people, ideas or circumstances (and all of them appear as characters in *Traces*) – are subversive and suspend or estrange the ordinary arrangements of reality. On the one hand, Bloch portrays himself, on the other, he gives form to the affective and the metaphysical elements of his utopian philosophy: to the unexpected nature of the instant, surprise and hope. Literature helps to question the familiar forms of existence. Bloch seems to invite the reader to partake in this artistic act, using an irregular textual rhythm and vague imagery.

These images are not necessarily visual, Bloch finds the mystical revelation in the sound, and shifts the metaphysical attitude into the realm of listening (especially in his philosophy of music). The sound appears to be more adequate than the word, even later Bloch devotes a separate essay to the poetic of everyday speech and to anacoluthon – intentional distortion of syntax that creates an immediacy of a lively, vocal speech (LA, pp. 560-7; Ueding 2009, p. 47). The sound is the first attempt to escape from the natural immediacy and to express oneself. The rhythm objectifies internal intensity and places it in a spatial context. Together they form music, and music sets the rhythm of revelation. It is an art based on productive indeterminacy, on the acute internal sense of time, inseparable either from internal emotion, crucial for the mystical experience, or from the apocalyptic mood constituted by the style of the expressionist epoch. It is no accident that Rosenzweig in his doctrine of revelation refers to music as a blessing of the mute self of the language and its transformation into the uttering soul (1988, p. 221).

I mentioned the connection between the mystical and the inexpressible. By comparing life with utopia, Bloch argues, we compare it with something not yet existent, not yet expressed. Both Bloch and Benjamin recurrently touch upon the questions, which balance on the edge of expressibility. They appeal to experience, which cannot be precisely or exhaustively described, they resist logical rigour, cannot relinquish their propensity to the paradoxical or deny the incommensurability between common forms of perception and messianic meanings.

Such was their idea of a philosophy adequate to their historical situation, and they believed that it was impossible to conceive of the ultimate matters otherwise, the old forms of knowledge were simply not up to scratch anymore. They both developed an extreme *sensitivity* towards these mysterious subjects, these gentle touches of meaning which implied being both receptive *and* productive. Primarily in their literary work they were inspired by *the mysticism of things and everyday occurrences*. Mystical knowledge is directed at something which is too close, barely noticeable in our own shadow (PH, p. 343) and therefore invisible. This is what Benjamin writes about this in his article on Surrealism:

> Any serious exploration of occult, surrealistic, phantasmagoric gifts and phenomena presupposes a dialectical intertwinement to which a romantic turn of mind is impervious. For histrionic or fanatical stress on the mysterious side of the

mysterious takes us no further; we penetrate the mystery only to the degree that we recognize it in the everyday world, by virtue of a dialectical optic that perceives the everyday as impenetrable, the impenetrable as everyday. (OWS, p. 237)

For Bloch this immanent proximity was a part of the utopian logic: the transcendent emerges in a simple story or an anecdote thus demonstrating that it is closer than might seem, but this immanent transcendency is poeticized and sublimated in order to be transformed, to turn it into a part of the labile utopian universe (Cf. Dubbels 2011, p. 152f.).

The key figure both for Bloch and for Benjamin is given by the wise expression of 'a rabbi' invoked in *Traces*:

To bring about the kingdom of freedom, it is not necessary that everything be destroyed, and a new world begin; rather, this cup, or that bush, or that stone, and so all things must only be shifted a little. Because this "a little" is hard to do, and its measure so hard to find, humanity cannot do it in this world; instead this is why the Messiah comes. (S, p. 201f.; T, p. 158)[57]

The legend of a minimal, imperceptible displacement, after which our world becomes the messianic kingdom, was later discussed by Adorno (1966) and Agamben (1993). Bloch notes a mystical principle here: it would not be easy to understand that everything has changed, but one shall be able to grasp the secret contours of the new world in a single – happy – moment. Each thing has its own name that has not yet been found, and the subject can grant it its name, having suddenly experienced it. In Bloch's poetics (especially in *Traces*) this moment is often marked as a kind of mismatch, a defect in reality, a source of anxiety, but also of anticipation and hope, that is, the beginning of the path.

The 'mystical' lack of identity with oneself in Bloch's prose implies that

the empirical "I", the psychological "I", and even the person's character is not the Self intended for each man, the secret Name with which alone the notion of rescue is concerned. . . Security is not to be had, there is no ontologically embellished *Befindlichkeit* [state-of-mind (Heidegger)] in which one can live; instead, Bloch notes the way it should be but is not. (Adorno 1991, p. 205)

However, I should repeat, there is no predefined route to this path – Bloch does not believe in its existence simply because, following the words of rabbi, there is no regularity to be found in this unnoticeable displacement. The more obscure and the vaguer the traces, the more we are sure that this is precisely where to look (Adorno 1991).

The hidden contours of the future open up to us not only in astonishment, but also through the images of the higher life, that possess 'moral-mystical' obviousness (GU2, pp. 256–62). Ethics is something that prevents the mystic from enclosing within the shell of his own self and becoming obsessed with his own contemplation. Importantly, the 'moral-mystical' openness and the visionary power of comprehending the Other became the foundational experience in the philosophies of Buber, Rosenzweig, Lévinas and early Bakhtin.

In the first edition of *The Spirit of Utopia* Bloch concludes the essay on Kant and Hegel with the pathetic coda:

> The aim will be achieved when we can bring together what we never could: glossolalia[58] and prophecy, soul and the cosmic totality so that . . . the powers of liberation coming from society and the powers of upbringing and theurgy coming from the church were carefully, objectively built and thought over – and only then to derive systematically from these great observatories the inner, the soul as a genuine cosmos, self-encounter, as a content of all the cultural values, the enemies and geniuses of the universal, absolute self-encounter in the apocalypse which alone can represent the mechanism of awakening and the mystical fulfilment of the self in totality. (GU1, p. 294)

In other words, Bloch's mysticism is not only ethical, but also *political*. What does this imply? First of all, it means that the lost absolute returns in *The Spirit of Utopia* in the new form of the not-yet-realized utopian kingdom and community. This mysticism is the lot of those who live in the god-forsaken world and have neither the mythical energy nor the fullness and completeness of being any more. God is replaced by the coming kingdom, which is just another name for the mystical encounter with oneself – that theurgical 'magic of the subject' that helps to identify inward movement, going deeper within oneself, with the outward impulse and the realization of the messianic kingdom. The soul having not yet encountered itself, the commitment to the utopian brotherhood of souls engaging one another into immediate communication – this is the locus of accomplishing the messianic idea and setting ablaze the sparks each of us are holding. It is this internal intensity of the utopian subject that makes politics mystical – because in Bloch, a mystic is always a rebel and a heretic.

The political element in Bloch's writing is emphasized by Adorno who deals with the connection between 'the occult' and 'the superstitious' stories, on the one hand, and alienation, on the other. These stories, so the Adornian argument goes, are listened to by someone who does not believe in them and thus can enjoy 'freedom from myth'. They are able to recognize – with the help of the narrator – how small and how cramped the unemancipated world is (Adorno 1991, p. 210).

Bloch's revelations are radically democratic, this is an important political message of his mysticism. They are not performed to discover just another hierarchy, previously unknown, concealed or forgotten, but always pre-existent, compulsive in its unmediated externality. Then the mystical would be closer to the political theology of Carl Schmitt, constructed from a combination of authority, revelation and conformity (cf. Meier's definitions quoted in Dubbels 2011, p. 203). This is not Bloch's style, and the critical energy of the Not-yet serves as an antidote here. He, rather, consciously engages in the deeply problematic pursuit of God's rule without God and without the rule; or the state of God, atheistic and anarchic at the same time. This is, ultimately, a struggle in this world against it (Bolz 1997).

Another important point in the mysticism of early Bloch is the doctrine of the transmigration of the soul. In *The Spirit of Utopia* he discusses death and immortality and insists on the irreducibility and phenomenological obviousness of the internal, mental life, that cannot be reduced to physical phenomena, and on the absurdity of the notion of absolute death. The existential 'core', once having appeared, cannot be fully dissolved. Metempsychosis at that moment seemed to be the very doctrine that could unite the two metaphysical 'puzzles' – memory and hope – to understand that motion and life exist not only in this world. He finds (in accordance with the esoteric literature contemporary to him) the idea of metempsychosis in the major religious traditions, being also impressed by Lessing's *tractatus* on the education of the human race.[59]

This idea allows us to see the earthly existence as a part of a broader plan, as a moment in the tacit movement, thus giving the historical process wholeness and meaning. Even the incarnation of Christ is interpreted by Bloch as a kind of reincarnation of the divine, as transmigration of God to earth, akin to a transmigration of the soul (GU1, p. 425). This doctrine brings before us a gnostic landscape (and gnostic metaphoric): the whole world, all of the things are bound in a cage, immured within the flesh/matter and awaiting liberation. An individual is redeemed from the tormenting, absurd limitations of worldly existence, from the thrownness and the given social obligations, with which one has to tolerate the total meaninglessness of this short life. Living here and now and trying to solve the mysteries of his limited being, he can take part in the events of the past and the future, bear witness to different epochs, breathing the air of world history. This, however, does not imply predestination, for over and above any determining of the manifest world by the latent one, history is led by the anticipation of the absolute – but not preordained with certainty! – encounter of the completely purified souls with themselves, of messianic redemption, which is the absolute centre of reality (GU1, p. 430).

Eric Jacobson contrasts Benjamin's and Bloch's theories of immortality, claiming that for Bloch *restitutio in integrum* is conceived almost as a materialistic notion. Commenting on a passage from *The Spirit of Utopia* (where before the end of times, when the whole world is unravelling, the house of men must remain unharmed and illuminated from the inside, so that God could inhabit it and help people (GU1, p. 429)), Jacobson says that in this transition from the doctrine of the transmigration of the soul to the 'true social and political ideology', Bloch becomes a 'materialist', losing the 'spiritual' dimension of redemption, whereas Benjamin talks about the self-liquidation of the mundane, and not of the self-destruction of the sacred (Jacobson 2003, pp. 49, 252). However, I have already drawn attention to Bloch's commentary on Lukács's essay (see 'Episode One: Metaphysics of Tragedy'). God must leave the scene but remain a spectator. This formula from Lukács can hardly be considered as an elimination of the sacred.

Benjamin also called himself a materialist, and at times a 'historical materialist' – in the sense that in particular things and events, in the transient impressions he saw the contemporaneity, like Baudelaire's flâneur, felt it physically and tried to respond to this 'innervation' of the historical being.

> The collective is a body, too. And the physis that is being organized for it in technology can, through all its political and factual reality, only be produced in that image sphere to which profane illumination initiates us. Only when in technology body and image so interpenetrate that all revolutionary tension becomes bodily collective innervation, and all the bodily innervations of the collective become revolutionary discharge, has reality transcended itself to the extent demanded by the *Communist Manifesto*. (OWS, p. 239)

But what could designate or stand for the mystical in Benjamin's writings, apart from the mysterious image in the *Fragment* that shows how the profane is linked to the messianic? One of the main mystical figurations in Benjamin is the metaphor of awakening (*Erwachen*) – awakening from dreams, attributed often to whole social classes imparting a new direction to their historical fate. The 'dissolution of mythology into the space of history', Benjamin claims, is possible only 'through the awakening of the not-yet-conscious knowledge of what has been' (GS V, 1. S. 571f.; AP, p. 458).[60] (Note that Benjamin uses Bloch's terminology here!) Awakening is this very 'short circuiting' between the past and the present, that is imprinted in the frozen dialectical image, a painful state, a break between the world of dreams and the real world in which all things suddenly fall into their places and the moment of truth comes, when humanity awakes from its slumber of the nineteenth century, rubs its eyes, and an historian interprets its dreams (GS, V, 1, p. 580).

This metaphor is, to be sure, important for Bloch as well, though in a slightly different manner: his hero is always vigilant (PH, p. 143), even dreaming, even in a daydream, and his dream is an integral part of the utopian path. An interesting parallel here could be represented by the vigilance and soberness of conservative mobilization as an attitude proclaimed by Ernst Jünger. The stylistic proximity (in which a common attempt to master the time and to experience its fullness can be discerned)[61] should not, however, conceal the decisive contradictions: Jünger's primary aim is the restoration, and it was this conservative messianism that both Bloch and Benjamin tried to avoid by describing themselves as Marxists in the 1930s and by continuously attacking various forms of 'irrationalism', without, however, becoming 'rationalists'.

However, this did not prevent them from dealing with the irrational in various cultural domains. Given the state of contemporaneous academic philosophy they probably regarded it as an important challenge. For Bloch, the sobriety of the neo-Kantians, as well as the chthonic trance of the conservative revolutionaries, was representing a desire to keep things as they were. When he was writing his first messianic book, Benjamin already had in his desk *On the Program of the Coming Philosophy* and *On Language as Such and on the Language of Man*, the manuscripts proposing to reconsider the Kantian theory of experience and the instrumental doctrine of language, instead of which another philosophy was envisaged, in which its author gave credit to the intellectual audacity of the old and the new mystics.

Things and communities – these are the subjects of Bloch's and Benjamin's secular mysticism; allegories and symbolization (permanently problematized) are for them the most adequate methods of grasping the time of an individual life and of historical time. If one calls Bloch and Benjamin mystics, then one does not do so in terms of an apophatic theology, of absolute exorbitance and inaccessibility of hidden knowledge to a human being. On the contrary: most important and most mysterious in human life is immediate experience, the blink of an eye, demonstrating all the historical monumentality in the small things, a world in a grain of sand, as William Blake put it. This is another, non-traditional mysticism, for it is revealed to the world that has lost the immanence of mystery, the vividness and transparency of the Adamic language. In this context mysticism itself becomes ironic and can, as in *Traces*, emerge out of anecdote. Its fate now is to deal with the debris, the ruins, the fragments of the former perfect universe and of absolute time, in short, with the world after the Fall.

In German culture romanticists were the first to resort to mysticism as a means of concentrating intellectual resources in such a historical situation. In some sense Benjamin and Bloch could be considered their heirs.

Time is intrinsic for both the melancholic experience and the experience of hope. For Bloch and Benjamin, secular mysticism was inseparable from their being-in-time, and hence, their *messianism*. In fact, the inclination to the small and insignificant that inspired Bloch and Benjamin is hardly distinguishable from the messianic *inversion* praised by Paul (1. Cor. 1:27; cf. Agamben 2005). *Montage is also a messianic category* enabling heterogeneous splits of time to conjoin and tremble with a new intensity. I shall allow myself another reprise of this topic to sharpen its contradictions, to show a way of working with them and to provide an exercise in understanding – all of which should bring us closer to the project of utopian philosophy and its foundations.

Recapitulation: Tensions of messianism and the ways through them

Jewish messianism of the 1920s was counterposed to the Hegelian philosophy of history. The linear law-governed unfolding of historical time was attacked in the name of symbolic time (Rosenzweig), in which there is a people (or, as Lukács claimed, a social class), who seem to have been pulled out of the overall historical movement, capable of looking at this history from the outside, of judging history.

Rosenzweig discovered in the Jewish world view and put in the service of the twentieth century the synchronicity of the Jewish time perception, and the notion that the Messiah can arrive without any mediation by the historical process, regardless of whether his time has objectively come, or whether he is in the schedule of the world spirit. Benjamin stating that it is necessary to slow down the movement of history is partially inheriting these ideas. But after the 1920s neither Scholem (Mosès 2006, p. 328) nor Bloch with Lukács, nor Benjamin, were satisfied with an image of a religious community, within which the fullness of time is attained through symbolic ritual. This doctrine was for them politically insipid, and they did not suppose it to be relevant in the contemporaneous world. However, it was clear that the linear model of historical regularity is equally impotent. Jewish symbolism had to be augmented with the Christian sense of history, while mysticism was expected to become a part of the apocalyptic doctrine.

Any attempt to conceive messianism as a philosophical programme immediately runs into a number of difficult questions, in part mentioned above. We now can return to them on a new level, in the context of Benjamin's philosophy, for he was among those who defined the horizons of the messianic idea.

It is not easy to formulate these paradoxes since, in general, they are reducible to one another, or perhaps inscribed into one another like geometric figures. To be sure, they all naturally translate into the language of Bloch's doctrine of utopia.

Properly speaking, the central nerve of messianism is formed by the question of the time when the Messiah will arrive – a question essentially lacking an intelligible answer. Should we await this coming *at any moment* or should we continually postpone it and live due to and in the expectation that itself acquires the absolute meaning[62]? In Blochian terms: should we wait for utopia in the very centre of the present or should we move it away into the future, to the end of times? It was reiterated that Bloch dealt with the traces of utopia in the present. This search implies that the Messiah will not come at a particular moment of homogenous historical time – 'sometime'. But the modus of a *promise* is retained, moreover this structure of deferral imparts the dynamics to the utopian idea.

In the discussion of messianism one can hear an echo of the old disputes around chiliasm and eschatology, in which, on the one hand, there were people like Justin the Martyr and Saint Irenaeus, who postponed the Kingdom of Christ into the future, and others like Origen and Saint Augustine who saw this Kingdom embodied in the church itself and thus *already realized* on earth (Bulgakov 1993, p. 418f.). The second view does not merely oppose sensory intuition, but rather urges us to search for a path to the self-encounter and to penetrate into the absolute event here and now.

Should we analyse the logic of discontinuity further, we are faced with a no less difficult question on this transcendent intrusion into history that ruptures its course. The very nature of the discontinuous or the arithmological element (A. Bely) remains unclear. Are we dealing with human freedom, with the essential unpredictability of the choice that each of us faces in our personal and in world history? Or is it, rather, the issue of divine intervention?

What is the nature of the dialectical solution envisaged by Bloch? Apparently, the crucial point is that he substitutes *religious* practice propagated by Rosenzweig with *the political and the literary* one, as having the last word in the constitution of our own history. And while Rosenzweig solves the messianic paradoxes through the complementarity of Judaism and Christianity, finding its expression in the symbolic life of a religious community, in a collective aim, passed on from generation to generation, Bloch eliminates the contradictions through *praxis* instituting and cultivating the utopian element, through praxis as the primary medium of the utopia even prior to Bloch's more or less 'final' conversion to Marxism.[63]

Art defines both the matter and the form of the coming world, it is both the key method and the key reference, and therefore, obviously, is not 'just' a fancy. Bloch's messianic idea transforms the religious into the *poetic*. Of course, Bloch does not make any strict distinctions; however, even the sources of intuitions are important, and in *The Spirit of Utopia* they are arranged around music and expressionist art; furthermore, the texts themselves, written at times like prophecies, do not lack an intentional artistic suggestion and resemble an alchemical laboratory, where the new forms are being forged.

But before appraising Bloch's messianism let us proceed a bit further in this labyrinth. Messianism always had difficult relations with the past. And it is no less difficult in Bloch: utopia often turns into a suspicion towards the past or its underestimation. Such reasoning runs the risk of losing the past, and with it – the future. The Blochian way of referring to the past tends to discover there everything but the past itself, its authenticity lies in its unfulfilled promise. Bloch never engages in recollection for its own sake.

In particular, Bloch's position turns out to be ambiguous with regard to the symbolic time of the sacred calendar, where the mythical past overlaps with the present, pointing to an entirely *different* world, beyond the limits of modernity, but which needs to be constantly reborn in the symbolic act so that the flow of time is not broken. This point differentiates Rosenzweig's understanding of the other and the new from the philosophy of 'revolutionary gnosis' (Mosès 2006, p. 125).

In Rosenzweig's vision of Judaism shared by Benjamin and Scholem, a sudden interruption of time exposes to us the very distant future. In the Jewish religion time seems to be cancelled, Jews get pulled out of time and live as though among the ancestors. This ceasing of time corresponds to its infinite acceleration, and the proximity of redemption is reinterpreted as the return to the origins. Were we to formulate this in terms of the dialogue between mysticism and eschatology mentioned earlier, we could say that the extreme concentration on the moment as on the 'actual present' can be conceived as a necessary condition of the messianic promise, for otherwise we cannot understand what is promised to us.

This extreme tension, in which the whole of the historical process resides in a compressed form, preoccupied Benjamin in his *Theses* on the philosophy of history. The *Theses* problematize the relations both to eternity and the ancient past. Bloch, on his part, devised his own specific vocabulary to deal with this backward-looking attitude. His perspective bears the mark of suspicion towards the idea of an original state, it is seen as a mere recurrence. Thought, which tries to return to its origins, could turn reactionary and thus politically defective. But the real question is how to understand these origins and this fundamental novelty that is essential for utopia. Bloch, as mentioned earlier, ensures the integrity of the messianic idea not by the common origin, but by the common goals, the homeland is placed not in the beginning of times, but at the end. However, he also conjures a darkness of the *Augenblick*, and this also makes him a thinker devoted to messianic temporality.

What solution can we then find in Benjamin? He interprets the messianic redemption as gathering up everything that was supposed to come true (Mosès 2006, p. 194). Paradoxically, the Benjaminian return to the origin means coming back to something that was always there *and* the attainment of the entirely new and unexpected. In this context Benjamin's critique of eternal recurrence is characteristic: 'It is the inherent tendency of dialectical experience to dissipate the semblance of eternal sameness, and even of repetition, in history. Authentic political experience is absolutely free of this semblance' (GS V, 1; p. 591; AP, p. 473).

But can one not see within this paradox any more or less accurate a statement of the finitude common to any human life, each time beginning from scratch? Can one not discern here an *aesthetic model of an original work of art*?

A good illustration for this dialectic is provided by the interaction between the idea and the empirical world. It's not just that within the idea one can find a contradictory combination of the sensuous and the supersensible. Realization, concretization, unfolding of an idea is the source of renewal of the original principle. Without such concretization and realization there would be no principle to begin with, and this is, of course, extensively argued by Hegel.

A similar reasoning could be applied in the philosophy of language. The original word, a pre-structure, the Adamic tongue, in which our contemporary language is rooted, is a basis for the infinite number of combinations. In *The Task of the Translator* an elegant scheme is laid out: a return to the original language – the mission of a genuine translator – is also a verbal creativity, every time, in every epoch beginning the job anew. Translations change, and so do the originals, and each time in a special way they expose and highlight that original, literal language, existing before any particular meaning. This authentic language is revealed in the form, in genuine *poetry* that emerges from what always existed and what never was before.

One could proceed likewise in a historical speculation. The original principle, a hidden meaning of history does not exclude the appearance of new possibilities, the processes here are open-ended. Benjamin uses a remarkable image: the unfolding of history is like a flame of a lamp, its fire flickers and glimmers, and the specks of its light are changing permanently, but the lamp continues to burn (GS I, 3. p. 1245). This flame is the point where the contact between the eternal and the transient occurs (the same point is also made for the structure of allegory in the book on tragic drama).

Bloch had a similar problem in reconciling his empirical symbolic mysticism with the overarching universality and absoluteness of a utopian dream (Cf. Dubbels 2011, p. 157). In quite a Hegelian fashion, notwithstanding his critical attitudes, he makes the whole weight of his work dependent upon resolving a tension between the simple experience of the everyday and the all-encompassing vision of the utopian future.

The messianic interruption of history as a concept and as a figure of philosophical discourse requires further clarification. Taking dialectics seriously, one could just as well consider the notion that the moment is valuable in itself, the uniqueness of each instant, the intensity experiencing the temporality of the here and now and, finally, the intrusion of eternity and overcoming uniformity as *depending on the progressive model* as an opposing principle. How can we write history at all, if there is nothing significant in it but the ruptures? Even if we make provisions, that there are also periods of dull, tedious and rather meaningless existence and flow of time, which are interrupted suddenly and without any reason by the flashes of eternal meaning, and it is those flashes that captivate us, containing all the meaning of historical hermeneutics – then in any case, in conceiving the ruptures, we cannot do without the scheme of continuity, and here the Kantian *a priori* constructions are of relevance. Is it not the case that our notions of time, including historical time, are based on some principle of continuous and progressive movement, into which then *the rupture is implanted*?

Of course, messianism is not that simple. Benjamin and Bloch maintain that the historical *as historical* is recognized precisely in the moment of sudden interruption and arrest. Any other history is too simple, and therefore – a fortiori, a lie. But the difficulties of such explanation persist. And in general, it is difficult to combine the historicity of redemption with its absolute transcendence, but if we make the redemption throughout historical we shall lose the radical moment on which both early Bloch and Benjamin along with Rosenzweig insist, each in their own way.

Benjamin interpreted his critique of a progressivist philosophy of history in a political and activist sense, meaning a revolutionary when talking of a 'historical materialist'. Bloch's position is even more explicit politically. But the notions of progress, even in their most plain and traditional forms that go back to the French Enlightenment, also contain energy, *they also inspire action*, quite possibly with a greater effect, than the sophisticated version of historical hermeneutics advanced by the new Marxist theorists. Bloch himself noted on many occasions, echoing Marx, that without heroic illusions, the French revolution would have been impossible to enact (TL, p. 365).

We know that the construction of linear historical regularity was abandoned not only on metaphysical grounds; however pragmatically from the viewpoint of action here and now, Bloch's and Benjamin's political engagement left many problems unsolved. The perpetual historical movement, which Benjamin wanted to stop, gives birth not only to the monsters of fascism, but also to saints, martyrs, prophets of the revolutionary time and, what is more, to time itself.

There is another difficulty related to the compatibility of political activism and messianic philosophy. If *we ourselves* are the creators of history, if the future depends on us (and this is the position to which Bloch gravitates after having read *History and Class Consciousness*), then our thinking is *projective*. The precarious nature of utopia and, to a larger extent, the absolute *unpredictability* of the messianic event are hard to combine with this projective approach,[64] and so new paradoxes arise.

To these paradoxes the main one is added: messianism can be maintained only in the *anticipation* of the Messiah. After his coming it abolishes itself, and if life continues afterwards, we become tormented by the suspicion: was it perhaps a deception? Our spirit dashes around between the continual postponement of the event, messianic procrastination, apophasis and the striving for the apocalyptic end. This constitutes the tragedy of the messianic idea, its political and philosophical failures, exemplified by the numerous discussions of the 'false' Messiah embodying the universal fraud. This image is common not only for Jewish culture. It is also present, for instance, in Vladimir Soloviev's *A Short Tale of the Antichrist* or in Thomas Mann's *Mario and the Magician*. But most importantly: the history of twentieth-century totalitarianism has demonstrated that the false Messiahs dwell not only in literature. Even the founder of the first Jewish state would hardly be called a 'true' Messiah today.

When (if at all) should we wait for the new Messiah and how could we tell the 'true' Messiah from the 'false' one? Where should we seek political clarity and where is the evidence for the ethical impeccability of the messianic idea itself? On another level the problem of eschatology arises, that is the form of *participation in history*: should we wait for the complete congruence of the Is to the Ought only with the coming of the Messiah, noting the omens of the apocalypse and relying on the utopian promises, or should we act here and now?

Without intending to give a satisfactory solution to all of these difficulties, which remain not only the tensions of messianism, but also the paradoxes of Bloch's utopian thinking, I shall try to illuminate just one of them in the hope it could shed light on the other issues raised here.

What I mean relates to *the problem of the messianic subject*. Already Andrei Bely's nervous aesthetic essayism attempts to find a 'way from the symbolics of the individual to the symbolics of the collective, that is to the ultimate transforming religion', where '*symbolics* becomes an *embodiment*, and symbolism – a *theurgy*' (Bely 1994, p. 238). So, who is the agent of messianic history? What is the locus of the messianic event? We have seen that these questions can be answered either with reference to the community, or insisting on the singularity of individual experience, which makes such a personal redemption possible. Bloch's messianism combines these two positions, without indicating the contradiction (while later Bloch would, for instance, reproach R. Bultmann for the subjectivism and an appeal to a 'private' eschatology). But this theme has a significance of its own, because the demarcation between the individual and the collective entails different logics of the messianic happening.

Scholars are far from unanimity on this point. Anson Rabinbach (1997, p. 123) insists that messianic critique never originates in a particular individual; Christina Ujma (1995, 281ff.) claims that for Benjamin, collectives and things play a central role in the messianic, while Bloch introduces a certain expressive subject as a key actor here; Gérard Raulet (2008, p. 158) distinguishes Bloch from Adorno and asserts that Bloch's 'strong' subject of history is always the collective subject, inspired by *History and Class Consciousness*. How, then, could we decide who is the subject of anticipation, in what space does the messianic event occur? And if the messianic idea claims to be universal, where can we find the link between the individual human being and the whole of humanity?

The Spirit of Utopia deals extensively with subjectivity, but when it comes to pronouns, Bloch uses 'I' and 'we' interchangeably without making any difference. Such a neglect of details is hardly due to the certainty of the arrival (meaning that the kingdom of freedom has come and there is no more difference between the utopian community and individuality). Even the innermost, the unique experience is meaningful for Bloch only when it is directed at the utopian whole (Münz-Koenen 1997, p. 54), which in the early philosophy is the kinship of souls, which saw the mysteries and encountered their selves.

However, this does not mean that Bloch gives immediate preference to the utopian intersubjective whole – it has not yet been realized, and it remains meaningless if it is not rooted in very basic and intimate phenomena, if there is no subjective, moral obviousness of an infinite effort (Bouretz 2010) apart from the apocalyptic vision of the redeemed world (see one of the first formulations of this point in GU1, p. 358). Small wonder that Bloch approvingly, though imprecisely, quotes Kant: 'God and the other world are the single goal of our philosophical investigations, and *if the concepts of God and the other world did not relate to morality, they would be useless*' (GU2, p. 250; SU, p. 198).

I think that the break between individuality and universality, between the personal and the collective is overcome aesthetically. *Literature* is a realm in which looking at oneself can be rephrased to account for humanity as a whole (GU1, p. 66), of which Faust was so eager to bear witness. It is the literary hero who can with ease, naturally – and visibly, symbolically! – combine collective aspirations with the most intimate emotions, living through both. It is in the metaphorical language of literary expression that one can find ways to transubstantiate religion into politics and back again (Dubbels 2011, p. 211). And it is literature that could saturate a certain moment of time with the totality of historical happening.

This is why Adorno (1991) could easily show how in *Traces* Bloch, following the path of aesthetic appearance (*Schein*), does not see the barriers between the finite and the infinite, the phenomenal and the noumenal, and, finally, between reason and faith – without mediating them in a consistently Hegelian fashion, preferring the theological instead. To grasp the unconditional, without mediating it, to grasp it in the way it is by itself, is the task of 'literary' philosophy. It reveals the paradox of the everlasting youth of utopia, its inexhaustible energy, that makes utopia the *perpetuum mobile* of critical thought.

Significant here, is, of course, not the systemic nature, but the expressivity, not just the logic, but also the persuasive power, the intensity of the effect on minds and hearts (Simons 1983). Early Bloch is an aesthete, in *The Spirit of Utopia* the aesthetic is, in fact, the sole possible kind of experience, it is given a special priority in illuminating the dark instant (despite religious rhetoric) and in it – through music, which approaches religion in its celebration of the hidden – an individual subject and a community open up to one another.

Bloch combines aestheticism with his critique of Benjamin, but there is no contradiction here, for they are both aesthetes; however, their style and their taste are different, although kindred. Bloch does not speak – he proclaims, and this prophetism is valuable in itself, owing to a large extent to the style of his prose. Bloch makes this style consonant to his subject – mysterious, having not yet occurred, formless yet, a subject that can hardly be called a subject, which can only be distorted by any epistemological optics, eluding the fishing net of perception and often disappearing in the darkness, from which it just began to show through.

But Bloch's style is also messianic in another sense which is quite straightforward. He never could build a complete and self-sufficient system, and the temporality of his prose is also organized around the happy instances of expression (see Voßkamp 1994). These flashes of meaning cannot be integrated in an evolving and progressive narrative with an expected and well-considered finale. Instead, the text is composed of enigmatic ruptures, repetitions and glimpses, it often returns to itself, struggling with reluctance in its reflective attitude inwards. Implosions of style put the present on trial.

It is difficult to say how seriously Bloch took Benjamin's esoteric reflections on the nature of the intentionless truth, and on the ideas carrying within them the source of their own manifestation. However, the performative significance of aesthetic action was also obvious to him. That is, he was aware that art itself creates the preconditions of its political efficacy. Philosophical ideas or musical compositions and all other media of utopian truth must also possess an expressive power. And Bloch himself proceeded in a similar fashion, quite in line with Benjamin's early philosophy, according to which language is not just a means of expression, but the expression *is* language itself, and in any manifestation language *only communicates its own self*. Why is Benjamin's dialectical image *an image*? Because the figurativeness helped formulate the 'inconstruable question' in all its absolute purity, as Bloch wanted it to be. It is only by means of this self-conscious fictionality that early Bloch could also overcome the well-known difficulty of apocalyptics, to claim the status of witness by performing the event it is supposed to describe (see Dubbels 2011, p. 129 with the reference to Böhme 1988). It is by recognizing this aesthetic gesture that one is never left wondering whether Bloch is serious in his pathetic appeals.

There is a danger of seeing this resolution of the messianic as a 'mere' aestheticism, as a detached, contemplative attitude towards the object. This sort of critique was advanced by Taubes (2004) with respect to Adorno's last messianic aphorism of the

Minima Moralia. Apart from Adorno's own considerations,[65] one should take into account the nature of Bloch's style in order to appreciate this aesthetic redemption. Bloch's poetic expressivity that sublimates the ordinary is aimed at overtaking the reader, who must be seized by puzzling feelings reaching the existential core. If this strategy does not succeed, no real redemption can take place. *Messianic philosophy should turn in/to literature to get coherence*, otherwise it will be stuck in the inextricable tensions and its political relevance will be diminished as well. Moreover, the literary experience Bloch was engaged in can hardly be interpreted differently. We will simply fail to grasp this kind of writing, if it is approached as an aesthetic contemplation precluding any consequences. This was certainly not the kind of work Bloch and Benjamin praised or produced themselves.

This aesthetic gesture is salient in *The Star of Redemption* that takes up a classic succession of epic, lyric and dramatic poetry to argue that the tripartite rhythm defines the logic of messianic occurrence. Beyond the 'figure' of the plastic art and 'melos' in music Rosenzweig envisages their dialectical synthesis in the 'tonality' of the poem. Indeed, poetry sets the stage for this messianic speculation. The same happens in the recent version of messianism in *The Time That Remains* (Agamben 2005) that renders the poem a means of how ordinary temporality is transformed into messianic time. The time of the poem abstains from itself and this difference, this yawn defines messianic temporality as '*the time that time takes to come to an end*' (p. 67). Agamben's messianic remnant corresponds quite well to the utopian one because it 'prevents divisions from being exhaustive and excludes the parts and the all from the possibility of coinciding with themselves', as 'an excess of the all with regard to the part and of the part with regard to the all' (p. 56). It is the poetry bearing the index of the utopian non-identity and revealing the intensity of the Not-yet that keeps messianism alive.

Finale: Penultimately

In a letter to Alfred Cohn in February 1935 Benjamin passes judgement upon *The Heritage of our Times*. He considers it misplaced and argues that Bloch looks like an affluent lord, who came to inspect a territory ravaged by an earthquake and could not find anything better than to order his servants to give away his luxurious – though moth-eaten – Persian rugs and expensive – though time-tarnished – golden and silver jugs. The book's best aspirations and intentions are suppressed by his excessive ambition: the extravagant goblets will be molten, and the rugs will have to be used as blankets.[66] 'Non-simultaneity' turns out to be both ill-timed and inappropriate.

Benjamin was right in that Bloch's book (like, however, Benjamin's own work) had no political impact and could only ensure that its author would end up in a concentration camp, if he remained in Berlin or Prague, or in NKVD prison, would he decide to escape to the East. Thus the question of who was more 'efficacious' politically is hardly relevant today.

The century of Bloch and Benjamin bore witness to the loss of confidence in bourgeois values and the self-determinant individual freely orienting in history. They were looking for an exit and found it in messianic thinking, gravitating towards the

Judeo-Christian synthesis and Marxism. Their messianism was a protest against the current political situation and a search for intellectual and political alternatives. In the 1930s Marxism began to play an ever-increasing role in Benjamin's work – not without Bloch's influence, who drew Benjamin's attention to *History and Class Consciousness*. They both saw Marxism and theology as the ways 'to disrupt the cool surfaces of established discourses, to break the thrall of the everyday' (Kaufmann 1997, p. 47). Both were ignited by the spirit of Jewish obstinacy and the will to emancipation (bequeathed to them by Buber and Landauer). But both ended up recurrently as outcasts[67] and heretics, though creating new forms of historical metaphysics.

Their vision of history ceases to conform to the Kantian model of perpetual self-perfection or to the Hegelian notion of progressive unfolding of the spirit. Baudelaire, whose prophetic words were quoted in the beginning of this chapter, foresaw in such a logic of history the horrors of world wars and catastrophes. Bloch and Benjamin could no longer satisfy themselves with prophecies, history both outside their windows and inside their works became a heterogeneous and unpredictable energy field. They endowed the historian and the interpreter with enormous will and abilities, charging them with hope. Bloch's hope, the sparks of which we must painstakingly collect, is aimed at the realization of 'the Not-yet-realized', especially in the perspective of the ultimate end of times. Benjamin, perceiving himself to be a witness of such an end, collected the quotations of the forgotten authors, implying that a sudden gleam of memory can tie them to the absolutely unexpected events of the present.

Benjamin shared Bloch's attempt to suspend the authority of the transcendental and to oppose any political hierarchy. But whereas Benjamin did it with the subtle figures of the eternal passing away and divine violence, Bloch stayed within the simple logic of the Not-yet, reshaping and relocating this figure in the literary form and taking it back into metaphysical speculation.

Of course, inherent in Bloch's vision is a certain kind of optimism. Yes, the world has become meaningless, but not because it is lost forever, not because it once was and will never return. There are, simply, no final, settled meanings. Allegories are not harbingers of death, but the seeds of the utopian in historical movement itself, in the vortex of literary mediations. What do they bring? Both the bad and the good. But through this vortex hope continues to shine – hope that perhaps, was that 'weak messianic force' desperately invoked in Benjamin's *Theses* of 1940.

One should not, however, think that Bloch was an optimist *tout court*, blindly forbidding himself to think otherwise. He shared the Baudelairean perspective by sending his hero on a journey into the unknown. His early eschatological reflections give even less occasion to such evaluation. The apocalypse is coming, welcomed by Bloch simply because the world, as it persists now, is unbearable. It has to be abolished, regardless of whether the end brings all or nothing. And of course, the journey is all the more cheerful if there is a horizon and if it is, here and there, illuminated by the flashes of the utopian images. The militancy of this 'militant optimism' implies that we are not simply going with the flow, we participate in this process, and to a large extent it is up to us where to turn, even though we might not know for sure what awaits us there.

Benjamin's tragic apocalyptic wisdom was born in a time of crisis and despair. The secularized ideas of the Fall and messianic redemption gave a guideline when none of the hopes were left unbetrayed, when the horizon lay waste, when there was no more confidence left in the symbolic integrity of the universe, and it seemed that only suffering lay ahead. Melancholic sigh among the ruins, the stoic and resolute angel of history, carried away by a blast of the wind, hope with wings on its back, in the absolute despair lifting its hands to the skies – these were the images of Benjamin's texts that imparted a particular tragic element to the instant, and a particular significance to the coming of the Messiah, even if in the end he never comes.

Notes

1 See Herodotus. *History*. III, 14. The same history is recounted by Montaigne in Book I of the *Essais* (*Of Sorrow*), and then – by Benjamin himself in *The Storyteller*, where he uses it to show the path-breaking difference between a genuine story and contemporary information messages, which are short-lived and quick to lose their freshness. Benjamin's claim is that even today this narration, with its lack of complete articulation, its mysteriousness and absence of a straightforward commentary, may be stimulating enough to create new forms of genuine thinking.
2 The paradox is that this clarity is achieved through vague, unreliable, questionable means (see Gekle 1986, p. 15f.).
3 According to Bloch's recollection – in 1918 (*Über Walter Benjamin*, p. 16). The editors of Bloch's correspondence hold the same opinion (Br II, p. 651).
4 I had access to these marginalia owing to the courtesy of the employees from the Israel National Library in Jerusalem.
5 And on Hugo Bergmann, Buber's friend and colleague in Prague's circle of Jewish Studies *Bar Kokhba*. See: Bergmann 1913.
6 Particularly, the notion and the terminology of the 'motoric' world view as a proper basis for Jewish culture – meaning the desire not only to grasp and to coincide with oneself, but also to transform the world around – is taken from Buber's *Three Speeches on Judaism* (See Mendes-Flohr 1991, p. 104 and ch. 3 above).
7 In *The Spirit of Utopia* Bloch mentions *Corpus Christi* only once – as a target of movement 'to oneself, to the Body of Christ' (GU1, p. 336) – in a discussion of internal life and its dynamics.
8 This text is considered to be lost. However, Wunder (1997, p. 86) suggests that what could be meant is *The Theological-Political Fragment*.
9 In *The Principle of Hope* Bloch documents the wonderful experiences of an opiomane (interpreted as a premonition of Heaven, anticipating the fulfilment of cherished desires) and mentions that contemporary opiomanes in their visions watch Dante and Petrarch immersed in a conversation. The narcomaniac, whose desire was a conversation like this, is none other than Benjamin himself (PH, 98–101, Unseld 1965, p. 353; Korngiebel 1999, p. 34f.).
10 See, for instance, a letter to his classmate Alfred Cohn dated from 18 July 1935, where Benjamin says that he does not send his work (implying *The Arcades Project*) to any of his friends, for 'It is at a stage in which it would be particularly vulnerable to all conceivable trials and tribulations, not least of all to theft. You will understand that Bloch's "hieroglyphs of the nineteenth century" have made me somewhat skittish' (CWB, p. 493). Bloch's text was included in *The Heritage of Our Time* (EZ, pp. 381–7). See also an earlier letter to Scholem dating from

3 October 1930, which was cut in the two-volume publication of correspondence, published in Bloch's lifetime, where the book *Traces* is characterized as 'traces of intrusion into the world of my thoughts' (Benjamin 1997, p. 541f.). However, Bloch quoted Benjamin extensively, and considered the return to Benjamin's legacy as a key task of postwar intellectual life (also in East Germany), while his own reception of Benjamin's texts was quite specific. All this gives no reason to doubt Bloch's originality. Mutual influence certainly took place, but to say that Bloch 'copied' everything from Benjamin would be unfair (Ujma 1995, p. 272f.). 'If this story is nothing... it belongs to the one who told it; if it is something, it belongs to all of us' (S, p. 127; T, p. 96) – Bloch was guided by this motto both when he wrote *Traces* and when he collected the material for his philosophical books.

11 As though Bloch tried to avert hostility which could potentially result from this review, of which Adorno had written to him before. He repeated, that immediately after the publication of *One-way Street* he had shown his – at the time rather critical – review to Benjamin, and having received no objections, published it.

12 Bloch's letters are published (Br II, 649–68), Benjamin's letters were lost by Bloch during his changes of residence, only a draft version of one letter remains, which indicates that Benjamin tried to maintain friendly relations with Bloch (Walter Benjamin 1990, pp. 96–7).

13 A clear reference to Aristotle with his notions of aim (*telos*) and potentiality-actuality (*dynamis*).

14 Cf.: «History has an end, but not an aim» (GS VI, p. 94).

15 This image used by Benjamin hints at a number of completely different traditions – from Kantian analytics of the sublime to Hegelian 'cunning of reason'. Commentators also refer to Benjamin's work on Kafka, where Benjamin quotes Plutarch from Bachofen's work *Essay on the Tomb Symbolism of the Ancients*: '"At mysteries and sacrifices, among Greeks as well as barbarians," writes Plutarch, "it is taught that there must be two primary essences and two opposing forces, one of which points to the right and straight ahead, whereas the other turns around and drives back."' (IER, p. 138; Wunder 1997, p. 107).

16 Benjamin's erotic imagery of a subversive masculine power that is able to blow up the status quo of conventional history reminds of Buber's early Nietzscheanism that also resisted the linear model of historical progression (in the form of evolutionary ideas fashionable at that time) as avoiding an authentic heroism. See the analysis of Buber in Dubbels 2011, p. 226f.

17 However, Jacobson, for instance, shows that Bloch criticized not the political theology of Zionism (Zionism itself as a theocratic movement is only a recent phenomenon), but the desire to 'rest', to curb the messianic spirit and to settle down on the Promised Land (2003, p. 29). Bloch saw in this the banalization, the forgetfulness of the world-historical mission of the Jewish people, but definitely not an attempt to link theology to politics. It is another issue that the very idea of otherworldliness of the Messiah and the attempt to overturn the secularization of messianic prophecy hints at certain real features of Jewish apocalyptics, where the Messiah is a king, who establishes the new state and defeats the enemies of Israel.

18 Cf. GU1, p. 434f., where Bloch actually writes that not aspiring to become like Jesus is a second and the genuine original sin. In the later work Bloch favourably refers to Cohen, but, siding with Buber, denounces Cohen's misunderstanding of Christianity: Jesus stayed for Bloch the best example of realizing the messianic idea (AC, p. 85f.).

19 It has to be mentioned that at the same time a similar movement, linked to the criticism of mediation between God and the world, appeared in theology: in the two editions, of 1919 and of 1922, of Karl Barth's *The Epistle to the Romans* – a commentary that marked a new era in European theological thought, close in spirit to the critique of political theocracy.
20 Burghart Schmidt even thinks that it was owing to Bloch that Benjamin realized the defective nature of progressist ideology (1985, p. 87). Of course, this is not the whole truth, but it is still meaningful to make correlations such as these. In any case, even if Benjamin actually reproached Bloch for being imprecise, he would never accuse him of historical determinism – the Marxist intellectuals of their circle had long gotten over this stage.
21 Czajka argues that Bloch took the notion of symbolic intention from Husserl, in a sense of different symbolic forms, giving rise to the feeling of wonder and prompting us to clarify the darkness of the moment (S, p. 97).
22 Cf. *Critique of Pure Reason* (B 836), where Kant talks about *corpus mysticum* of the sentient beings, to which the idea of the 'moral world' refers.
23 Indeed, Hegel writes in section VI.C of *The Phenomenology of Spirit*: 'Here once again we see *language* as the existence of spirit. . . . The content that language has acquired here is no longer the inverted and inverting, disrupted self of the world of cultural development. Rather, it is spirit which has returned into itself, is certain of itself, certain within itself of its truth, that is, certain of its recognition and certain as the spirit which is recognized as this knowledge. . . language emerges as the middle term between self-sufficient and recognized self-consciousnesses. . . . The content of conscience's language is the *self knowing itself as the essence*. This alone is what it expresses, and this expression is the true actuality of the activity, that is, is what makes action valid'. (652–3).
24 For Simons this open game is *the* philosophical project of Bloch, as distinct from the unsuccessful versions of the latter in the form of an ontological materialistic system, for which Bloch was criticized by Adorno, among others. On this see Chapter 5 below.
25 Bloch selectively cites Sections 27–9 of the first chapter of Böhme's *On Election of Grace* (Böhme 1842, p. 472f.).
26 Another analogy comes to mind here – a Kabbalistic notion of 'tzimtzum', a 'contraction' of God within Himself, as a result of which He frees up space for the creation by His own free will.
27 This eschatological notion, which implies both the resurrection of the dead and the return of all things into their initial perfect state, seems to have been borrowed by Benjamin from Bloch (Löwy 1992, p. 102) or from the Jewish tradition with its notion of *Tikkun* (Dubbels 2011, p. 292).
28 Deuber-Mankowsky also invokes Benajmin's rather characteristically favourable opinion of Salomo Friedlaender's review, where the latter reproaches *The Spirit of Utopia* with excessive and inadequate asceticism.
29 Cf. the 'salvation of the specific' in Bloch's later aesthetics (TE, p. 178).
30 It was precisely this dimension that Sergei Bulgakov had in mind, when he wrote: 'Eschatologism can only be a personal perception of the world, a personal attitude, and not a historical programme' (1993, p. 432).
31 The German text of the Bible includes both *Heil* (salvation) and *Erlösung* (redemption) (Isaiah 49: 25). But in the religious-philosophical context of the beginning of the twentieth century the word *Erlösung* can be translated both as 'salvation', 'deliverance' and 'redemption' (the latter may be closer to Christian reading). Of course, one could view salvation as an individual event, imbued

with personal characteristics, while attributing an historical dimension to deliverance, making it the possession of the many, but it is undesirable to create a terminological confusion here. See, however: Jacobson (2009). Translating *Erlösung* as 'salvation' to a certain extent reconciles Christian and Jewish connotations. It is also important to note that *Heil* (*salus*) is a state, while *Erlösung* (*redemptio*) is a process that leads to it.

32 Dubbels 2011, traces the impersonalization of the Messiah in the contemporaneous German-Jewish context.
33 Interestingly, the 'external' magic and theurgy in Lurianic Kabbalah was overcome through the notion of the individuality of *kavanah* (a mystical prayful intention) for each and at every new moment.
34 Here and further *The Arcades Project* will be quoted not only because in the 1930s it was Benjamin's primary occupation, but also based on the assumption that Bloch was clearly familiar with most of Benjamin's ideas. Ujma (1995, p. 256f.) shows, referring to Benjamin's letters, that Bloch knew almost all of his works.
35 The motif of a prophetic book was, incidentally, very familiar both to Bloch and to Benjamin, for instance, from Novalis's novel *Heinrich von Ofterdingen*. Cf. also in Márquez an episode with the execution of the workers – a classic example of an historical event, which is supplanted and almost erased from memory by those who won the victory (1970, pp. 292–6).
36 'The act of remembrance is no longer the gaze of the subject from the present into the past but the *gaze of the past* at the subject and at his present situation (Magun 2013, p. 208).
37 The same criticism appears in Lukács, who correlated the epopee with such an abstract understanding of time.
38 In the light of what has been said above, it seems inappropriate to reduce the disagreements between Bloch and Benjamin to a difference between historicism and theological nihilism, to an alleged aspiration on Benjamin's part to altogether abandon the notion of the course of history – and this is exactly what, for instance, H. Thielen does (2005, p. 146).
39 Cf. also a critique of the linear historical development model and of the pre-givenness of historical situation, including a discussion of Benjamin, in: TE, pp. 119, 152f., 200.
40 This notion appears in Section 81 of Heidegger's *Being and Time*, where it characterizes a popular conception of time, measured as a sequence of the 'now' moments, captured by clocks.
41 In the 14th thesis (*On the Concept of History*) Benjamin invokes Ancient Rome, which for Robespierre was that very past that was charged with the actual present. Cf. also Bloch's discussion of *Jetztzeit* in: PA, p. 481.
42 In *The Heritage of Our Times* Surrealism is not equated with its canonical historical manifestation – Bloch spoke not as much of Breton, as he did of Joyce and Picasso, who were important for him in their use of montage (See: Kessler 2006, p. 209). However, the aesthetic and political preferences of Bloch and Breton are at times quite similar (Ujma, p. 203f.). Ujma, however, shows that for Bloch Surrealism, unlike Expressionism, was a bunch of 'cold', frozen dreams, devoid of utopian dynamics.
43 By 'revue' Bloch means a theatrical play, patching of different scenes and episodes, following one another without a visible logical coherence.
44 Montage is 'the hollow space' of the late bourgeoisie's world (EZ, p. 228; HT, p. 208), the hollowness of which is something unacceptable and at the same time a starting

point of a potential revolution. The montage technique is correlated by parataxis in Bloch's texts – a stylistic device implying a special syntactical structure, deliberately abandoning subordinating conjunctions in complex sentences (Cf.: Ueding 2009, pp. 48–50).

45 Curiously, many years later in *Die Eigenart des Ästhetischen*, giving a generally favourable appraisal of Benjamin's work on tragic drama, Lukács criticizes him precisely for such a fetishization.

46 Having shown the review to Benjamin, Bloch then softened some sharp qualifications and published it in the *Vossische Zeitung*. Afterwards, the edited version of the text, in a much more complimentary tone (particularly, with an addition of the last sentence, reconciling Benjamin to Bloch's militant optimism), was included in *The Heritage of Our Times*, and later reprinted in 1956 in East Germany (where, as Ujma asserts, it was supposed to help Benjamin's popularization and reception). For a more detailed account, see: Ujma (1995, pp. 96–9).

47 'The truth exists not of the thing, but in it' (GS VI. S. 50). The elements of this conception of truth can be found in Bloch as well, if we accept, for instance, G. Ueding's interpretation (2009, p. 178).

48 Benjamin on his part 'has witnessed that moment of the contemporary European consciousness, where the notion of "progress" was reduced to that very little, which remains here (in the IX thesis *On the Concept of History* – I. B.), that is progress as a kind of forcedness, as a kind of inability to stop, and no more' (Mikhailov 2000, p. 762).

49 Cf. similar passages in Bloch's manuscript of the 1930s, where he writes that 'the doctrine of the categories is not an abstract dragging-on, but an incessantly recommencing effort: to direct oneself to the goal, to the many variable goals' (Bloch 2000, p. 254) and in *The Principle of Hope*, where he says that the being of the Not-Yet-Being constantly grounds itself anew (PH, p. 274). Both versions can be traced at least to Friedrich Schlegel with his notion of philosophy as an experiment in which anyone has to start from the very beginning. Kessler draws an interesting parallel between Bloch and Benjamin, finding in Benjamin's book *The Concept of Criticism in German Romanticism* a Blochian notion of the not-yet-conscious knowledge in the characteristic of Schlegel and his idea that only in an unaccomplished world is there room for understanding and action (see: Kessler 2006, p. 119).

50 For Bloch this is the symbol of a frozen, petrified thinking, stuck in the labyrinth of endless repetitions. Cf., for instance: GU2, pp. 37, 115–6, 270.

51 B. Hansen contrasts Benjamin's surrealistic 'dreams' with real historical experience and traces how the notion of instantaneous 'awakening' evolved (2006, p. 11). However, already in the 1928 essay on Surrealism Benjamin recognized and promoted an activist, revolutionary potential of art.

52 Cf. Bloch's eschatological call: 'To open the Gate of Christ everywhere, in all the regions and domains of the world' (GU1, p. 388). Benjamin's messianic pathos is so close to that of Bloch, that Ujma's argument that Benjamin was alien to practical dreaming, which he allegedly associated with Bloch, and that he was more radical in his political conclusions (and therefore closer to *Realpolitik*?) in the light of his theological orientation seem to me hardly adequate (see Ujma 1995, p. 284f.).

53 Interestingly in the first edition of *The Spirit of Utopia*, in 1918, long before Benjamin's book was published, Bloch defended the ideas of baroque aesthetics, seeing in it a utopian element, a vividness of ornamentation, brightness of colours,

flexibility of lines and images – all of what the new revolutionary art needed to inherit (GU1, p. 50ff.).
54 Benjamin uses the word 'Einfall' – 'a sudden idea', 'an insight'.
55 Here Benjamin understands metaphors primarily as elements of symbols. See: Korngiebel 1999, p. 119.
56 M. Zerlang (1985) shows that this sovereign gesture of an allegorist could be also attributed to Bloch as an author of *Traces*.
57 Cf.: See also: GS IV. S. 419. 'The great rabbi with the profound dictum on the messianic kingdom who appears in Bloch is none other than I myself; what a way to achieve fame!! It was one of my first ideas about the Kabbalah'. (Scholem to Benjamin, July 1934. CWB, p. 446).
58 *Zungenreden*, that is glossolalia, incomprehensible speech (see, for instance: 1 Cor. 14:9) or the ability to talk in different languages (Acts 2: 4).
59 At the time of Bloch's youth very different authors were interested in the idea of metempsychosis. See: Simmel 1997.
60 Another stylistic topos of equal importance – a lightning (*Blitz*), an instantaneous insight, a flash, which appears in Benjamin's thesis VI (*On the Concept of History*), and later is invoked by Bloch in a general metaphysical context (TE, p. 277, 365).
61 One could say that Bloch (abstracting from the early Gnostic radicalism of *The Spirit of Utopia*) described this conquest ever more often as *nonviolent* and tried to mediate it by reality, or, rather, overreach the reality by the utopian impulse. Cf. also the idea of 'sacred soberness' in Benjamin (GS II, 1, p. 125) and Ujma's commentary on this issue (1995, p. 122ff.).
62 Rosenzweig associates the former position with Judaism, and the latter – with Christianity (Mosès 2006, p. 122), which, in my view, is an oversimplification.
63 And on this point, unlike all the others, one cannot agree with V. Marzocchi (1985), who considers Bloch's early metaphysics to be an example of contemplative world view, later rejected in favour of Marxism – no, activism was peculiar to Bloch from the very beginning, it is just that Marx himself held a subordinate position in this doctrine.
64 On this issue, Bloch invariably invokes the argument that however blurred the utopian dreams may be, they provide a solid ground beneath the feet – courage and hope – and moreover, unlike the dark and vague romantic and chthonic dreams, – they give an impulse to transform reality (PH, p. 85f.).
65 See a characteristic passage from Adorno's letter to Benjamin, written at the time of their polemic around the dialectical image: 'We are all the more close to reality, the more faithful we are to its aesthetic origins and we are just aesthetes when we denounce them '(Adorno T. W./W. Benjamin. Briefwechsel. Fr.a.M.: Suhrkamp, 1994. S. 113. Cit. in: Wohlfahrt 2006, p. 264).
66 In a letter to Kracauer Benjamin also reproaches Bloch for the narrowness of his context (Ujma 1995, p. 277). Ujma argues (p. 279) that this criticism is unjust, because the texts collected in the book were mostly written before Hitler's coming to power and were already then known to Benjamin.
67 For instance, neither of them had a successful academic career. Benjamin did not manage to habilitate, while Bloch, also without defending the second thesis received his professorship at the age of 64, only to lose it and to acquire it again in another country already at the age of 76.

5

The Void of Utopia and the Violence of the System: Bloch contra Adorno

Interestingly, the young critics are continually rethinking the relationship between you, me, Benjamin and Bloch. For them we are a group that stands out from the substance of time. It seems to me that we should only welcome this.
(Siegfried Kracauer to Theodor Adorno)[1]

Bloch and Adorno constitute the last constellation of thought we need to clarify. Apart from their uneasy friendship and their mutual influence, Adorno provided an insightful critique of Bloch illuminating some of the ideas discussed above.

Their personal relations always remained ambivalent: in the beginning Bloch felt himself a 'senior' and was annoyed by the self-confidence and misinterpretation of his work on Adorno's part; later Adorno and Horkheimer could not find a position for Bloch in the Institute for Social Research (in 1938 Bloch was trying to leave Prague with his family quite promptly, and getting this position was a question of life and death for him). All of the time spent in emigration Adorno kept a distance from Bloch, leaving him in total isolation for many years. Adorno called Bloch's metaphysical improvisations irresponsible, and his indiscriminate critique of established philosophical notions illegitimate. He even labelled him 'Buber without [a] beard' and was uncomfortable with his messianic arrogance (Claussen 2008, pp. 293–6).

Bloch was much more enthusiastic about the 1968 protests than Adorno and subsequently called the position of the Frankfurt School defeatist and philistine, attacking its pessimism and debunking them as false Marxists. (However, Bloch's own 'militant optimism' did not prevent him from constantly appealing to Schopenhauer's sombre wisdom, in order to measure all the absurdity and illusiveness of the world, to feel the burden of negativity.) (Schmid Noerr 2001; Schiller 1991).

Adorno came from a different generation, but his biography and his philosophical destiny inevitably led him to Bloch. Despite the fact that it was Benjamin, who, as it is widely known, had the decisive influence on Adorno, even before meeting Bloch, the young philosopher read *The Spirit of Utopia* and, according to his own testimony, became fascinated by its apocalyptic style, which seemed to have come from the pen of Nostradamus. Adorno recalled that he immediately felt the heterodoxy in this philosophy and saw how this prophetic tone stood out from the chorus of his philosophy teachers, how alien this thinking was to the officially preached philosophical scientism, to 'what there is'. Bloch's style of thinking became one of the main reference points for Adorno, which he himself admitted with rare frankness, and of which Bloch knew very well.[2] The energy of protest, Bloch's literary style (it is telling that the critical essay on *Traces* appeared as a part of *Notes to Literature*), philosophy paired with mimesis, and Bloch's resolute inclination towards the inner, the authentic – all this had an enormous appeal for Adorno. And, again, it was (a certain kind of) literature that allowed for the transcendence of authoritarian philosophy. Adorno recalls that he perceived Bloch's book as a rebellion against the renunciation (*Versagung*) of thought, that is, against its intellectual deficiency and inability to dare (Schiller 2011). 'Prior to any theoretical content, I took this motif so much as my own that I do not believe I have ever written anything without reference to it, either implicit or explicit' (Adorno 1992, p. 212).

Adorno inherited from Bloch and Benjamin not only suspicion towards the Hegelian ideology of progress and totality, but also the notion of the radical otherness of art, of its eccentric nature with respect to the world as it is. And of course Bloch's pungent, sarcastic attacks on Spengler and Heidegger were fundamentally in concert with Adorno's critique of right-wing existentialist philosophy (primarily of Heidegger) and in denouncing the conservative myth.

Certainly, the critique of popular culture in Adorno today may seem outdated. His attempts to separate 'high-brow' art from the 'popular' may seem strange. On the one hand, Adorno ridicules the 'jargon of authenticity', an attempt to carry science and poetry to the point of indiscernibility, burdening the language so that it cannot articulate words any more, to forget oneself in the dark chthonic substance of the mythological element, which abolishes critical reflection. On the other hand, he sees in the attempt to *separate* scientific discourse from art the very same propensity for totalization. He is unwilling to postulate the totality, the internal relation, yet he despises the analytical vivisection, decomposing the world into clear and simple elements. In this honest ambivalence, in the lightness of speech and gravity of intentions, in the reluctance to compromise – today the negative dialectics stands before us as an aim, both philosophical and political.

The details of the relationship between Bloch and Adorno are well researched. Some periods in communication can be distinguished (Schmid Noerr 2001). In 1920–28 Adorno was under the influence of *The Spirit of Utopia*, but assimilated only the critical and revolutionary pathos, not the idea of a religious community. They met personally, most probably, in 1928, apparently through Kracauer or Benjamin (Münster 2008). In 1928–31 Bloch and Adorno mingled in Berlin as close friends, discussing for the most part (but not exclusively) musical topics. Adorno published Bloch's articles in the musicological journal *Anbruch (Dawn)*, and Bloch was trying to ensure the support of his young friend in the debates around Expressionism. In 1931–37 there was a certain coolness, primarily due to Benjamin's suspicions noted before. Schmid Noerr accurately notices how complex was Adorno's attitude not only to Bloch, but also to Benjamin and Kracauer. They were all friends, but also rivals. In this sense it was much easier to deal with enemies than with friends, especially when they were gifted writers engaged in similar subjects; at times it was difficult to work together, without suspecting plagiarism or without the desire to mark off from each other, to find differences (even if unsubstantial). Evidently, this, and not Bloch's courting of Adorno's future wife Gretel Karplus, was the source of their difficult relations, particularly of the critical stance towards Bloch's *Heritage of Our Times* on the part of Adorno and Benjamin. Bloch's uneasy personality also played a role: like his friends, he was extremely sensitive to criticism and never had an inferiority complex. At the end of 1934, probably after having received Adorno's rather critical review of his book, Bloch wrote him a long letter full of bitterness, blaming Adorno for superficial, unfriendly and hostile criticism, clearly regretting that he remained a stranger to Adorno (and Benjamin).

In 1938–42 Adorno was averted by Bloch's Stalinist statements, considering Bloch's infamous support of the Soviet political trials unacceptable, but at the same time did not sever their relations completely, from time to time praising Bloch's work and providing him with certain minimal support. In 1942–59 they almost never communicated, and in 1959 met at a conference in Frankfurt where, according to Adorno, Bloch came mainly for a reconciliation with him. Friendly if reserved relations were resumed and continued until Adorno's death in 1969. Subsequently Bloch did not change his attitude towards the Frankfurt School, Adorno remained for him an example of 'materialized despair' and 'bad negativity' (AC, p. 324).

Schmid Noerr shows how unjustified the accusations were that Bloch and some of his interpreters levelled against Adorno's critical ideology. Adorno never gave up on the possibility of changing the world; his negative dialectics never ceased to be revolutionary. And even though messianism (especially in the last years) was less and less an issue for him (Jimenez 1983; Münster 1986a), the experience of messianic philosophy remained important and in a transformed way was still a part of negative dialectics. What was *no longer* a part of it was, as Arno Münster (2008) notes, faith in Marxist activism.[3] Adorno's attitude towards the social reality that surrounded him was not similar to the rebellion of a plebeian revolutionary Thomas Müntzer. It was, rather, an aesthete's indignation, suffocating in the world of popular vulgarity; an aesthete, for whom hypocrisy and banality are not just counterrevolutionary – they mean death.

Adorno's first and most important essay on Bloch was written in 1959, when the new edition of *The Traces* appeared in the *Neue Deutsche Hefte*. Its title, *Große Blochmusik*, written by Adorno the musicologist, sounded rather contemptuous for it closely resembled *Blechmusik*, 'bad music' (the text was eventually republished under a different title, *Bloch's Traces*).

Adorno emphasized the experience Bloch tried to convey – the feeling of non-identity something one cannot speak of; of childhood reminiscence that once possessed fullness, now redundant. This is why for Adorno, Bloch's prose is an expression of certain impossibility, exacerbated by the fact that Bloch is a born narrator. But this art, Adorno claims, following Benjamin, has now passed away together with the epic forms. In dealing with Bloch's philosophy as a narrative, Adorno cannot criticize it from some standard viewpoint. The truth of the narrative is born and transformed in the irreversible flow of time and can hardly be taken apart into pieces, it is not susceptible to the analysis of its structure or epistemological status, leaving all of its interpretations behind itself. Such an analysis would be guided by the measure of what there is, without liberating itself from the authoritarian burden of facts. But Bloch, according to Adorno, exculpates market barkers and charlatans who conjure the philosopher's stone, for his texts preserve the great power of the appearance, elevating the expression above the content, closing the distance between the narrator and the world of objects around him, while his utopia dwells in the hollow space between this appearance and the simple givenness.

The source of Adorno's own radicalism is an avant-garde aesthetics as well as the non-conceptual and non-identical artwork. And it is precisely these moments that he inherited from Bloch, basing on them his understanding of history and politics. Adorno and Bloch did not have to deliberately seek or invent the examples of resistance to authoritarian practices and discursive formations. *History itself was this resistance*, and its name at first was – abhorrence of the war, but also – Expressionism, new music, the avant-garde. One could say that Bloch and Adorno tried to generalize and to integrate the new art into some kind of all-encompassing narrative, but, I think, we shall better understand their motives, interpreting them simply as a desire to *think* through history and together with history.

But Bloch, unlike Mannheim, never distinguished between utopia and ideology, viewing it as part of the ideological superstructure. In other words, utopia also 'deceives'. But this deception is germane to art, so dear to Adorno.

We saw that it was the search for form that proved decisive in Bloch's philosophical biography. Adorno showed that abandonment or conscious disregard for form, the fetishization of 'the real matter', turns out to be a mark of the most inveterate and lamentable dogmatism, and Bloch becomes the one who manifested a particular sensitivity to the embodiment of philosophical ideas in a text, to their commensurable representation (Adorno 1992).

However, there are problems in the utopian ideology, and the first one noted by Adorno is the threat of triviality. Similarly to the way in which in psychoanalysis anything can be a symbol for sexual desire, Bloch, unlike Benjamin, rephrases any symbolic phenomenon in the world into the symbolic intention, into a utopian trace. Hence, Adorno's primary complaint: he blames Bloch for *totalizing and instrumentalizing the utopian*. 'For the trace itself is involuntary, spontaneous, inconspicuous, intentionless. To reduce it to an intention is to violate it'. And further: 'Hope is not a principle' (Adorno 1991, p. 213). The latter aphorism became almost as famous as the thesis that the whole is false.

Adorno's own version is well known:

At the center of contemporary antinomies is that art must be and wants to be utopia, and the more utopia is blocked by the real functional order, the more this is true; yet at the same time art may not be utopia in order not to betray it by providing semblance and consolation. If the utopia of art were fulfilled, it would be art's temporal end. (2002, p. 32)

Adorno thus makes of Bloch (in his gravitation towards a system) a Hegelian of the worst kind, who is held captive by an 'irresolvable' antinomy, trying to construct 'the last philosophy' using the methods of 'the first philosophy', turning eschatology into a principle, an element of the world, ontologizing utopia, subsuming the diversity of its manifestations under a common basis. Adorno concludes that Benjamin, unlike Bloch, avoids such an absurd overgrowth of the systematic element, and the imperceptible remain imperceptible, without becoming the pillar of the utopian synthesis.[4]

For Adorno, Bloch has too much faith in this hopelessly corrupted world, but this is a world of despair where all that is left of German Idealism is an obscure noise. Adornian utopia, 'the unspeakable' can only be approached 'by virtue of the absolute negativity of collapse' (2002, p. 32). Following the logic explored earlier, we could say that Adorno is a radical gnostic (maybe that is why he liked *The Spirit of Utopia* so much in its original, gnostic version), and the Bloch he attacks is, rather, a Hegelian.

Burghart Schmidt suggests two arguments to disavow Adorno's critique. First, Bloch's turn towards ontology was conceived as a hypothetical project, which, given a rather peremptory style of Bloch's later texts, appears unconvincing. Second, and apparently more important, is the way Bloch, through his dialectical-materialist natural philosophy, glorifies human labour and the human subjective element, capable of transforming and augmenting reality (Schmidt 1985, p. 29). Instead of the radical non-identity which is oppressed by the identical, he brings to the fore the very process of identification, a problematic, historical, perpetually floundering and resurging pursuit (and articulation) of identity (Ibid., p. 69).

In fact, Adorno's position is no less problematic, because for him utopia turns out to be so fragile that, once having come into contact with reality, it inevitably becomes reified, turns into ideology and deception, becoming its own betrayal (Bahr 1978). His critique of rationality (initiated in collaboration with Horkheimer in *The Dialectic of Enlightenment*) stands in quite an ambivalent relation to his rational methodology and to his ideals, which he does not undertake to state explicitly. And critical theory becomes a no less paradoxical project than the philosophy of hope in hopeless times (Simons 1983).

Neither Adorno nor Bloch had a systematically constructed alternative conception of rationality, that new rationality, which they sought to oppose to the irrational myth and the instrumental ideological domination, each time blaming utopia and critical thought for 'not offering anything positive'. What is this rationality, that Michael Löwy (2008) calls Adorno's 'new Enlightenment'?

An interesting version is proposed by Max Blechman (2008), who shows that the contradictions entangling Adorno's negative dialectics can be resolved if his position is interpreted as a *speculative materialism*. A subject has to take a critical stance towards the social totality, but to do this he has to simultaneously be both inside and outside of it. And critical attack on the system results in a danger of contamination, a critique can easily be fetishized. Therefore, apart from negativity, from the infallible sense for injustice and falsity, one also needs an idea of the 'Not-yet', that is the self-overcoming of the negative consciousness, which stems not from its social and historical but from its natural organic texture. Blechman refers to Bloch's conception of *the natural right* (NW) as a certain material basis of human action, which finally becomes the source of genuine immanent negativity and of utopian energy, resistant to the diseases of social 'positivity' and putting away the boundary between physical and moral suffering. Natural right was, in fact, Bloch's own version of the subversive line of thought, and its history is interpreted as a history of the utopian remnant.

The fact that Adorno disliked the systematic ambitions of utopian philosophy is clear from a letter that he wrote to Peter Suhrkamp, who intended to publish *The Principle of Hope* in West Germany and asked Adorno for an unofficial review. The Frankfurt philosopher started by saying that Bloch was one of his closest friends in the decisive years of his youth and he could only welcome any publication of his works. However, he had found *The Principle of Hope* intellectually impoverished, overloaded with encyclopaedic material in the absence of speculative content.[5] Various conceptual disagreements could stand behind this: Adorno's discomfort with the Blochian critique of psychoanalysis (Adorno and other members of the Frankfurt school saw a much greater potential in it than did Bloch). There is also for Adorno a far less optimistic appraisal of technology and of its role in building the future, as well as aesthetic disputes.[6]

However, the utopian impulse was significant for Adorno as well. He recalls Benjamin's words, reporting that he warmed himself off Bloch's thoughts. Adorno is repelled by the systematic ambition, present in *The Principle of Hope* (and becoming even clearer in *The Tübingen Introduction in Philosophy* and especially in *Experimentum Mundi*), but he is clearly attracted by the paradoxicality, the radical elusiveness of Bloch's utopian prose, the situation in which Bloch becomes not an idealist *malgré lui*, but a player, who first exposes all of philosophy as charlatanry, and then – maybe as joke, maybe earnestly – stating that this is not the whole truth, leaving traces, which look rather like fabrications, intentionally forged in order to foul the trail and to confuse the pathfinder, as exemplary figures of silence (Massalongo 2008, p. 95). Why was this position so dear to Adorno? Most likely because his own project of negative dialectics is another version of the paradoxical balance between the one-sided self-assertion of individuality, which does not realize its relation to the whole, and the critique of Hegelian totality, which, in its objectivism, subordinates critical individuality and therefore disavows genuine dialectics. Adorno does not claim to have uncovered the paradoxes of utopian philosophy. On the contrary, he emphasizes and transposes them in his own critical project, seeking, like Bloch, to show the dead ends of various intellectual forms. Critique in *Traces* is the way to conceal 'the whole' truth and an urge to live and act as if the utopian apparition were true (let us remember that precisely in this gesture of 'as if', transformed into the 'Not-yet', Bloch saw the entire significance of Kant's critical thought).

Again, Bloch's ambivalent position, so readily emphasized by Adorno, is present in critical theory as well. In 1964 Bloch and Adorno gave a joint television interview, which turned into a dialogue about utopia.[7] To a large extent this was a friendly gesture on Adorno's part and here his tone is nowhere near as peremptory and derisive as in private letters.[8] Adorno's remarks show how important the idea of utopia was for him; utopia, interpreted closely to the Blochian understanding. Adorno also deals with utopia as a kind of being-in-potential, and this possibility is total, but not in the sense of Hegelian totalization, but as a complete, all-encompassing transformation of the status quo. Adorno and Bloch agree that the utopian idea only makes sense if this change is radical.

One of the obvious forms of this radicality is the possibility of overcoming death. But Adorno stressed that a utopia that would simply depict a society of immortals would not be genuine. The essence of a utopian idea is in its paradox; it envisions the overcoming of death in the middle of death, from within the unbearable and compulsory situation of mortality. To overcome death is to overcome unfreedom. It is this overcoming that becomes the most eloquent example of that which Adorno and Horkheimer call 'the radical other'. But only because of this, the essence of this theory is the prohibition to *depict* the utopian, close to the Jewish taboo on depicting God and on uttering His name (Horkheimer 1970, p. 81).

Interestingly, Bloch had the same intention in *The Spirit of Utopia*, attaching the special role to music, which took over the role of divination and did not presuppose the objectified images, fraught with reification. Music becomes the utopian medium, impervious in the face of the alienated reality. The world's instability, the inability to articulate one's thoughts to the end, this critical pathos of suspicion, the 'something's missing' (the motif Bloch and Adorno cite from Brecht), brings us closer to music, in which there is this explicit moment of dynamic production (see an interesting analysis in Richter 2006). Something is amiss, and however close we are, we feel that our destination is far away. Is it not the same in any hermeneutic undertaking, in any translation from one language to another or of thought – to word? The utopian philosophy aspires to become commensurate to the dream-world, to erase the boundary between sleep and wakefulness, without falling completely asleep. We see dreams of revolution – dreams, in which everything is entangled, but it is good, for if it is entangled, then it is not the same, hence it can be *different*.

Adorno's utopia can only be negative – that is, as he says, even though we cannot depict it, just as we cannot know what is the right way, we still can be sure what we should fight against (TL, p. 362f.). And in the very insistence of this thought coming to us – that everything could have been different, that 'something is missing' – *in this very insistence there is already a moment of reality*. Were utopia completely impossible, the thought of it appears again and again. The situation of lack, the feeling that something is not right with the world is always around in Bloch's texts. We could recall his metaphysics of comedy, written as a critique of Lukács, where it is laughter that guides this feeling. It is no accident that this context reminds one of Schlegel's theory of romantic irony and of his notion of wit (*Witz*) – a 'fragmentary genius' (Schlegel 1993, p. 2) – that, just as Bloch's hope, grants ease and freedom without providing any warranties or obligations,[9] does not preach the past or foretell the predetermined future.

In his characteristic of Hegelian thought, Adorno asserts that 'the ray of light that reveals the whole to be untrue in all its moments is none other than utopia, the utopia of the whole truth, which is still to be realized' (1993, p. 88). This shining and vividness are necessary for the transformation of the world, and Bloch felt this need more than Adorno, not fearing the objectivation and reification of the utopian desire while feeling deeply, as Adorno did, the inner falsity of the world, in which nobody waits for anything anymore, in which everything is clear to everyone.

Philosophy, as Benjamin put it, continually searches for the adequate form of exposition. But what is it that the philosopher needs to express? And why is this search so persistent? In order to answer these questions one has to correlate the problematization of form with the compulsory, irreversible texture of historical time, which defines the possibilities of figurative expressivity, anticipating even the most unprecedented experiments. Thus poetics meets the philosophy of history and discerns a vague and shapeless figure approaching that emerges from the darkness. It finally stumbles upon the thought that it may be facing its own reflection.

Bloch was the one who deliberately set out to establish a tension between aesthetics and historical temporality by making the dark moments that prefigure the utopian the moments of aesthetic expression. As Voßkamp (1994, p. 301) notes, this tension that emerged due to reconfiguring the utopian moments in the moments of aesthetic contemplation enables the art of writing as such. I would add that it ultimately enables the working of history as well. It is salient in Bloch's elaboration of particular literary *forms* that, by themselves, were repositories of this historical energy.

For Adorno, Bloch was a master of the *essay*. In his 1965 article he compares Bloch to his teacher Simmel. The teacher was famous for his brief essayistic sketches, one of which – *The Handle* – has drawn Adorno's attention.[10] He contrasts Simmel's detached, aesthetical gaze with the energetic and impatient opening in *The Spirit of Utopia*, *An Old Pitcher*. Unlike Simmel, Bloch immediately closes the distance between the spectator and the artwork, trying to reveal in the unpretentious object that essential thing that he is searching for throughout his book – the identity, the intensity of the I. *The Spirit of Utopia*, comprising essays on art, architecture, music and concluding with an apocalyptic cadenza, was one of the books that inspired Adorno to reveal the meaning of a *form* he himself tried to follow and in which he sought the very historical language which it seeks to redeem – *the form of the essay*.

Adorno (1991) characterized the essay as a genre, which resists the work ethic of the philistine intellectual trade, as an exemplary form, into which *critique* can become invested. An essayist does not seek to create a coherent structure of thought, he is relieved from the burden of exhaustive expression, from having to follow the once-and-for-all specified definitions, from the ennui of completeness, which neither he nor his reader need.[11] An essayist plays, he writes on different occasions, without an ambition to create a system. He is radical in refusing to go to the end. He does not divide the world into the eternal and the transient. He is carefree and does not trouble to safeguard himself against mistakes beforehand, by enamouring himself into the shell of precise descriptions and orderly conclusions. As Adorno puts it, coordination of concepts replaces their subordination. And the essential – *the experience* – acquires a characteristic universality due to its *historical embeddedness*. This experience is completely alien to the deductive constructions and pettiness of an analyst, who approaches history with gloves on, scrupulously separating the abstract from the concrete, who sees his goal in closing the system, by eliminating contradictions to calm his impoverished mind and to praise the common sense. An essayist treats concepts as he treats the objects of everyday life; he perceives them as engulfed in the life of the language, he takes them up and responds to their life.

> The specific moments are not to be simply derived from the whole, nor vice versa. The whole is a monad, and yet it is not; its moments, which as moments are conceptual in nature, point beyond the specific object in which they are assembled. But the essay does not pursue them to the point where they would legitimate themselves outside the specific object; if it did so, it would end up in an infinity of

the wrong kind. Instead, it moves in so close to the *hic et nunc* of the object that the object becomes dissociated into the moments in which it has its life instead of being a mere object (Adorno 1991, p. 14).

But this response should be appropriate as well, it needs to strike the right note. And in order to do this the essayist has to be ready to see his words fly away, as wind or music, with the flow of time. History, which did not originate in him, but in which he partakes, will carry him, and the essay itself will become a part of this movement.

In Adorno's phrases and in the gestures of his thought one can recognize a reader of Bloch. For instance, he criticizes 'the technisation' of art, the primacy of the constructive over the expressive. But it is precisely this opposition that became decisive in Bloch's *Production of Ornament* written under the influence of Wilhelm Worringer. Bloch affirmed a new decorativeness, glorified the transcendent aspiration of Gothic architecture and declared war against the 'cold' constructivism embodied in the callous exterior of Egyptian pyramids, which symbolized the unbearable nature of the mundane, a stasis disguised as order. Bloch's ornamental images form a carpet (*Teppich*) – the concept used by the untimely deceased Leo Popper, an art critic and a friend of Lukács (who dedicated to Popper the first essay of *The Soul and Form*). In Adorno the moments of the essay are also intertwined like in a carpet, while his method reveals 'a utopian intention' (Adorno 1991, p. 13). An essayist 'thinks in fragments, just as reality is fragmentary, and finds its unity in and through the breaks and not by glossing them over' (p. 16). We have before us the key element of Bloch's philosophy: the immanence of the utopian that prevents its witnesses from writing otherwise. These incompletenesses attract one another through a symbolic and a metonymic relation. If the world has no boundaries, why should I set one for myself and for my thought? Adorno inherits from Bloch this heretical question.

Taking stock we have to come back to another question Adorno posed, now directed at anyone who attempts to understand Bloch: can we separate the later system from early expression, the doctrine of categories in *Experimentum Mundi* from the literary figurations of *Traces*? Does Bloch not turn the expressionist 'cry' into a system of concepts, does he not transfigure the experience of darkness and the search for the self into something entirely different, putting it into the fetters of ontological schemes? Is such transformation possible at all, does it not *betray* the initial utopian experience? Finally, how can this experience be grasped? Does it pertain to the 'radical other' or, as Bloch claims, to something that is closest to us (PH, p. 1417)?

Eberhard Simons argued that Bloch's solution is a montage, joining the systematic and the expressive elements, whereas no explanation as to whether it is successful or not is ever given. And an explanation cannot be given, it should be said, for such evaluations are essentially aesthetic judgements of taste and can only be made *a posteriori*. Simons believes that in the end Adorno was right, and the system, instead of 'protecting' the sensitive and fragile expressive-prophetic experience from misunderstandings and distortions (Simons 1983), totalizes and betrays it.

In this Adornian criticism, not even on behalf of negative dialectics, but proceeding from the internal requirements of the utopian project, as though appealing to the critical conscience of the 'philosopher of hope', lies the main lesson of their polemic, which does not by any means abolish their internal affinity.

What unites Adorno and Bloch is what reconciles utopian and critical thinking. This is the reason why Bloch is so vigilant against the dangers of reification and ossification of images reflecting the future. The rejection of utopia or its instrumentalization leads to totalitarianism – we either completely banish visions of otherness from our lives or replace them with a discussion of purely technical issues and the utopia becomes 'blurred', turning into a dictatorship and the suppression of the individual.

Adorno's favourable remarks include everything that was said at the end of the previous chapter: Bloch authored subtle philosophical prose, and the stories that he narrated *are* his philosophy (Mayer 1965, p. 25). Certainly, it would be historically accurate to say that having created a 'system', Bloch became a hostage of his own concepts, forced to defend and clarify them until their philosophical significance and their revolutionary potential would be exhausted.

However, it may just be that the banal instrumentalism of the later ontological constructions, the searching for the 'Not-yet' in any given being, the transformation of any artistic or intellectual expression into a sign of the utopian truth – all of these are no more than symbols which had to be overcome within utopian philosophy itself, preliminary stops, on which one catches one's breath. For it is infinitely hard to balance between the fetishization of the utopian ideal and the swampy 'reality' (where we seem to stand 'on solid ground'). And it is on this brink that our hero attempts to walk, when he problematizes the basis of his own thinking, when, diffusing cultural forms boldly, he finds in the artistic and the social experience that vanishing remnant of the utopian, which is orthogonal to the system of ordinary things and teaches one to live in the world that fell to the lot of German intellectuals after the war.

Notes

1. Kracauer's letter to Adorno, from 1 April 1964 in *Theodor W. Adorno — Siegfried Kracauer. Briefwechsel 1923–1966* (Fr.a.M.: Suhrkamp, 2008), p. 658f. cited in Schopf 2009, p. 129.
2. See Bloch's letter of congratulation on the occasion of Adorno's 60th anniversary (Br II, p. 450f.).
3. Münster refers to the first page of *Negative Dialectics* where Adorno writes that *praxis* has turned into a way of 'strangulating' critical thought.
4. See historical criticism of Adorno, based on Bloch's texts from the 1920s to the 1930s in Ujma 1995, p. 95.
5. See the main passages from Adorno's letter in Schopf 2009, pp. 111–12.
6. For instance in musical aesthetics and, in particular, in the appraisal of Wagner. See Münster 1982, pp. 170–80; Lilienfeld 1987.
7. 'Etwas fehlt. . . . Uber die Widerspruche der utopischen Sehnsucht' in TL, pp. 350–68.
8. A commentator writes that during the interview Adorno clearly tried to smooth out the contradictions (David 2008, p. 57). This can also be heard in the recording available on the internet.
9. It is worth reminding that danger belongs to the very essence of hope, for it can always be mistaken and disappointed.

10 Implied is a handle of a jug or a vase as an intermediate stage between the self-sufficient, completed in itself reality of the artwork and the bustling outwards-directed reality external to it. See Simmel 1919.
11 Bloch also described a similar feeling as a *melancholy of fulfilled desires* (in PH, p. 348ff.; PHE, p. 295ff.).

Conclusion: Drawing the Utopian Line

Perhaps the best example of thinking that debunks Bloch's utopian philosophy was given by Franz Kafka in his sketch *The City Coat of Arms*, a story about the construction of the Tower of Babel. Justifying that 'one simply could not build too slowly', the dwellers of the city of builders, occupied with ideological constructions, reasoned as follows:

> The essential thing in the whole business is the idea of building a tower that will reach to heaven. In comparison with that idea everything else is secondary. The idea, once seized in its magnitude, can never vanish again; so long as there are men on the earth there will be also the irresistible desire to complete the building.

This insane utopian goal, necessary to bind humanity together and elevate it to the sky, towards which all of its thoughts should be directed, was deemed nonsense by later generations, but they could not leave the city anymore. The higher aim was replaced by the intermediary and the construction remained incomplete – they simply did not get around to it.

The story of the tower is remarkable, not only in that it shows how easily the utopia can become impoverished, ossified, meaningless, how quickly people fall into the trap of a big idea. Something else is also important: in Kafka's story, the builders, be it secretly or openly, desire to break free of this trap. They await *the apocalypse*, the day, 'when the city would be destroyed by five successive blows from a gigantic fist. It is for that reason too that the city has a closed fist on its coat of arms' (trans. W. and E. Muir). In some sense Bloch chose an opposite, but parallel path – from the anticipation, even invocation of the apocalypse and from the dreary hopelessness of the mundane world – to the utopia that at no place and at no time can be fully realized, but cherishes the hope that Kafka's heroes have long lost.

Following the traces that Bloch left in the history of thought, we certainly learnt a lot. In his polemic with Lukács he instituted the communicative space between avant-garde art and Marxist criticism. Under the influence of *The Theory of the Novel* he searched for the descriptive languages of the philosophy that would recognize itself in literature. Bloch's early thinking became the touchstone on which the Judaic messianism tried itself in all of its tensions between the new trembling and the awkward monumentality of its own ambition, between the search for spiritual freedom and the thousands and thousands, who did not even have time to realize why and to what end they were crushed by history. This messianism is revealed to us not only in the apocalyptic passages of *The Spirit of Utopia* or *The Theological-Political Fragment*; the messianic rhythm guides the heroes of tragedy, of the novel, of the baroque 'tragic drama', the genres refer to history in a messianic way.

We have to ask what, in our times, can grow out of Bloch's heritage with its obsessive notion that all dreams will someday come true, with his strange optimism and his sermon of humanistic values on behalf of Marx? Can the philosophy of utopia today, when the apocalyptic consciousness asserts itself with renewed force, become for us a suitable descriptive language and a stylistic reference point?

The important philosophical lesson that is infinitely repeated in Bloch is that *there is no absolute instance that can judge utopian thought*, that the rational sobriety, attempting to denounce the utopia as 'castles in the sky' or Aristophanes's 'clouds', itself becomes helpless facing the instability of the world that we inhabit. The completeness of forms, the precision of concepts and definitions can not only mark perfect beauty or progressive science, but also can be characteristics of the dogmatic, authoritarian consciousness. Bloch managed to articulate this thought with utmost determination in the language of his age, and it – consciously or not – became the guiding stone not only for contemporary art, in which the search for and the very possibility of the form is constantly questioned or even abandoned, but also for the many currents of contemporary philosophy. And here Benjamin's experience proved decisive.

Certainly, it was Bloch who became one of the first in the twentieth century for whom Marxism and theology could be freely combined in one conceptual context. But with the appearance of Benjamin's works, Bloch's style also changed – from apocalyptic mysticism he went to the mysticism of the secular and together with Benjamin he began to testify to the world in which the immanence of meaning has passed away forever (PH, p. 354), leaving only the remnants of utopia. Benjamin, apparently, revealed to Bloch the inexhaustibility of these traces. The lightning on the stormy sky of history can, of course, for a brief moment, illuminate the dark landscape of truth, but this experience cannot be repeated at will, and the next day nothing will be left of this landscape. The reverse side of such a paradox, inherent in the utopian project, turns out to be precisely the fibrillation of the vague, opaque instant; the fundamental perplexity in the face of the experience of time and the search for solutions, which could help mark our way in this time.

In Bloch's philosophy, utopia was, undoubtedly, a living medium, located at the very centre of history. This had an impact on aesthetics as well: supporting Expressionism, Bloch critiqued the idea of the autonomous, 'pure' art, free of politics and not interacting with the historical situation in any way. The fulfilment of oneself, of which he constantly and on different levels speaks in his work, is also historical. This historicity was for him closely linked with the notion of praxis, 'saving' utopia and simultaneously threatening to shatter its already fragile foundations – for despite the fact that for Bloch the utopia was never reducible to the social technology of attaining a better future (Ueding 2009, p. 58), the temptation to think of it as of a 'project' in the traditional sense remained. And the 'inflation' of the utopian idea (Schmidt 1985, p. 102) in the demand for constant innovation still remains a danger. I mean the everyday intensity of actuality, the notorious 'openness to change', from which there is only one step to cynicism and indifference to the present situation, fraught with the obliviousness and shallowness that belong to the 'age of the feuilleton'.

We saw that Bloch's philosophical and political ideas are no less vulnerable than a banal, abstract utopia. Bloch did not want to fetishize the utopian element, maintaining that it is precisely what allows us to partake in the present (PH, p. 366f.), and insisting that the deep and the desired social transformations always require daydreaming. Nonetheless, he himself, apart from the penetrating characterizations of his own time, often demonstrated, like many of his contemporaries, an inexcusable political short-sightedness. When the mass repressions began in the USSR in 1937, he deliberately refused to condemn them referring sometimes to the lack of information, sometimes to the legitimacy of harsh measures in the face of possible civil war, which would weaken the only significant ally of European communists and anti-fascists. It turns out that even the dreams of a metaphysician could be wicked, and the aspirations – monstrous.

However, this does not mean that utopia today is only remembered as a horrible dream, or an object of ridicule. Is it not the case that the leftist, the communist ideals were expelled from everywhere at the turn of the twentieth century? Can one not consider the history of communist movements throughout the world as the history of mistakes and failures, the history of the defeated, of those whose heritage Walter Benjamin called to preserve?

I tried to show that Bloch's ideal is by no means a helpless humanism, behind which lies a desire to embrace the drowsy mediocrity of a philistine, and his dull, insipid, long completed world together with it. Bloch's humanism is the realization of the mystery that was revealed to him in the new art, and the urge to clarify this mystery of humaneness and morality which unwittingly corresponds to Benjamin's definition of politics as 'the fulfillment of an unintensified humanity' (GS VI, p. 99).

The countless paradoxes comprise the formula of this nomadic philosophizing, for Bloch not only illuminates, but also *poeticises* his political situation. His utopia is as distant and unattainable as it is attractive, as a beautiful work of art. Bloch is a writer, whose philosophy demonstrates that an artistic effort is at times indistinguishable from the effort of thought and that the rigour of the artistic gesture, the indisputable aesthetic persuasiveness is not inferior to the traditional logic of philosophical argumentation. Much depends on whether we shall find the right interpretation for this gesture, on whether we shall hear the sound of utopia barely discernible in the roar of the universe – whether we shall sense when it is due, *when the time is right*.

Bibliography

Bloch's work is cited following the standard German edition of his collected works and using the abbreviations given after each volume. When quoting, I tried to use existing English translations also listed below. Although it is now common in Bloch scholarship to prefer the original editions of many texts to the more balanced and careful presentations in the last edition, I do not follow this practice (that otherwise I could only welcome) since I am not really concerned here with the evolution of Bloch's philosophy. Nevertheless I did try, where necessary, to refer to the texts and secondary sources documenting the shifts of Bloch's metaphysical and political positions. The years indicated refer to the appearance of the first edition and, in the case of some volumes, to the first republication within the corpus of the *Collected works*. The pagination of the subsequent re-editions of the volumes has not changed.

Gesamtausgabe in 16 Bänden + 1 Ergänzungsband, Frankfurt am Main: Suhrkamp, 1959–1978.
Vol. 1. *Spuren* (1930, 1969) (S)
Vol. 2. *Thomas Münzer als Theologe der Revolution* (1921, 1969) (TM)
Vol. 3. *Geist der Utopie. Zweite Fassung* (1923, 1964) (GU2)
Vol. 4. *Erbschaft dieser Zeit* (1935, 1962) (EZ)
Vol. 5. *Das Prinzip Hoffnung* (written 1937–1948, 1959) (PH)
Vol. 6. *Naturrecht und menschliche Würde* (1961) (NW)
Vol. 7. *Das Materialismusproblem, seine Geschichte und Substanz* (written 1936–1937, 1972) (M)
Vol. 8. *Subjekt-Objekt. Erläuterungen zu Hegel* (1951, 1962) (SO)
Vol. 9. *Literarische Aufsätze* (1965) (LA)
Vol. 10. *Philosophische Aufsätze zur objektiven Phantasie* (1969) (PA)
Vol. 11. *Politische Messungen, Pestzeit, Vormärz* (1970) (PM)
Vol. 12. *Zwischenwelten in der Philosophiegeschichte* (1977) (ZP)
Vol. 13. *Tübinger Einleitung in die Philosophie* (1963/64, new, enlarged edition 1970) (TE)
Vol. 14. *Atheismus im Christentum. Zur Religion des Exodus und des Reichs* (1968) (AC)
Vol. 15. *Experimentum Mundi. Frage, Kategorien des Herausbringens, Praxis* (1975) (EM)
Vol. 16. *Geist der Utopie. Erste Fassung* (1918, 1971) (GU1)
Supplementary volume: *Tendenz – Latenz – Utopie* (1978) (TL)
Briefe 1903–1975. Bände I–II, Karola Bloch et al. (eds), Frankfurt am Main: Suhrkamp, 1985 (quoted as Br, with the indication of the volume).
Kritische Erörterungen über Rickert und das Problem der modernen Erkenntnistheorie: Inauguraldiss. der Universität Würzburg. Lüdwigshafen, 1909.

'Das Faustmotiv der Phänomenologie des Geistes'. *Hegel-Studien* (1961), 1, 155–71
Durch die Wüste. Frühe kritische Aufsätze. Frankfurt am Main: Suhrkamp, 1964 (DW).
Vom Hasard zur Katastrophe. Politische Aufsätze 1934–1939. Frankfurt am Main: Suhrkamp, 1972.
Gespräche mit Ernst Bloch. Edited by R. Traub and H. Wieser. Frankfurt am Main: Suhrkamp, 1975 (Gespräche).
'Talking with Ernst Bloch: Korcula, 1968', in *Telos* 25, pp. 165–85. (Landmann 1975).
Tagträume vom aufrechten Gang. Sechs Interviews mit Ernst Bloch. Edited by A. Münster. Frankfurt am Main: Suhrkamp, 1977 (Tagträume).
'Interview with Ernst Bloch (Michael Löwy, trans. Vicki Williams Hill)'. *New German Critique* 9 (Fall 1976): 35–45 (Interview).
The Principle of Hope. Vol. I-III. Trans. by Neville Plaice, Stephen Plaice and Paul Knight. Cambridge, MA: MIT Press, 1986 (PHE).
The Utopian Functon of Art and Literature. Trans. by Jack Zipes and Frank Mecklenburg. Cambridge, MA: MIT Press, 1988.
Heritage of Our Times. Trans. by Neville and Stephen Plaice. Cambridge: Polity Press, 1991 (HT).
Literary Essays. Trans. by Andrew Joron, Jack Zipes, Frank Mecklenburg, and Helga Wild. Stanford: Stanford University Press, 1998 (LE).
The Spirit of Utopia. Trans. by Anthony A. Nassar. Stanford: Stanford University Press, 2000 (SU).
Logos der Materie. Eine Logik im Werden. Aus dem Nachlas 1923–1949, Edited by G. Cunico. Frankfurt am Main: Suhrkamp, 2000 (Logos der Materie).
Traces. Trans. by Anthony A. Nassar. Stanford: Stanford University Press, 2006 (T).

In citing the work of Walter Benjamin I also followed the standard German edition and, when it was accessible and seemed adequate, used the existing English translations.

Gesammelte Schriften. Bd. I–VII. Unter Mitwirkung von T. W. Adorno und G. Scholem hrsg. von R. Tiedemann und H. Schweppenhäuser. Frankfurt am Main: Suhrkamp, 1972–89 (cited as GS with the Roman number of volume and, if applicable, with the Arabic number of the half-volume).
The Correspondence of Walter Benjamin. Trans. by Manfred R. Jacobson, Evelyn M. Jacobson, and Gary Smith. Chicago and London: University of Chicago Press, 1994 (CWB).
One-Way Street and Other Writings. London: New Left Books, 1979 (OWS).
The Arcades Project. Trans. by Howard Eiland and Kevin McLaughlin. Cambridge, MA and London: The Belknap Press of Harvard University Press, 1999 (AP).
Origin of the German Tragic Drama. Trans. by John Osborne. London, New York: Verso, 2003 (OD).
Illuminations. Essays and Reflections. Trans. by Harry Zohn. New York: Schocken Books, 2007 (IER).

The three major works of Lukács dealt with are also abbreviated as follows:

Soul and Form. Trans. by Anna Bostock. Cambridge, MA: MIT Press, 1974 (SF).
The Theory of the Novel. Trans. by Anna Bostock. London: Merlin, 1971 (TN).
History and Class Consciousness. Trans. by Rodney Livingstone. Cambridge, MA: MIT Press, 1971 (HCC).

Adorno, T. W. (1966), *Negative Dialektik*. Frankfurt am Main: Suhrkamp.
—(1991), *Notes to Literature*, vol. 1. New York: Columbia University Press.
—(1992), *Notes to Literature*, vol. 2. New York: Columbia University Press.
— (1993), *Hegel. Three Studies*, Cambridge, MA, London: MIT Press.
—(2002), *Aesthetic Theory*, trans. R. Hullot-Kentor. London, New York: Continuum.
Agamben, G. (1993), *The Coming Community*. Minneapolis: University of Minnesota Press.
—(2005), *The Time that Remains*. Stanford: Stanford University Press.
Arndt, A. (2012), 'Geschichte(n) mit Paulus. Römerbrief und Geschichtsdenken von Schelling bis Agamben', in C. Breytenbach (ed.), *Der Römerbrief als Vermächtnis an die Kirche. Rezeptionsgeschichten aus zwei Jahrtausenden*. Neukirchen-Vluyn: Neukirchener Theologie, pp. 227–36.
Auerbach, E. (2003), *Mimesis: The Representation of Reality in Western Literature*, trans. Willard Trask. Princeton: Princeton University Press.
Badiou, A. (1999), *Manifesto for Philosophy*. Albany, N.Y.: State University of New York Press.
Bahr, E. (1974), *Ernst Bloch*. Berlin: Colloquium Verlag.
Bahr, H. D. (1978), 'Ontologie und Utopie', in B. Schmidt (ed.), *Materialien zu Ernst Blochs 'Prinzip Hoffnung'*. Frankfurt am Main: Suhrkamp.
Bakhtin, M. M. (1990), *Art and Answerability: Early Philosophical Essays*. Edited by M. Holquist and V. Liapunov, trans. Vadim Liapunov and Kenneth Brostrom. Austin: University of Texas Press.
Bartsch, G. (1969), 'Bloch und Lukács'. *Geist und Tat*, 3, 142–7.
Bataille, G. (1985), 'The Psychological Structure of Fascism', in A. Stoekl (ed.), *Visions of Excess: Selected Writings 1927–1939*. Minneapolis: University of Minnesota Press, pp. 137–60.
Baudelaire, Ch. (1955), *The Mirror of Art: Critical Studies*, trans. Jonathan Mayne. New York: Phaidon.
Becker, R. (2003), *Sinn und Zeitlichkeit. Vergleichende Studien zum Problem der Konstitution von Sinn durch die Zeit bei Husserl, Heidegger und Bloch*. Würzburg: Königshausen & Neumann.
Bely, A. (1994), 'Krisis soznanija i Henrik Ibsen', in L. A. Sugaj (ed.) Bely, A., *Simvolizm kak miroponimanie* ['The Crisis of Consciousness and Henrik Ibsen', in *Symbolism as a World-View*] Moscow: Respublika.
Benjamin, W. (1997), *Briefe*. Bd. 3. Edited by Ch. Gödde and H. Lonitz. Frankfurt am Main: Suhrkamp.
Benseler, F. (2002), 'Freundschaft in der Pestzeit. Ernst Bloch und Georg Lukács'. *Sinn und Form*, 54(4), 485–98.
Berdyaev, N. A. (1995), 'Opyt eshatologicheskoj metafisiki', in P. V. Alexeev (ed.) Berdyaev, N. A., *Tsarstwo Duha i tsarstwo kesarja* ['An Essay in Eschatological Metaphysics', in *The Kingdom of God and the Kingdom of Caesar*]. Moscow: Respublika.
Berghahn, K. (1985), 'L'art pour l'espoir. Literatur als ästhetische Utopie bei Ernst Bloch', in K. L. Arnold (ed.), *Ernst Bloch. Sonderband Text + Kritik*. München: Edition Text+Kritik, pp. 5–20.
Bergmann, H. (1913), 'Die Heiligung des Namens (KIDDUSCH HASCHEM)', in *Vom Judentum. Ein Sammelbuch,* hg. vom Verein jüdischer Hochschüler Bar Kochba in Prag. Leipzig: Kurt Wolff, pp. 32–43.
Bianchi, U. (ed.) (1970), *The Origins of Gnosticism/Le Origini dello Gnosticismo*. Leiden: Brill.

Blechman, M. (2008), '"Not yet". Adorno and the utopia of consciousness', *Cultural Critique*, 70 (Fall), 177-98.
Blumentritt, M. (1999), 'Das Dunkel des gelebten Augenblicks und das präreflexive Cogito', in R. E. Zimmermann and K.-J. Grün (eds), *Existenz & Utopie*. Cuxhaven&Dartford: Junghans, pp. 23-38.
Böhme, H. (1988), 'Vergangenheit und Gegenwart der Apokalypse', in *Natur und Subjekt*. Frankfurt am Main: Suhrkamp.
Böhme, J. (1842), 'Von der Gnadenwahl, 1623', in K. W. Schiebler (ed.), *Jakob Böhme's sämmtl. Werke*. Bd. 4. Leipzig: Barth.
Bolz, N. (1984), 'Erlösung als ob. Über einige gnostische Motive der Kritischen Theorie', in J. Taubes (ed.), *Religionstheorie und Politische Theologie. Bd. II: Gnosis und Politik*. Paderborn etc.: Schöningh, pp. 264-89.
—(1985), 'Der Geist der Kapitalismus und die Utopie', in M. Löwy, A. Münster, N. Tertullian (eds), *Verdinglichung und Utopie. Ernst Bloch und Georg Lukács*. Frankfurt am Main: Sendler, pp. 48-59.
—(1987), 'Mystische Theokratie', in J. Taubes (ed.), *Theokratie* (Religionstheorie und Politische Theologie, 3). München u.a.: Fink, Schöningh, pp. 293-320.
—(1997), 'Das Gottesexperiment', in J. R. Bloch (ed.), *'Ich bin. Aber ich habe mich nicht. Darum werden wir erst'. - Perspektiven der Philosophie Ernst Blochs*. Frankfurt am Main: Suhrkamp, pp. 36-50.
Bouretz, P. (2010), *Witnesses for the Future. Philosophy and Messianism*. Baltimore: Johns Hopkins University Press.
Brecht, B. (1992), 'Kehren wir zu den Kriminalromanen zurück!', in W. Hecht (ed.), *Große kommentierte Berliner und Frankfurter Ausgabe*. Bd. 21. Frankfurt am Main: Suhrkamp, pp. 128-32.
Buber, M. (1916), *Vom Geist des Judentums. Reden und Geleitworte*. München, Leipzig: Kurt Wolff.
—(1963), *Der Jude und sein Judentum*. Köln: Melzer.
—(1966), *Moses*. Heidelberg: Lambert Schneider.
Bulgakov, S. (1993), 'Apokaliptika i socialism,' in *Sochineniia v 2 tt*. T. 2 ['Apocalyptics and Socialism', in *Collected works in 2 volumes*. Vol. 2]. Moscow: Nauka.
Christen, A. (1979), *Ernst Blochs Metaphysik der Materie*. Bonn: Bouvier.
Claussen, D. (2008), *Adorno. One Last Genius*, trans. R. Livingstone. Cambridge, MA, and London: The Belknap Press of Harvard University Press.
Czajka, A. (2003), 'Das "Gespräch" der Religionen und der Messianismus. Margerete Susman und Ernst Bloch'. *VorSchein. Jahrbuch der Ernst-Bloch-Assoziation*, 22/23, 98-116.
—(2006), *Poetik und Ästhetik des Augenblicks. Studien zu einer neuen Literaturauffassung auf der Grundlage von Ernst Blochs literarischem und literarästhetischem Werk*. Berlin: Duncker&Humblot.
David, C. (2008), 'Adorno et la conception blochienne de l'utopie'. *Europe*, Mai, 55-64.
Denecke, A. (1993), 'Jüdisch-marxistischer Messianismus bei Ernst Bloch und der christliche Messiasglaube'. *Bloch-Almanach*, 13, 61-76.
Derrida, J. (1981), *Positions*, trans. Alan Bass. Chicago: University of Chicago Press.
—(1999), Marx&Sons, in M. Sprinker (ed.), *Ghostly Demarkations. A Symposium on Jacques Derrida's Spectres of Marx*. London: Verso, pp. 223-69.
Deuber-Mankowsky, A. (2002), 'Walter Benjamin's *Theological-Political Fragment* as a response to Ernst Bloch's *Spirit of Utopia*'. *Leo Baeck Institute Yearbook*, 47(1), 3-20.
Dietschy, B. (1988), *Gebrochene Gegenwart. Ernst Bloch, Ungleichzeitigkeit und das Geschichtsbild der Moderne*. Frankfurt am Main: Vervuert.

Dietschy, B., Zeilinger, D., and Zimmermann, R. E. (eds) (2012), *Bloch Wörterbuch. Leitbegriffe der Philosophie Ernst Blochs*. Berlin, Boston: De Gruyter.
Dilthey, W. (1992), *Gesammelte Schriften. Bd. 7. Der Aufbau der Geschichtlichen Welt in den Geisteswissenschaften*. Göttingen: Vandenhoeck&Ruprecht.
Dmitriev, A. (2004), *Marksizm bez proletariata: Georg Lukács i ranniaia Frankfurtskaia shkola, 1920—1930-e gg*. [Marxism without Proletariat: Georg Lukács and the Early Frankfurt School in 1920–1930s.] Saint-Petersburg and Moscow: European University of Saint-Petersburg Press; Letniy Sad.
Dobbins, J. and Fuss, P. (1982), 'The silhouette of Dante in Hegel's *Phenomenology of Spirit*'. *Clio*, 11(4), 387–413.
Dostoyevsky, F. M. (1974), *Polnoe Sobranie Sochinenii v 30 tt., t. 11* [Collected Works in 30 Vols., vol. 11]. Leningrad: Nauka.
Dubbels, E. (2011), *Figuren des Messianischen in Schriften deutsch-jüdischer Intellektueller*. Berlin, Boston: Walter de Gruyter.
Eidam, H. (1992), *Strumpf und Handschuh. Der Begriff der nichtexistenten und die Gestalt der unkonstruierbaren Frage. Walter Benjamins Verhältnis zum 'Geist der Utopie' Ernst Blochs*. Würzburg: Königshausen & Neumann.
Eisenstein, S. (1998), *Montage* [in Russian]. Moscow: VGIK.
Eßbach, W. (1994), 'Radikalismus und Modernität bei Jünger und Bloch, Lukács und Schmitt', in M. Gangl and G. Raulet (eds), *Intellektuellendiskurse der Weimarer Republik. Zur politischen Kultur einer Gemengelage*. Frankfurt am Main: Campus, pp. 145–59.
Faber, R. (2006), *Politische Dämonologie: über modernen Marcionismus*. Würzburg: Königshausen & Neumann.
Fahrenbach, H. (1986), 'Marxismus und Existentialismus – im Bezugsfeld zwischen Lukács, Sartre und Bloch', in G. Flego and W. Schmied-Kowarzik (eds), *Ernst Bloch – Utopische Ontologie. Bd. II des Bloch-Lukács-Symposiums 1985 in Dubrovnik*. Bochum: Germinal Verlag, pp. 45–69.
Falke, G.-H. H. (1996), *Begriffne Geschichte. Das historische Substrat und die systematische Anordnung der Bewußtseinsgestalten in Hegels Phänomenologie des Geistes. Interpretation und Kommentar*. Berlin: Lukas.
Fehér, F. (1980), 'The pan-tragic vision: the metaphysics of tragedy'. *New Literary History*, 11(2), 245–54.
—(1985a), 'Lukács and Benjamin: parallels and contrasts'. *New German Critique*, 34(Winter), 125–38.
—(1985b), 'Lukács, Benjamin, theatre'. *Theatre Journal*, 37(4), 415–25.
Franz, T. (1985), 'Philosophie als revolutionäre Praxis', in K. L. Arnold (ed.), *Ernst Bloch. Sonderband Text + Kritik*. München: Edition Text+Kritik, pp. 239–73.
Garcia Marquez, G. (1970), *The One Hundred Years of Solitude*, trans. G. Rabassa. New York: Harper & Row.
Gekle, H. (1986), *Wunsch und Wirklichkeit. Blochs Philosophie des Noch-Nicht-Bewußten und Freuds Theorie des Unbewußten*. Frankfurt am Main: Suhrkamp.
Geoghegan, V. (1996), *Ernst Bloch*. London: Routledge.
Gethmann-Siefert, A. and Stemmrich-Köhler, B. (1983), 'Faust: die "absolute philosophische Tragödie" – und die "gesellschaftliche Andersartigkeit" des West-östlichen Divan. Zu Editionsproblemen der Ästhetikvorlesungen'. *Hegel-Studien*, 18, 23–64.
Gluck, M. (1985), *Georg Lukács and His Generation*. Cambridge, MA and London: Harvard University Press.
Goethe, J. W. (1864), *The Auto-Biography of Goethe. Truth And Poetry: From My Own Life*. Trans. John Oxenford, Esq. London: Bell&Daldy.

Goldmann, L. (1973), *Lukács et Heidegger*. Paris: Denoël-Gonthier.
Göschel, K. F. (1832), *Hegel und seine Zeit, mit Rücksicht auf Goethe*. Berlin: Duncker & Humblot.
Habermas, J. (1971), 'Ernst Bloch, ein marxistischer Schelling', in J. Habermas (ed.), *Philosophisch-politische Profile*. Frankfurt am Main: Suhrkamp, pp. 141–67.
Hamacher, W. (2006), 'Das Theologisch-politische Fragment', in B. Lindner (ed.), *Benjamin-Handbuch*. Stuttgart, Weimar: Metzler, pp. 175–93.
Hanegraaf, W. J. (ed.) (2006), *Dictionary of Gnosis and Western Esotericism*. Amsterdam: Brill.
Hansen, B. (ed.) (2006), *Walter Benjamin and The Arcades Project*. London, New York: Continuum.
Harnack A. (1921), *Marcion: Das Evangelium vom fremden Gott*. Leipzig: J.C. Hinrichs.
Harth, D. (1985), 'Gesellschaftsdämmerung in Heidelberg. Zur Kritik der Moderne in Lukács' und Blochs Frühschriften', in K. Buselmeier, D. Harth, C. Jansen (eds), *Auch eine Geschichte der Universität Heidelberg*. Mannheim: Edition Quadrat, pp. 251–69.
—(1986), 'Georg Lukács in Heidelberg 1912–1918'. *Heidelberger Universitätshefte*, 38(74), 130–3.
Hegel, G. W. F. (1968), *Gesammelte Werke. Bd. 4*. Hamburg: Meiner.
—(1969), Johannes Hoffmeister (ed.), *Briefe von und an Hegel*, Bd. 2: 1813 bis 1822. Hamburg: Meiner.
—(1975), *Aesthetics. Lectures on Fine Art*, trans. T. M. Knox, Vols. I–II. Oxford: Oxford University Press for Clarendon Press.
—(1984), *The Letters*, trans. Clark Butler and Christiane Seiler. Bloomington: Indiana University Press.
—(1991), *Elements of the Philosophy of Right*. Edited by Allen W. Wood, trans. H. B. Nisbet. Cambridge: Cambridge University Press.
—(2010), *The Science of Logic*, trans. G. di Giovanni. Cambridge: Cambridge University Press.
Heidegger, M. (1962), *Being and Time*. Oxford: Blackwell.
—(1977), *Hegels Begriff der Erfahrung. Gesamtausgabe. Abt. I. Bd. 5. Holzwege*. Frankfurt am Main: Klostermann.
—(1998), 'A Letter on "Humanism"', in W. McNeil (ed.), *Pathmarks*. Cambridge: Cambridge University Press.
Hofmannsthal, H. v. (2008), *The Whole Difference: Selected Writings of Hugo von Hofmannsthal*. Edited by J. D. McClatchy. Princeton: Princeton University Press.
Holz, H. H. (1968), 'Prismatisches Denken', in *Über Walter Benjamin*. Frankfurt am Main: Suhrkamp, pp. 62–110.
—(1975), *Logos spermatikos. Ernst Blochs Philosophie der unfertigen Welt*. Darmstadt, Neuwied: Luchterhand.
Honneger, R. (1925), 'Goethe und Hegel'. *Jahrbuch der Goethe-Gesellschaft*, 11, 38–111.
Hörisch, J. (1982), 'Objektive Interpretation des schönen Scheins', in N. Bolz, R. Faber (eds), *Profane Erleuchtung und rettende Kritik*. Würzburg: Königshausen & Neumann, pp. 37–55.
Horkheimer, M. (1970), 'Was wir Sinn nennen wird verschwinden'. *Der Spiegel*. 1–2, 79–84.
Horster, D. (1987), *Ernst Bloch. Eine Einführung*. Wiesbaden: Panorama.
Jacobson, E. (2003), *Metaphysics of the Profane. The Political Theology of Walter Benjamin and Gershom Scholem*. New York: Columbia University Press.
—(2009), 'Locating the Messianic: In Search of Causation and Benjamin's Last Message'. *Journal for Cultural Research*, 13(3), 207–23.

Jameson, F. (1971), *Marxism and Form: 20th Century Dialectical Theories of Literature.* Princeton: Princeton University Press.

Jay, M. (1984), *Marxism and Totality: The Adventures of a Concept from Lukács to Habermas.* Berkeley, Los Angeles: University of California Press.

—(1986), 'Lukács, Bloch et la lutte pour un concept marxiste de totalité', in P. Furlan, M. Löwy, A. Münster, N. Tertulian (eds), *Réification et utopie. Ernst Bloch et György Lukács. Un siècle après.* Arles: Actes Sud, pp. 59–68.

Jimenez, M. (1983), *Vers une esthétique négative. Adorno et la modernité.* Paris: Klincksieck.

Jonas, H. (1975), 'Typologische und historische Abgrenzung des Phänomens der Gnosis', in K. Rudolph (ed.), *Gnosis und Gnostizismus.* Darmstadt: Wissenschaftliche Buchgesellschaft.

Jung, W. (1988), 'The early aesthetic theories of Bloch and Lukács'. *New German Critique*, 45(Autumn), 41–54.

Kambas, Ch. (1996), 'Hugo Ball, Ernst Bloch, Walter Benjamin. Die Jahre bei der "Freien Zeitung"', in B. Wacker (ed.), *Dionysius DADA Areopagita. Hugo Ball und die Kritik der Moderne.* München: Schöningh, pp. 69–92.

Karadi, E. (1986), 'Bloch et Lukács dans le cercle de Weber', in P. Furlan, M. Löwy, A. Münster, N. Tertulian (eds), *Réification et utopie: Ernst Bloch et György Lukács, un siècle après.* Arles: Actes Sud, pp. 69–87.

Kaufmann, D. (1997), 'Thanks for the memory: Bloch, Benjamin, and the philosophy of history', in J. O. Daniel and T. Moylan (eds), *Not Yet. Reconsidering Ernst Bloch.* London: Verso, pp. 33–52.

Kessler, A. (2006), *Ernst Blochs Ästhetik. Fragment, Montage, Metapher.* Würzburg: Königshausen & Neumann.

Korngiebel, W. (1999), *Bloch und die Zeichen. Symboltheorie, kulturelle Gegenhegemonie und philosophischer Interdiskurs.* Würzburg: Königshausen & Neumann.

Korstvedt, B. M. (2010), *Listening for Utopia in Ernst Bloch's Musical Philosophy.* New York: Cambridge University Press.

Koselleck, R. (1979), 'Begriffsgeschichte und Sozialgeschichte', in R. Koselleck (ed.), *Vergangene Zukunft.* Frankfurt am Main: Suhrkamp.

Kracauer, S. (1965), 'Zwei Deutungen in zwei Sprachen', in S. Unseld (ed.), *Ernst Bloch zu ehren.* Frankfurt am Main: Suhrkamp, pp. 145–55.

—(1990), 'Prophetentum', in S. Kracauer and I. Mülder-Bach (eds), *Schriften. Bd. 5, 1.* Frankfurt am Main: Suhrkamp, pp. 196–204.

Krochmalnik, D. (1993), 'Ernst Blochs Exkurs über die Juden'. *Bloch-Almanach*, 13, 39–58.

Lacoste, J. (2008), 'Ernst Bloch et Faust. La lecture paradoxale'. *Europe*, Mai, 84–95.

Lacoue-Labarthe, Ph. (2002), *Poétique de l'histoire.* Paris: Galilée.

Landmann, M. (1982), 'Das Judentum bei Ernst Bloch und seine messianische Metaphysik', in M. Landmann (ed.), *Jüdische Miniaturen. Bd. I. Messianische Metaphysik.* Bonn: Bouvier, pp. 161–82.

Lehmann, G. (1985), 'Stramin und totale Form: Der Kunstphilosoph Georg Lukács und sein Verhältnis zu Ernst Blochs Ästhetik der Hoffnung'. *Weimarer Beiträge*, 31, 533–57.

Lellouche, R. (2008), *Les juifs dans l'utopie* (with the French translation of Bloch: *Symbole: les Juifs*). Paris: Éditions de l'éclat.

Letschka, W. (1999), '"Geburt der Utopie aus dem Geist der Destruktion": Anmerkungen zu allegorischen Strukturen in der Geschichtsphilosophie Blochs und Benjamins'. *Bloch-Almanach*, 18, 43–69.

Lévinas, E. (1976), 'Sur la mort dans la pensée de Ernst Bloch', in G. Raulet (ed.), *Utopie-Marxisme selon Ernst Bloch. Un système de l'inconstructible*. Paris: Payot, pp. 318-26.

—(1993), *Dieu, la mort et le temps*. Paris: Grasset.

Lilienfeld, R. (1987), 'Music and society in the 20th century: Georg Lukács, Ernst Bloch, and Theodor Adorno'. *International Journal of Politics, Culture, and Society*, 1(2), 120-46.

Löwith, K. (1941), *Von Hegel zu Nietzsche: Der revolutionäre Bruch im Denken des neunzehnten Jahrhunderts*. Zürich, New York: Europa-Verlag.

Löwy, M. (1986), 'Le romantisme revolutionnaire de Bloch et Lukács', in P. Furlan, M. Löwy, A. Münster, N. Tertulian (eds), *Réification et utopie. Ernst Bloch et György Lukács. Un siècle après*. Arles: Actes Sud, pp. 102-14.

—(1992), *Redemption and Utopia. Jewish Libertarian Thought in Central Europe. A. Study in Elective Affinity*. Stanford: Stanford University Press.

—(2008), 'Lumières du romantisme chez Adorno et Bloch'. *Europe*, Mai, 96-108.

Lukács, G. von (1911), 'Metaphysik der Tragödie: Paul Ernst'. *Logos*, 2, 79-91.

Lukács, G. (1912), 'Von der Armut am Geiste. Ein Gespräch und ein Brief'. *Neue Blätter*, 5/6: 67-92.

—(1916-17), 'Solovjeff, Wladimir: Die Rechtfertigung des Guten. Ausgewählte Werke. Band II. Jena 1916. Eugen Diederichs'. *Archiv für Sozialwissenschaft und Sozialpolitik*, 42: 978-80.

—(1968), 'Faust-Studien', in G. Lukács (ed.), *Faust und Faustus. Vom Drama der Menschengattung zur Tragödie der modernen Kunst*. Berlin: Rowohlt.

—(1970), 'The Old Culture and the New Culture'. *Telos*, 5(Spring), 21-30.

—(1972), *Political Writings*. London: New Left Books.

—(1973), *Marxism and Human Liberation: Essays on History, Culture and Revolution*. New York: Dell Publishing Co.

—(1974), *Heidelberger Philosophie der Kunst. Werke. Bd. XVI*. Darmstadt, Neuwied: Luchterhand.

—(1977), 'Bolshevism as a Moral Problem', trans. Judith Marcus Tar. *Social Research*, 44(3), 416-24.

—(1981), *Entwicklungsgeschichte des modernen Dramas*. Darmstadt, Neuwied: Luchterhand.

—(1982), *Briefwechsel. 1902-1917*. Edited by Eva Karádi and Eva Fekete. Budapest: Corvina Kiadó.

—(1985), *Dostojewski. Notizen und Entwürfe*. Edited by J. C. Nyíri. Budapest: Akadémiai Kiadó.

—(1998), 'Das Problem des untragischen Dramas', in *Lukács 1997 (Jahrbuch der Internationalen Georg-Lukács-Gesellschaft. Bd. 2)*: 13-16.

Luther, A. (1984), 'Variationen über die Endzeit. Bloch kontra Benjamin'. *Bloch-Almanach*, 4, 57-73.

Lyotard, J.-F. (1993), 'An Answer to the question, what is the Postmodern?', in J.-F. Lyotard, *The Postmodern Explained. Correspondence 1982-1985*. Minneapolis: University of Minnesota Press.

Magun, A. (2013), *Negative Revolution. Modern Political Subject and its Fate After the Cold War*. London and New York: Bloomsbury.

Mandelstam, O. (1965), *The Prose of Osip Mandelstam*, trans. Clarence Brown. Princeton: Princeton University Press.

Mann, Th. (1955), 'Die Kunst des Romans', in Th. Mann, *Gesammelte Werke in zwölf Bänden. Bd. XI*. Berlin: Aufbau-Verlag.

—(1968), 'Culture and Socialism' (1927), in Th. Mann, *Past Masters and Other Papers*, trans. H. T. Lowe Porter. Freeport, New York: Books for Libraries Press, pp. 201-14.

Marcuse, H. (1934), 'Der Kampf gegen den Liberalismus in der totalitären Staatsauffassung'. *Zeitschrift für Sozialforschung*, 3(2), 161–94.
Marotzki, W. (1987), 'Der Bildungsprozess des Menschen in Hegels "Phänomenologie des Geistes" und Goethes "Faust" '. *Goethe Jahrbuch*, 104, 128–56.
Marx, K. (1998), *The German Ideology*. New York: Prometheus Books.
Marzocchi, V. (1985), 'Utopie als "Novum" und "letzte Wiederholung" bei Ernst Bloch', in K. L. Arnold (ed.), *Ernst Bloch. Sonderband Text + Kritik*. München: Edition Text+Kritik, pp. 194–207.
Massalongo, M. (2008), 'Die Entdeckung schmaler Kontinente. Spuren eines topographischen Denkens', in E. Locher (ed.), *Spuren. Lektüren*. Innsbruck: Studienverlag.
Mayer, H. (1959), *Von Lessing bis Thomas Mann*. Pfullingen: Neske.
—(1965), 'Ernst Blochs poetische Sendung', in S. Unseld (ed.), *Ernst Bloch zu ehren*. Frankfurt am Main: Suhrkamp.
Mendes-Flohr, P. R. (1983), '"To Brush History Against the Grain": The Eschatology of the Frankfurt School and Ernst Bloch'. *Journal of the American Academy of Religion*, 51(4), 631–49.
—(1991), *Divided Passions: Jewish Intellectuals and the Experience of Modernity*. Detroit, Mich.: Wayne State University Press.
Menninghaus, W. (1980), *Walter Benjamins Theorie der Sprachmagie*. Frankfurt am Main: Suhrkamp.
Mikhailov, A. V. (2000), Iz lekciy, in D. R. Petrov, S. Yu. Khurumov (eds), A. V. Mikhailov *Obratnyi perevod* ['From the lectures,' in *Reverse Translation*]. Moscow: Yazyki russkoj kultury.
Moltmann, J. (1964), *Theologie der Hoffnung*. München: Chr. Kaiser.
Mosès, S. (2006), *L'Ange de l'Histoire*. Paris: Gallimard.
Munich, D. (2008), 'Ernst Bloch et la théologie de l'action'. *Europe* (Mai), 109–18.
Münster, A. (1982), *Utopie, Messianismus und Apokalypse im Frühwerk von Ernst Bloch*. Frankfurt am Main: Suhrkamp.
—(1986), 'Le navire de la mort de la philosophie: Ernst Bloch et Martin Heidegger', in P. Furlan, M. Löwy, A. Münster, N. Tertulian (eds), *Réification et utopie. Ernst Bloch et György Lukács. Un siècle après*. Arles: Actes Sud, pp. 241–51.
—(1986a), 'Positive Utopie versus negative Dialektik', in G. Flego, W. Schmied-Kowarzik (eds), *Ernst Bloch – utopische Ontologie*. Bochum: Germinal.
—(2008), 'De l'amitié à la polémique. À propos de correspondence Adorno-Bloch (1928–1968)'. *Europe*, Mai, 15–35.
Münz-Koenen, I. (1997), *Konstruktion des Nirgendwo. Die Diskursivität utopischen Denkens bei Bloch, Adorno, Habermas*. Berlin: Akademie.
Nancy, J.-L. (1991), *The Inoperative Community*. Minneapolis and Oxford: University of Minnesota Press.
Negt, O. (1972), Nachwort zu: E. Bloch. *Vom Hasard zur Katastrophe*. Frankfurt am Main: Suhrkamp.
Oittinen, V. (2001), 'Die "ontologische Wende" von Lukács und seine Faust-Interpretation', in F. Benseler, W. Jung (eds), *Lukács 2001. Jahrbuch der Internationalen Georg-Lukács-Gesellschaft*. Bielefeld: Aisthesis, pp. 67–99.
Osterkamp, E. (1978), 'Utopie und Prophetie. Überlegungen zu den späten Schriften Walter Benjamins', in G. Ueding (ed.), *Literatur ist Utopie*. Frankfurt am Main: Suhrkamp, pp. 103–28.
Paetzold, H. (1974), *Neomarxistische Ästhetik I: Bloch-Benjamin*. Düsseldorf: Schwann.
Pauen, M. (1992), 'Dithyrambiker des Untergangs. Gnosis und die Ästhetik der Moderne'. *Deutsche Zeitschrift für Philosophie*, 40(8), 937–61.

—(1992a), 'Apotheose des Subjekts. Gnostizismus in Blochs "Geist der Utopie"'. *Bloch-Almanach*, 12, 15–64.
—(1994), *Dithyrambiker des Untergangs: Gnostizismus in Ästhetik und Philosophie der Moderne*. Berlin: Akademie.
—(1997), 'Der apokalyptische Augenblick. Kontinuität und Umbruch in den geschichtsphilosophischen Vorstellungen des jungen Bloch'. *Bloch-Almanach*, 16, 11–44.
Pelletier, L. (2008), 'Bloch a-t-il plagié Landauer?' *Bloch-Almanach*, 27, 74–120.
—(2009), 'Ernst Bloch à la rencontre de la phénoménologie'. *Bloch-Almanach*, 28, 201–76.
Popper, K. (1945), *Open Society and its Enemies*. London: Routledge.
Rabinbach, A. (1997), *In the Shadow of Catastrophe: German Intellectuals Between Apocalypse and Enlightenment*. Berkeley and Los Angeles: University of California Press.
Radnóti, S. (1975), 'Bloch and Lukács: Two radical critics in a "Godforsaken" world'. *Telos*, 25(Fall), 156–66.
Raulet, G. (1997), *Le caractère destructeur*. Paris: Aubier.
—(2008), 'La mélancolie de l'exaucement'. *Europe*, Mai, 157–84.
Richter G. (2006), 'Bloch's Dream, Music's Traces', in J. Hermand, G. Richer (eds), *Sound Figures of Modernity. German Music and Philosophy*. Madison: University of Wisconsin Press, pp. 141–80.
Riedel, M. (1993), 'Gewaltrecht des Guten? Moraldämonismus und das ursprüngliche Problem der Moral bei Bloch und Lukács'. *Sinn und Form*, 3, 423–35.
—(1997), 'Krug, Glas und frühe Begegnung. Zum Auftakt von Blochs Philosophie', in J. R. Bloch (ed.), *'Ich bin. Aber ich habe mich nicht. Darum werden wir erst.' - Perspektiven der Philosophie Ernst Blochs*. Frankfurt am Main: Suhrkamp, pp. 225–37.
Rockmore, T. (1992), 'Fichte, Lask, and Lukács's Hegelian Marxism'. *Journal of the History of Philosophy*, 30(4), 557–77.
Rosenkranz, K. (1844), *Georg Wilhelm Friedrich Hegels Leben*. Berlin: Duncker & Humblot.
Rosenzweig, F. (1988), *Der Stern der Erlösung*. Frankfurt am Main: Suhrkamp.
—(2005), *The Star of Redemption*. Trans. Barbara E. Galli. Madison: University of Wisconsin Press.
Safranski, R. (1999), *Martin Heidegger. Between Good and Evil*. Cambridge, MA: Harvard University Press.
Sandkaulen, B. (2004), 'Hegel G. W. F.', in B. Witte, T. Buck, H.-D. Dahnke, R. Otto (eds), *Goethe-Handbuch, Bd. 4/1*. Stuttgart, Weimar: Metzler, pp. 468–71.
Scheler, M. (1991), *Die Stellung des Menschen im Kosmos*. Bonn: Bouvier.
Schelsky, H. (1979), *Die Hoffnung Blochs. Kritik der marxistischen Existenzphilosophie eines Jugendbewegten*. Stuttgart: Klett-Cotta.
Schiller, F. and Goethe, J. W. (1845), *Correspondence between Schiller and Goethe from 1794 to 1805*, trans. George H. Calvert. New York and London: Wiley and Putnam.
—(1890), *Correspondence between Schiller and Goethe. From 1798 to 1805*. Trans. L. Dora Schmitz, Vol. II. London: George Bell and Sons.
Schiller, H.-E. (1982), *Metaphysik und Gesellschaftskritik. Zur Konkretisierung der Utopie im Werk Ernst Blochs*. Königstein/Ts.: Forum Academicum in d. Verl.-Gruppe Athenäum, Hain, Scriptor, Hanstein.
—(1991), *Bloch-Konstellationen. Utopien der Philosophie*. Lüneburg: zu Klampen.
—(2011), 'Tod und Utopie: Ernst Bloch und Georg Lukács', in R. Klein, J. Kreuzer, S. Müller-Doohm (eds), *Adorno-Handbuch*. Stuttgart: Metzler, pp. 25–35.
Schlegel, F. (1993), *Philosophical Fragments*. Minneapolis: University of Minnesota Press.
Schmid, Noerr G. (2001), 'Bloch und Adorno. Bildhafte und bilderlose Utopie'. *Zeitschrift für Kritische Theorie*, 13, 25–55.

Schmidt, B. (1985), *Ernst Bloch*. Stuttgart: Metzler.
Schmitt, C. (1996), *Roman Catholicism and Political Form*, trans. G. L. Ulmen. Westport, CT: Greenwood Press.
Schmitt, H.-J. (ed.) (1978), *Der Streit mit Georg Lukács*. Frankfurt am Main: Suhrkamp.
Scholem, G. (1955), *Major Trends in Jewish Mysticism*. London: Thames and Hudson.
—(1975a), *Walter Benjamin – die Geschichte einer Freundschaft*. Frankfurt am Main: Suhrkamp.
—(1975b), 'Wohnt Gott im Herzen eines Atheisten? Zu Ernst Blochs 90. Geburtstag'. *Spiegel*, 28, 110–14.
—(1986), 'Zum Verständnis der messianischen Idee im Judentum', in G. Scholem (ed.), *Judaica I*, Frankfurt am Main: Suhrkamp, pp. 7–74.
—(1999), *Briefe. Bd. 3*. Edited by I. Shedletzky. München: Beck.
Schopf, W. (2009), 'Auf den "Spuren" Blochs zu Suhrkamp'. *Bloch-Almanach*, 28, 105–29.
Schweppenhäuser, H. (1985), 'Reale Vergesellschaftung und soziale Utopie', in K. L. Arnold (ed.), *Ernst Bloch. Sonderband Text + Kritik*. München: Edition Text+Kritik, pp. 165–74.
Shaffer, E. S. (ed.) (1987), *Comparative Criticism: Volume 9, Cultural Perceptions and Literary Values*. Cambridge: Cambridge University Press.
Siebers, J. (2011), 'Aufenthalt im Unerhörten. Ernst Bloch's reading of Hegel'. *Oxford German Studies*, 40(1), 62–71.
—(2012), 'Front', in Dietschy, B., Zeilinger, D., and Zimmermann, R. E. (eds), *Bloch Wörterbuch. Leitbegriffe der Philosophie Ernst Blochs*. Berlin, Boston: De Gruyter, pp. 161–4.
Siep, L. (2000), *Der Weg der Phänomenologie des Geistes. Ein einführender Kommentar*. Frankfurt am Main: Suhrkamp.
Simmel, G. (1918), *Lebensanschauung. Vier metaphysische Kapitel*. München, Leipzig: Duncker und Humblot.
—(1919), 'Der Henkel', in G. Simmel (ed.), *Philosophische Kultur*, 2nd edn. Leipzig: Alfred Kröner Verlag, pp. 116–24.
—(1997), 'The Adventure', in D. Frisby and M. Featherstone (eds), *Simmel on Culture. Selected Writings*, pp. 221–32.
Simons, E. (1981), 'Hoffnung als elementare Kategorie praktischer Vernunft. Kants Postulatenlehre und die kritische Verwandlung konkreten Handlung- und Gestaltungsverständnisses durch Hegel und Bloch'. *Philosophisches Jahrbuch*, 88, 264–81.
—(1983), *Das expressive Denken Ernst Blochs. Kategorien und Logik künstlerischer Produktion und Imagination*. Freiburg, München: Alber.
Speight, A. (2001), *Hegel, Literature, and the Problem of Agency*. Cambridge: Cambridge University Press.
Spinoza, B. (2002), 'Short Treatise on God, Man, and His Well-Being' Ch. 25 ('On Devils'), in *The Complete Works*, trans. S. Shirley. Indianapolis, Cambridge: Hackett.
Steiner, G. (1978), 'Träume nach vorwärts', in B. Schmidt (ed.), *Materialien zu Ernst Blochs «Prinzip Hoffnung»*. Frankfurt am Main: Suhrkamp.
Taubes, J. (1996), 'Vom Kult zur Kultur. Baustein zu einer Kritik der historischen Vernunft', in A. and J. Assmann (eds) Taubes, J., *Gesammelte Aufsätze zur Religions- und Geistesgeschichte*. München: Fink.
—(2004), *The Political Theology of Paul*. Edited by A. Assmann, J. Assmann, H. Folkers, W.-D. Hartwich, and Ch. Schulte, trans. D. Hollander. Stanford: Stanford University Press.
—(2006), 'Walter Benjamin – ein moderner Marcionit?' in *Der Preis des Messianismus. Briefe von Jacob Taubes an Gershom Scholem und andere Materialien*, Edited by E. Stimilli and A. Ment. Würzburg: Königshausen & Neumann, pp. 53–65.

Thaler, J. (2003), *Dramatische Seelen. Tragödientheorien im frühen zwanzigsten Jahrhundert*. Bielefeld: Aisthesis.
Thielen, H. (2005), *Eingedenken und Erlösung: Walter Benjamin*. Würzburg: Königshausen & Neumann.
Thompson, P. and Žižek, S. (eds) (2013), *The Privatization of Hope: Ernst Bloch and the Future of Utopia*. Durham, NC: Duke University Press.
Tihanov, G. (2000), *The Master and the Slave. Lukács, Bakhtin, and the Ideas of Their Time*. Oxford: Oxford University Press.
Tillich, P. (1932), *Hegel und Goethe. Zwei Gedenkreden*. Tübingen: Mohr.
Über Walter Benjamin. Frankfurt am Main: Suhrkamp, 1968.
Ueding, G. (2009), *Utopie in dürftiger Zeit. Studien über Ernst Bloch*. Würzburg: Königshausen & Neumann.
Ujma, Ch. (1995), *Ernst Blochs Konstruktion der Moderne aus Messianismus und Marxismus. Erörterungen mit Berücksichtigung von Lukács und Benjamin*. Stuttgart: M & P, Verl. für Wiss. und Forschung.
Valéry, P. (1957), 'Lettre sur Mallarmé', in *Œuvres*. Vol. 1. Paris: Gallimard.
Vidal, F. (2010), 'Ernst Bloch', in S. L. Sorgner and O. Fürbeth (eds), *Music in German Philosophy. An Introduction*. Chicago and London: University of Chicago Press.
Vogt, J. (1985), 'Nicht nur Erinnerung: "Hitlers Gewalt"', in K. L. Arnold (ed.), *Ernst Bloch. Sonderband Text + Kritik*. München: Edition Text+Kritik, 1985.
Voßkamp, W. (1985), '"Höchstes Exemplar des utopischen Menschen": Ernst Bloch und Goethes Faust'. *Deutsche Vierteljahrsschrift für Literaturwissenschaft und Geistesgeschichte*, 59(4), 676–87.
—(1994), ' "Wie könnten die Dinge vollendet werden, ohne daß sie apokalyptisch aufhören." Ernst Blochs Theorie der Apokalypse als Voraussetzung einer utopischen Theorie der Kunst', in K. Bohnen (ed.), *Aufklärung als Problem und Aufgabe*. Kopenhagen, München: Fink, pp. 295–304.
Walter Benjamin (1990), *1892–1940. Marbacher Magazin 55. Katalog der Ausstellung*. Marbach: Marbacher Literaturarchiv.
Weber, M. (1958), 'Religious Rejections of the World and Their Directions', in H. H. Gerth and C. Wright Mills (eds), *From Max Weber: Essays in Sociology*, New York: Oxford University Press.
—(2005), *The Protestant Ethic and the Spirit of Capitalism*. London etc.: Routledge.
Weissberg, L. (1992), 'Philosophy and the Fairy Tale: Ernst Bloch as Narrator'. *New German Critique*, 55(Winter), 21–44.
Widmer, P. (1974), *Die Anthropologie Ernst Blochs*. Frankfurt am Main: Athenaeum.
Wieland, R. (1992), *Schein, Kritik, Utopie. Zu Goethe und Hegel*. München: Edition Text+Kritik.
Wizisla, E. (1990), 'Ernst Bloch und Bertolt Brecht: Neue Dokumente ihrer Beziehung'. *Bloch-Almanach*, 10, 87–105.
Wißkirchen, H. (1987), 'Die humane Kraft des Denkens. Zur frühen Philosophie Blochs und Benjamins'. *Bloch-Almanach*, 7, 53–79.
Wohlfahrt, I. (1986), '"Immer radikal, niemals konsequent"', in W. Bolz and R. Faber (eds), *Antike und Moderne: Walter Benjamins Passagen*. Würzburg: Königshausen&Neumann.
—(2006), 'Die Passagenarbeit', in B. Lindner (eds), *Benjamin-Handbuch*. Stuttgart: Metzler, pp. 251–74.
Wolin, R. (1982), *Walter Benjamin: An Aesthetic of Redemption*. Berkeley and Los Angeles: University of California Press.
Wołkowicz, A. (1985), 'Der frühe Bloch und der literarische Symbolismus', in K. L. Arnold (ed.), *Ernst Bloch. Sonderband Text + Kritik*. München: Edition Text+Kritik.

—(1988), 'Der hohe Ton', in K. Sauerland (ed.), *Melancholie und Enthusiasmus; Studien zur Literatur- und Geistesgeschichte der Jahrhundertwende*. Frankfurt am Main etc.: Peter Lang, 109–19.

Wunder, B. (1997), *Konstruktion und Rezeption der Theologie Walter Benjamins: These I und das 'theologisch-politische Fragment'*. Würzburg: Königshausen & Neumann.

Wurth, M. (1986), *Antizipierendes Denken. Ernst Blochs Philosophie und Ästhetik des Noch-Nicht-Bewußten im Zusammenhang seiner Freud-Kritik*. Frankfurt am Main etc.: Peter Lang.

Zerlang, M. (1985), 'Ernst Bloch als Erzähler. Über Allegorie, Melancholie und Utopie in den "Spuren"', in K. L. Arnold (ed.), *Ernst Bloch. Sonderband Text + Kritik*. München: Edition Text+Kritik, pp. 61–75.

Ziegler, L. (1902), *Zur Metaphysik des Tragischen. Eine philosophische Studie*. Leipzig: Dürr'sche Verlagsbuchhandlung.

Žižek, S. and Milbank, J. (2009), *The Monstrosity of Christ. Paradox or Dialectic?* Cambridge, MA: MIT Press.

Zudeick, P. (1980), *Die Welt als Wirklichkeit und Möglichkeit. Die Rechtfertigung der Utopie in der Philosophie*. Bonn: Bouvier.

—(1987), *Der Hintern des Teufels. Ernst Bloch – Leben und Werk*. Baden-Baden, Moos: Elster.

Zyber, E. (2007), *Homo Utopicus: Die Utopie im Lichte der philosophischen Anthropologie*. Würzburg: Königshausen & Neumann.

Index

Abulafia, Abraham   105
Adorno, Theodor   1, 4–5, 8, 11, 26–8, 35, 37, 80, 82, 88, 123, 128, 139, 145, 147–8, 156–8, 161–2, 165, 167–77
   Dialectic of Enlightenment   28
   The Notes to Literature   168
Agamben, Giorgio   121, 147, 151, 158
   The Time That Remains   158
Alain   86
allegory   4, 11, 13, 18, 82, 86, 96–7, 105, 141–3, 150, 154, 159
Althusser, Louis   136
anarchism   4, 37, 49, 53, 99, 102–3, 109, 115, 122, 124, 129, 148
anticipation   11, 13, 23–4, 26, 31, 33, 35, 45, 50, 56, 75, 89, 92, 98, 103–6, 111, 120, 127, 131, 134, 147, 149, 155–6, 179
anticipatory illumination (*Vor-Schein*)   2, 11, 13
Apokalypse, apocalyptics   11, 24, 40, 47, 49–50, 52–3, 58, 65, 87, 94, 96–100, 103–4, 106, 108–10, 120, 123, 130, 132, 146, 148, 151, 155–7, 159, 161, 174, 179–80
Arendt, Hannah   27
Aristophanes   180
Aristotle   6, 10, 37, 41, 50, 135, 161
atheism   1, 8, 11, 23, 30–1, 94, 106–7, 111, 148
Auerbach, Erich   53, 58, 110, 144
Augustine   152

Baader, Franz   12, 25, 78, 92, 108
Baal Shem Tov   101, 104
Badiou, Alain   32
Bakhtin, Mikhail   11, 57–8, 147
   Author and Hero in Aesthetic Activity   57
Ball, Hugo   115
Bar Kokhba, Simon   106

Barth, Karl   39, 87, 122, 162
   The Epistle to the Romans   162
Basilides   93
Bataille, George   27
Becher, Johannes   8–9
Bely, Andrei   98–9, 152, 155
Benjamin, Walter   1, 3–4, 6, 8, 11, 13, 16–17, 27, 30, 39, 41, 43–4, 46, 50, 62, 66, 82, 85–6, 91, 99–100, 102–3, 111, 102–47, 149–51, 153–65, 167–73, 180–1
   Arcades Project   114, 118, 133, 140–1, 160, 163
   Epistemo-Critical Prologue   117, 130, 138, 140
   One-Way Street   118, 133, 136–9, 161
   The Task of the Translator   153
   The Theological-Political Fragment   4, 44, 119–25, 128–30, 132–3, 150, 160, 179
   Theses (On the Concept of History)   4, 13, 117, 120, 123, 129, 134, 140, 153, 159
Benn, Gottfried   9
Berdyaev, Nikolai   31
Bergmann, Hugo   160
Blake, William   150
Bloch, Karola   136
Böhme, Jakob   13, 19, 22–3, 37, 107–8, 128–9, 144, 157, 162
   On Election of Grace   162
Brecht, Bertolt   8, 11, 30, 66, 144, 173
Breton, André   163
Brod, Max   8
Bruno, Giordano   10
Buber, Martin   2–3, 85, 97, 100–5, 107, 109, 111–12, 116–17, 122, 124, 129, 132, 147, 159, 161, 167
   Three Speeches on Judaism   160
Bulgakov, Sergei   29, 162
Bultmann, Rudolf   156

Chagall, Marc   63
chiliasm   96, 109, 126, 152
Christ, Christianity   1, 3–4, 11, 23, 34, 44,
    47–8, 58, 94–5, 101, 103, 105–10,
    112, 116–17, 121–2, 131–2, 149,
    151–2, 159–65
Claudel, Paul   45
Clement of Alexandria   111
Cohen, Hermann   101–3, 111, 121–2,
    126, 132, 161
Cohn, Alfred   158, 160
communism   12
community   3, 11, 18, 23, 26, 28, 36, 49, 52,
    60, 66, 84, 99, 102–3, 109–10, 121,
    126, 132, 148, 151–2, 155–7, 168
Creuzer, Friedrich   142
Curtius, Ernst Robert   85

daydreams   26, 114, 150, 181
Derrida, Jacques   88, 111
Diderot, Denis   67
Dilthey, Wilhelm   17
Döblin, Alfred   8, 63
Dutschke, Rudi   9

Eckhart von Hochheim (Meister
    Eckhart)   19, 47, 102, 106–7,
    109, 122, 144
    On Eternal Birth   107
Eco, Umberto   11
Eisenmenger, Johann Andreas   99
    Judaism Unmasked   99
Eisenstein, Sergei   14, 49
Eisler, Hanns   66
Engels, Friedrich   29, 63–4, 76
    *The Development of Socialism from
    Utopia to Science*   29
Epicurus   21
Ernst, Paul   41, 45, 50, 57
eschatology   3, 22, 94–112, 121, 130,
    152–3, 155–6, 159, 162, 164, 170
estrangement   15, 50, 96, 140
Expressionism   2–3, 9, 28, 37, 40, 49–50,
    61, 66, 93, 97–8, 114, 116, 146,
    152, 163, 168, 170, 175, 180

Fichte, Johann Gottlieb   61, 86
Flaubert, Gustave   55
    Sentimental Education   55

Foucault, Michel   136
Freud, Sigmund   22, 25–6, 38
Friedlaender, Salomo   45, 162
Fromm, Erich   11
Front   24

Gehlen, Arnold   22
George, Stefan   28, 47, 138
gnosticism   2–3, 30, 39, 52, 63, 92–6, 99,
    104, 106, 108, 122–3, 129, 133,
    144–5, 149, 165, 171
Goethe, Johann Wolfgang von   3–4, 10,
    21, 41, 51, 59, 67–8, 70–5, 77–85,
    87–8, 136, 138, 141
    Poetry and Truth   88
Grabenko, Elena   52
Gundolf, Friedrich   138

Hamsun, Knut   16
Harnack, Adolf von   93–6
    *Marcion: The Gospel of the
    Alien God*   94
Hartmann, Eduard von   7, 10, 37
Hartmann, Franz   92
Hasidism   101, 109, 112
Hebbel, Friedrich   45, 52, 85
Hebel, Johann Peter   31, 68
Hegel, Georg Wilhelm Friedrich   10, 32,
    38–9, 41, 58–64, 67–89, 109–10,
    125, 127, 132, 139–40, 148,
    153, 162
    The Phenomenology of Spirit   2, 10,
    63, 67–9, 71–5, 78, 81–4, 87–9,
    126–7, 139, 144, 163
    The Science of Logic   22
Heidegger, Martin   2, 31–3, 36, 58, 66, 76,
    87, 163, 168
    Being and Time   32, 163
    Letter on 'Humanism'   32
    *The Question Concerning
    Technology*   32
Herodotus   115
Herzen, Alexander   33
Hesse, Herrmann   11
Heym, Georg   9
Hitler, Adolf   27, 165
Hobsbawm, Eric   11
Hofmannsthal, Hugo von   16
    The Letter of Lord Chandos   16

Hölderlin, Friedrich   28, 31–2, 88, 134
homeland   24–5, 34–6, 103, 153
Honigsheim, Paul   108
hope   1, 2, 8–10, 17, 22–3, 25, 30, 33–4,
    55–6, 75, 77, 83, 85, 100, 106,
    125, 127–9, 133, 143, 145–7, 149,
    151, 159–60, 165, 170–1, 173,
    176, 179
Horkheimer, Max   26, 28, 167, 171, 173
Husserl, Edmund   33, 37, 162

Ibsen, Henrik   51, 98
inconstruable question   20–1, 100, 124,
    133, 140, 157
instant   2, 4, 11, 14–21, 23–4, 30–1, 34,
    36, 39, 42–4, 46, 58–9, 62, 74,
    82–5, 98–9, 102–3, 107, 129, 140,
    146, 154, 157, 160, 165, 180
  darkness of the lived   14–21, 46, 58–9,
    62, 82, 102, 140, 157
  fulfilled   11, 74, 82–5
inwardness   20, 65, 99, 125, 145
Irenaeus   152
Ivanov, Vyacheslav   98

Jacobi, Friedrich Heinrich   67, 88
Jameson, Fredric   11, 55, 67
Jetztzeit (Now-time)   4, 135, 140–1, 163
Joyce, James   144, 163
Jung, Carl Gustav   118
Jünger, Ernst   60, 150
Justin the Martyr   152

Kafka, Franz   16–17, 77, 100, 161, 179
kairos   15, 24
Kandinsky, Wassily   116
  Concerning the Spiritual in Art   116
Kant, Immanuel   19, 62, 87, 99, 125–9,
    148, 150, 156, 162, 172
  Idea for a Universal History   126
Karplus (Adorno), Gretel   169
Keyserling, Hermann   101
Kierkegaard, Søren   19, 21, 31, 43, 80, 82
Koselleck, Reinhart   28
Kracauer, Siegfried   11, 84, 112, 124,
    165, 168
Kropotkin, Peter   102
Kuhn, Thomas   136
Külpe, Oswald   7, 37

Landauer, Gustav   3, 102–3, 159
  The Revolution   102
  Scepticism and Mysticism   102
Leibniz, Gottfried Wilhelm von   10
Lenin, Vladimir Ilyich   37
Lessing, Gotthold Ephraim   149
Lesznai, Anna   108
Lévinas, Emmanuel   11, 147
Lichtenberg, Georg Christoph   67, 136
Lipps, Theodor   7
Lukács, György   1–2, 5, 7, 9, 11, 26–9,
    36, 39–69, 71–80, 83–8, 91, 93,
    97, 100, 110, 114, 124, 129, 135,
    145–6, 149, 151, 163–4, 173,
    175, 179
  Heidelberg Aesthetics   40
  Heidelberg Philosophy of Art   40
  History and Class Consciousness
    30, 59–67
  *The History of the Development of
    Modern Drama*   44, 86
  *The Old Culture and the
    New Culture*   59
  On Poverty of Spirit   28, 53
  Soul and Form   40–51, 59, 85
  The Theory of the Novel   51–9, 86
Luria, Isaac   131, 144
Luxemburg, Rosa   29, 61
Lyotard, Jean-François   11, 42

Mach, Ernst   7, 79
Mann, Klaus   11
Mann, Thomas   11, 28, 54, 87, 155
  Culture and Socialism   28
  Mario and the Magician   155
Mannheim, Karl   12, 170
Marcion   93–5, 98, 111, 121
Marcuse, Herbert   38
Marx, Karl   12–13, 26, 28–30, 60–2, 76,
    84, 94, 120, 155, 165, 180
  The German Ideology   12
  The Holy Family   13
Marxism   2, 9, 11, 26–31, 33, 36, 39, 59,
    61–7, 72, 75–6, 83, 87, 92, 94,
    101–4, 110–11, 114, 123–4,
    129, 135, 140, 152, 159,
    165, 180
  'warm' and 'cold'   25, 27, 29–30,
    61, 102

materialism   10, 13, 23, 29–30, 32, 59, 63, 65, 75–6, 135, 140, 149, 154, 162, 171
   dialectical   10
   historical   29–30, 32, 59, 63, 65, 135, 140, 149, 154
   speculative   171
   vulgar   76, 135
matter   10, 13, 22–5, 37, 62, 131, 149, 152
May, Karl   8
Mechthild of Magdeburg   144
Messiah   3–4, 22, 24, 30, 48, 60, 65, 92, 97, 100, 103–5, 107–8, 110, 119–22, 125, 131, 140, 143, 147, 151–2, 155, 160–1, 163
   true and false   155
messianism   1–5, 14, 22–3, 28, 39–40, 44, 52–3, 59–60, 92, 95–9, 101–4, 108–11, 119–25, 128–31, 133, 136, 147–61, 163, 165, 169, 179
Michaux, Henri   11
Molitor, Franz Joseph   92, 108, 111–12
Montaigne, Michel de   115, 150
Montesquieu, Charles-Louis de Secondat   8
Müntzer, Thomas   53, 63, 65, 87, 92, 98, 109, 115, 169
Musil, Robert   8
mysticism   3–4, 8, 10, 15, 19, 36, 43–4, 46–7, 49, 52, 57, 73, 76, 78, 83–4, 91–2, 95, 97–102, 104–12, 119, 123, 125, 140, 144–51, 153–4, 180

Nancy, Jean-Luc   23, 50
nature   9, 13, 24–5, 29, 32–4, 56, 63–4, 82–4, 87–8, 92–3, 98, 107–8, 113, 119–20, 127–30, 142
negativity   3, 22, 69, 73, 76–82, 85, 167, 169, 171
Neo-Kantians   4, 7, 39, 57, 111, 125, 150
Nicholas of Cusa   7
Nietzsche, Friedrich   28, 41, 50, 85, 98, 126
non-contemporaneity   4, 11, 27–9, 49, 64, 108, 135
Nostradamus   167
Not   22–3

Not-yet (Not-Yet-Being)   2, 10, 22–5, 31, 33–4, 58, 65, 67, 70, 74, 92, 110, 125–6, 128, 132, 148, 158–9, 164, 171–2, 176
Not-Yet-Conscious   25–6, 150, 164
Novalis (Friedrich von Hardenberg)   14, 31, 36, 42, 163
Novum   24
Now (*Jetzt*)   14–15, 34, 59, 62–4, 82, 97, 115, 134–5, 154, 163

Origen   152
Otto, Rudolf   122

Paul the Apostle   45, 95, 105, 107, 121, 151
   The Epistle to the Romans   105
Picasso, Pablo   163
Piscator, Erwin   8
Plato   6, 10, 87–8
Plessner, Helmuth   22
Ponge, Francis   21
Popper, Karl   18
Popper, Leo   48, 85, 175
praxis   2, 31, 33, 60, 66, 85, 123, 127, 139–40, 152, 176, 180
Proust, Marcel   55, 86

Ratzinger, Joseph   11
redemption   13, 19, 22, 24, 30, 48, 52, 58, 82, 93, 95, 100, 103–4, 106, 109–10, 119–22, 129–33, 143, 149, 153–4, 156, 158–9, 162
remembrance (*Eingedenken*)   39, 50, 120, 134, 163
revolution   8–9, 12, 18, 24, 28–30, 32–4, 36–7, 46, 48, 52–3, 59–62, 65, 75, 84, 89, 94, 106, 110–11, 120, 134–5, 149, 154–5, 164, 173
Robespierre, Maximilien de   163
romanticism   42, 49, 55, 102, 144, 151, 173
Rosenstock-Huessy, Eugen   101
Rosenzweig, Franz   3–4, 39, 44, 80, 95, 99–101, 103–4, 110, 131–2, 146–7, 152–4, 158, 165
Rousseau, Jean-Jacques   32, 88

Sartre, Jean-Paul   14, 46, 142
Savinkov, Boris   52
   The Pale Horse   52

Scheler, Max   7, 74, 86, 95, 112
Schelling, Friedrich Wilhelm Joseph
   13, 22–3, 33, 37, 68, 71, 76, 78,
   88, 93, 105, 108–9
Schelsky, Helmut   11, 27, 49, 89
Schiller, Friedrich   67, 77, 88
Schlegel, Freidrich   35, 40, 164, 173
Schmitt, Carl   49, 60, 87, 92, 112, 148
   Political Romanticism   49
Schoen, Ernst   116
Schoenberg, Arnold   63
Scholem, Gershom   3–4, 50, 62, 100,
   104–5, 108, 110–12, 115–17,
   121–2, 132, 144, 151, 153, 160
Schopenhauer, Arthur   54, 64, 167
Seghers, Anna   66
self-encounter   4, 11, 18–19, 21, 34, 37,
   47, 55, 97, 102, 105, 115, 134,
   148–9, 152, 156
Shekhinah   104, 112, 131
Simmel, Georg   7, 14, 24, 39, 61, 85, 100,
   118, 126, 174
   Philosophy of Money   61
socialism   26, 28–30, 33, 36, 91, 98,
   101–3, 115, 135
Soloviev, Vladimir   53–4, 86, 155
   A Short Tale of the Antichrist   155
Sophocles   67
Sorel, Georges   26–7, 115
   Reflections on Violence   26
Spengler, Oswald   168
Spinoza, Benedict   78–9, 103, 120
   Tractatus Theologico-Politicus   120
Stalin, Joseph   9
Steiner, Rudolf   98
Stepun, Fyodor   53
Strindberg, August   50
subject   2–3, 13–15, 18–21, 23, 25, 30,
   34, 36, 48–50, 55, 58–63, 74, 76,
   80, 83, 87, 91, 93, 97, 101, 107,
   122, 125–7, 132, 139, 142–3, 148,
   155–7, 163, 171
   messianic   3, 18, 50, 59–61, 64, 122,
     126, 132, 139, 155–7
   and object   13–14, 23, 25–6, 34, 48, 59,
     61–4, 72–5, 88

subject-nature   13, 25, 112
Suhrkamp, Peter   172
surprise   16, 21, 30–1, 146
Susman, Margarete   86, 102
symbolic intention   21, 125, 162, 170

Taubes, Jacob   93, 121, 157
teleology   4, 35, 80, 88, 120, 123
temporality   17, 43–4, 55, 63, 72, 91, 107,
   119, 153–4, 157–8, 174
Tieck, Ludwig   17
time   1–4, 14–15, 17–18, 24, 33, 35, 37,
   39, 43–4, 46, 52–3, 72, 81, 86, 91,
   95, 98, 103, 108, 110, 120, 123,
   130, 134–5, 140–1, 150–5, 158,
   163, 169, 181
   messianic   3, 44, 52, 108, 130, 140,
     151–5, 158
   in the novel   55–6
   in tragedy   43–4, 72
Toller, Ernst   8–9
Tolstoy, Lev Nikolayevich   53, 56
   War and Peace   56
tragedy   40–51, 70, 85–6, 179

Ultimum   24, 34
utopia   1–2, 4–5, 8–15, 18–20, 23–4, 29,
   33–7, 45, 47, 50, 53–7, 62, 64–6,
   82, 87–8, 99, 102–3, 108, 111,
   122, 124–7, 135, 139, 146, 148,
   151–8, 170–6, 179–81
   concrete   12, 66, 87

Van Gogh, Vincent Willem   16, 97
Vattimo, Gianni   11

Weber, Max   2, 7–9, 29, 40, 61, 87,
   97, 108
   *The Protestant Ethic and the Spirit of
     Capitalism*   8
Windelband, Wilhelm   7
wonder   15–16, 21, 162

Ziegler, Leopold   42, 85
Zionism   102, 109, 121, 161
Žižek, Slavoj   1, 23

double sided tape

160

120

speaking objects — noise

text.

not-
yet